Conceived in Doubt

AMERICAN BEGINNINGS, 1500–1900

A series edited by Edward G. Gray, Stephen Mihm, and Mark A. Peterson

Conceived in Doubt

RELIGION AND POLITICS IN
THE NEW AMERICAN NATION

Amanda Porterfield

The University of Chicago Press   CHICAGO & LONDON

The University of Chicago Press, Chicago 60637
The University of Chicago Press, Ltd., London
© 2012 by The University of Chicago
All rights reserved. Published 2012.
Paperback edition 2015
Printed in the United States of America

21 20 19 18 17 16 15   2 3 4 5 6

ISBN-13: 978-0-226-67512-1 (cloth)
ISBN-13: 978-0-226-27196-5 (paper)
ISBN-13: 978-0-226-67514-5 (e-book)
DOI: 10.7208/chicago/9780226675145.001.0001

Library of Congress Cataloging-in-Publication Data
Porterfield, Amanda, 1947–
    Conceived in doubt : religion and politics in the new American nation /
Amanda Porterfield.
        p.   cm. — (American beginnings, 1500–1900)
    Includes bibliographical references and index.
    ISBN-13: 978-0-226-67512-1 (hardcover : alk. paper)
    ISBN-10: 0-226-67512-2 (hardcover : alk. paper)
    1. Church and state—United States.   2. United States—Church history—
19th century.   3. United States—History—19th century.   I. Title.
    II. Series: American beginnings, 1500–1900.
BR516.P67 2012
261.70973'09034—dc23
                                                            2011028786

To Keith

CONTENTS

ACKNOWLEDGMENTS

My interest in the early American republic began in graduate school at Stanford, where I was fortunate to study with several great Americanists—Bill Clebsch and Giles Gunn in religion; Al Gelpi and George Dekker in English; and David Tyack and David Kennedy in history. In a particularly memorable seminar led by George Dekker, the only other student was Jay Fliegelman, a wonderfully original thinker whose delight in the textual monuments of the early American republic was contagious. I am also indebted to Sidney Mead, who visited Stanford for a lecture. Sitting on the floor in a crowded living room one evening, I listen to Mead confess astonishment at the massive shift in the early republic from deism to evangelical religion. His wonderment over that change made a lasting impression; this book seeks to explain that puzzling change.

As a young professor at Syracuse University, I learned a great deal from Ralph Ketcham. His interest in the intellectual and religious issues embedded in the political history of the early republic captured my imagination, and his work on James Madison set a standard of scholarship I continue to admire. For several years at Syracuse, I participated in Ralph's team-taught course in American studies supported by the Maxwell School of Citizenship and Public Affairs. I have often thought back gratefully to Roger Sharp, Don Miekeljohn, Michael Barkun, and other colleagues in that course whose knowledge of American political history shaped my own.

After exploring other topics, I returned to the early republic at Florida State University (FSU), where I am surrounded by fine scholars who inspire and support my work. Chief among them is John Corrigan, whose interest in emotion advanced my thinking about the early republic. John supported this project from the outset, worked through a draft of the manuscript, and urged me to sharpen my argument about power and suppression of doubt at several crucial points. He also confirmed that argument by calling my attention to the echo of doubt in Barack Obama's winning campaign slogan, "Yes We Can."

Paul Erickson and the librarians at the American Antiquarian Society helped the project along at an early stage, as did Kyle Roberts, Phil Goff, Mark Silk, Larry Moore, and Dan Howe. Peter Williams at Miami University, Jennifer Reid at University of Maine at Farmington, and Kate Carté Engel at Texas A&M hosted lectures in which I tried out portions of my book on their colleagues and students. The Library of Congress provided fine resources, and librarians at Milsaps College went out of their way to assist me. The efficient and gracious staff of FSU's Interlibrary Loan Department expedited my work considerably.

Research assistants Todd Brenneman, Katie Hladkey, and Andy Polk aided my work through many newspapers and other primary documents. Daniel Dillard, Barton Price, and others in the graduate colloquium in American religious history at FSU asked insightful questions about a draft of chapter 3. In my graduate seminar on religion and politics, Anna Amundsen, Chris Blythe, Emily Clark, John Crow, Josh Fleer, Lauren Gray, Michael Graziano, Tammy Heise, Andy Polk, and Brad Stoddard talked over the whole manuscript. Randy Tarnowski and Adam Brasich helped me with the final editing.

Ed Blum, Tommy Kidd, and Matt Day responded to my request for a critical reading of the manuscript with great generosity of time and spirit. Simon Newman and Barney Twiss allowed me to read and cite from unpublished working papers. Ed Gray helped enormously by sharing his expertise on Thomas Paine, warning of pitfalls, and pressing me to spell out what I meant by "religion." Ed invited me to submit the manuscript to the University of Chicago Press (UCP) and offered judicious commentary and celebratory toasts as the process unfolded.

At UCP, Robert Devens has been a splendid editor. His delight in the project at an early stage inspired me, and I am grateful for his intelligent superintendence of the editorial process. Advice from Kirsten Fischer and a second reviewer enabled me to clarify my argument and develop it more fully. The book also benefited from the skills of Elissa Park, Laura Avey, Sandy Hazel, Jeff Waxman, and other members of the UCP team. Back at FSU, Lauren Gray applied her acumen to the index.

Last but not least, my husband, Keith Hull, lived with my research and writing, as well as with me, and happily joined in when the book and I became one. At the Library of Congress one morning, he found the envelope with John Breckinridge's scrawl noting five dollars to a Methodist minister. We often talked through one aspect or another of the project, and I queried him more than once at 3 a.m. on points that were keeping me awake. With skills honed as an English professor, Keith lavished my chapters with criticisms, ruminations, and grammatical chastisements. A wonderful partner in every way, Keith is this book's dedicatee.

As pastor in Avon, Connecticut, a village of about one hundred families, Rufus Hawley was dismayed at the prevalence of religious skepticism among his people in the late 1790s. Determined to pray for a revival, he and ministers from nearby towns convened in Avon during the spring of 1799 to raise alarm about the horrible consequences of religious laxity. Responding to the ministers' call for repentance, neighbors met in "conferences" to crack open the "hardness of their hearts." Pleased with the town's reaction, Hawley reported that "[b]alls, all merry meetings and public diversions were laid aside." In a collective wave of emotion, "[p]eople of all ages" confessed to ruin in "the abounding wickedness of their lives." Submitting to God and praying for divine mercy, many found themselves wonderfully "exalted to heaven." Though not everyone engaged in this emotional process maintained their trust in God, more than forty individuals did become new members of Hawley's church. Those already joined "were stirred to pray more fervently than usual for themselves and for the prosperity of Zion."[1]

Through cathartic rituals such as this, ministers in many parts of the United States at the turn of the nineteenth century tapped into a pervasive sense of self-doubt and mistrust of the world. The self-confidence manifest during the revolutionary era in skepticism of British authority had diminished, giving way to darker forms of doubt, ranging from cynicism toward policies enacted by the federal government to resentment of sharp traders and land speculators. People feared the miseries of debt, grew wary about counterfeit currency, suspicious of women who worked along waterways, and of Indians harboring revenge. Free blacks would work for almost nothing, and the problems associated with slavery were legion. The 1790s saw rising panic about how to get along in the new world of American liberty, where old traditions of decorum had broken down, stability was a memory about the past, and innocence an invitation to predators. As old traditions fell away, uncertainty about how to conduct oneself, cynicism with respect to other people, and ambivalence about the effects of American independence all contributed to the uneasy atmosphere of mistrustful doubt.

Religious institutions grew as much to manage mistrustful doubt as to relieve it. Trust in God did not save people from counterfeit bills, steep prices, or slavery. Instead, it offered hope and visualizations of a better world where problems were resolved or transcended. In many cases, engagement in these imagined worlds, as well as in the communities supporting them, helped people control their behavior and get through pain and difficulty. These communities expanded religious assistance to the poor and downtrodden, provided safety for some victims of abuse, and created new opportunities for individual leadership and community development. But reliance on religion to resolve doubt came at a price. Preachers insisted that the imagined worlds supported by religious communities were real, and that insistence required strategies and institutions to deflect the doubt it continued to generate.

Managing anxiety about American freedom, churches muffled skepticism about biblical revelation and the need for religious authority. Promoting the supreme authority of God's law, churches not only exerted moral authority as interpreters of divine governance but also fostered distrust of secular reason and government. Thus churches manipulated distrust as well as relieved it, feeding the uncertainty and instability they worked to resolve.

Absolute trust in God was the solution to life's problems that ministers always advocated, and many found respite in taking their advice. But even when individuals desperately wanted their faith to be genuine, they could not be entirely sure. Individuals celebrated for maintaining their religious edge went back and forth between doubt and trust, each tendency renewing intensity in the other. Thus Reverend Hawley of Avon praised one earnest convert who worried that "he might be deceived with regard to the state of his soul."[2] In nearby Killingworth, another model convert showed how mistrust could be harnessed to support religious determination. She hoped she trusted God but still worried—"I might be deceived by the treachery of my own heart." Assailed by "Doubts as to the existence of a God," she committed to pressing on in faith nevertheless. "Though he slay me," she told her minister, quoting the book of Job, "yet I will trust in him."[3]

The spike in religion's popularity around 1800 coincided with political upheaval and new forms of political organization. Popular participation in politics increased greatly in the 1790s with a profusion of partisan newspapers, political toasts, caucuses, parades, open-air speeches, and barbecues.[4] These activities expanded politics as a popular arena of public life, broadened the base of participation in government, and stirred up excitement about elections that, prior to 1800, had been relatively uncontested. In Massachusetts, for example, voter turnout rarely exceeded 20 percent prior to the 1790s, and in many towns, more than 90 percent of those who did vote cast their ballots for the same candidate. Whatever grudges people held outside that narrow corridor of political expression, earlier elections reflected powerful forces of social consensus and deeply ingrained habits of deference to social elites.[5]

Participation in mass politics swelled in the context of opposition to federal policies enacted during the presidencies of George Washington and John Adams. Federal taxes, restrictions on occupation of Indian lands, and the Alien and Sedition Acts of 1798 limiting free speech and allowing President Adams to deport politically troublesome immigrants all met with strong opposition. As public life in every region of the new republic became increasingly politicized, old habits of deference were publicly denounced, and political activists channeled mistrust along partisan lines. Dividing people into opposing groups whose caricatures of each other subverted honest debate, partisan politics organized and amplified mistrust. Taverns became headquarters for a new breed of political organizers who planned public events and worked to recruit voters. Alcohol flowed freely, and duels were common. As one French immigrant to America recalled the atmospheres of mistrust that pervaded American cities in 1798: "Everybody was suspicious of everybody else; everywhere one saw murderous glances."[6]

When the rowdy opposition movement headed by the Virginia slaveholder and religious insouciant Thomas Jefferson turned Adams and many of his supporters out of office in 1800–1801, promising to make government less restrictive, defenders of government responsibility for moral order were dismayed, some to the point of apocalyptic grief. Hostility to Jefferson was so extreme in Connecticut—where sin was the word for unrestricted liberty—that it is not surprising a convert in Killingworth would invoke Job; the true Christian's plight in libertine America, according to many proponents of religion, was victimization and unmitigated suffering. From newspapers, political conversations, and pulpits, residents of Connecticut had every opportunity to absorb dire assessments about the nation's descent into ruin and the punishments from God sure to follow. Urged on by their ministers, citizens intent on preserving Connecticut's reputation as "the land of steady habits"[7] looked to religion to manage their fears about the future. As the *Connecticut Courant* re-minded readers, "The leading Democrats in this country, are among the most shewy, the most extravagant, and the most despotic of our inhabitants." Beware of those French besotted scoundrels, the *Courant* cautioned ominously, "Look to your houses, your parents, your wives, and your children. Are you prepared to see your dwellings in flames, hoary hairs bathed in blood, female chastity violated, or children writhing on the pike or the halbert?" Invoking the violence of the French Revolution and its spillage in the Americas through Jefferson and his comrades, the *Courant* advised readers to make ready to defend everything they cherished: "Look at every leading Jacobin, as a ravening wolf, preparing to enter your peaceful fold, and glut his deadly appetite on the vitals of your country."[8]

Religious organizations grew on both sides of the partisan political divide, and revivals flourished even more exuberantly outside New England, in regions where Jefferson and his party were more popular. New Light Presbyterians from North Carolina ignited the Great Revival of 1801 in the Kentucky Cumberland, and that amazing event shaped religious expectations throughout the West and in many parts of the South. At Cane Ridge in Kentucky that summer, thousands of participants—estimates ranged from twelve to twenty-five thousand—attended a mass rally, with eighteen Presbyterian ministers and at least equal numbers of Methodist and Baptist preachers on hand to inspire extraordinary performances of religious enthusiasm, most notably the jerks, a convulsive exercise performed by men being purged of unbelief.

Though considerable variety existed at the level of individual inclination, overwhelming support for Jefferson's libertarian politics came from the West and South where the rate of evangelical growth was strongest. Mistrust was not less prevalent in these regions than in Connecticut, but it was directed more consistently toward the federal government and the religious elites of New England. Thus the upsurge in religious devotion around 1800 occurred on both sides of the political divide, with partisan activities contributing to animosity, religion often flowing along partisan lines, and evangelicalism growing fastest where government regulation was weakest.

New enthusiasm for religion reversed the nation's trend toward secularity. As historian Jon Butler showed, relatively few Americans participated in organized religion during the revolutionary era, many church buildings deteriorated, and patriotic idealism commanded greater interest than calls to Christ. America's most prominent citizens continued to observe Christianity's public rites, as historian David Holmes showed, but their devotions were mild and tended to avoid firm endorsement of Christianity's miraculous claims.[9]

Prior to the revivals that sprang up around the time of Jefferson's election, indifference toward religion, if not outright skepticism, was the norm at most American colleges. Reports of "infidelity" at William and Mary, lack of "fear of God" at Dartmouth, and similar concerns at Princeton reveal how the critique of monarchical authority in politics had spread to religion. Dartmouth's class of 1799 included only one professing Christian, the chapel at Yale counted only two full members, and prayer meetings at Princeton attracted only three or four students. As William Ellery Channing remembered from his years as a student at Harvard from 1794 to 1798, "The tendency of all classes was to skepticism." Yale alumnus Lyman Beecher recalled that "[t]he college church was almost extinct" in the mid-1790s.[10]

Skepticism of religious authority in the 1790s was not confined to educated young men. An Englishman traveling the Carolinas at the end of the century observed that "[r]eligion is at a very low ebb" throughout the region. And in 1797, Reverend Joseph Caldwell of North Carolina was sorry to say that in his state, where he taught mathematics at the state university, "every one believes that the first step he ought to take to rise into respectability is to disavow, as often and as publicly as he can, all regard for the leading doctrines of the scriptures." The Methodist advocate Devereux Jarratt declared "the prospect" of religion in Virginia in 1796 to be "gloomy and truly suspicious and discouraging." A British traveler in rural Virginia that year echoed that complaint, writing that "the people have scarcely any sense of religion, and in the country parts the churches are all falling into decay"; he had "scarcely observed one that was not in ruinous condition, with the windows broken, and doors dropping off the hinges, and lying open to the pigs and cattle wandering about the woods." The Presbyterian Synod of Virginia barely mustered a quorum in 1797, and in a pastoral letter of 1798, the Presbyterian General Assembly meeting in Philadelphia declared itself "filled with concern and awful dread" at the general disregard for biblical piety across the country.[11]

At a pivotal moment of religious and political formation in the United States, reaction against skepticism from both sides of the political divide secured a privileged place for religion in American society. Painting religious skepticism as a danger to the country, advocates for religion succeeded in muting religious skepticism by equating it with moral depravity. As the Kentucky revivalist James McGready explained, the "unrepentant" were "murderers, robbers, and distracted persons . . . spreading misery and destruction through the country."[12]

Preachers regarded people outside religious communities as immoral, living without the commitment to Christian revelation that produced virtuous behavior. Meant to shame and intimidate religious skeptics, claims for a causal link between religion and morality may have been exaggerated, simplistic, and manipulative, but they did bear out in certain situations. For blacks and women especially, participation in Christianity brought respectability and some protection against being treated as inherently degraded. For slaves, the advantages of organized Christianity were considerable, since biblical revelation held up a bar of divine justice against which human injustice could be described and measured. At a time when slavery was expanding inside the United States, operating as a powerful stimulant to the national economy, the policing of slaves grew harsher and opportunities for black freedom diminished. Subject to increasing suspicion and vulnerability to kidnapping, free blacks found themselves unwelcome at public events they had previously participated in, and their exercise of voting rights fell to zero. Christianity offered blacks protection and respect from whites as nothing else did.

For women, Christianity offered even greater respectability and social influence but these benefits entailed acceptance of women's lack of political rights. Previously, in the relatively tolerant, relatively secular society of the mid-1790s, Mary Wollstonecraft's *Vindication of the Rights of Women* had been widely discussed. By the end of that decade, however, arguments in support of women's rights came to seem increasingly dangerous and even repulsive, as religious moralists associated anyone who would uphold such arguments with sexual license. For evangelicals, the solution to the sufferings of women and their vulnerability to poverty was religion—not political rights. Suppressing the free thought associated with lax restraints on sexual activity, evangelicals argued that religion would enable women vulnerable to poverty to live respectably. When memoirs of the recently deceased Wollstonecraft, published by her husband William Godwin, appeared in 1798, revealing Wollstonecraft's adulterous relationships with the Swiss-born painter Henry Fuseli and the American painter Gilbert Imlay, critics linked her affirmation of women's rights to a debauched lifestyle. As the preface to the first American edition asserted, "our fair country women will feel, on perusing these memoirs, that virtuous indignation, which her perversion of talents and profligacy of sentiment must inspire, and that they will turn with horror from a detestable philosophy, which would degrade the sex to the lowest infamy."[13]

When religious growth and organization burst forward around 1800, overwhelming the trend toward skepticism of religious authority that had gained momentum in the 1790s, not only had mistrust gained ground, but the meaning of "religion" had shifted. In British colonial America, the codependence of religion and civil government was obvious. The British monarchy was a religious and political institution through which divine authority flowed; established Christianity was the religion authorized by the king and from which his authority drew. Even though the power of the king was constrained by the British parliament and mediated through colonial charters, American colonists felt its religious force, and that force was intrinsic to the political system they challenged in 1776 and overturned.[14]

Religion had an institutional presence in colonial America linked to monarchy and civil order. Though some colonists wanted the form of protestant Christianity upheld by the state to be different than it was, some wanted complete separation between church and state, and some considered religion a matter of individual opinion so inconsequential to public life as to allow belief in twenty gods, the religious authority of the state stood as the foil against which these desires and speculations came to expression. Whether people liked it or not, men in power imbued the state with the authority of God. That religious component of civic government was manifest during public elections and state events, when religious and civic leaders stood together and reminded people of their religious obligations to the state.

At the same time, however, civic government in eighteenth-century America was weak, and the religious institutions associated with it were often anemic, especially outside New England. The weakness of institutional religion in colonial and revolutionary America did not dampen popular interest in supernatural occurrences and occult phenomena or suppress metaphysical beliefs about the operations of nature. Though the boundaries between religion and nature were permeable, people often ascribed metaphysical forces outside the church to medicine, or the stars and planets—not to religion. Our categorization of these things under the rubric of "popular religion" or "lived religion"[15] is a later characterization based more on what "religion" has come to mean in the United States than on how people in colonial or revolutionary America understood the term. That older meaning of state religion was still very much in play in 1785, when Maryland's House of Delegates proposed a state tax to support Christian ministers, declaring "that the happiness of the people, and the good order and preservation of civil government, depend on morality, religion, and piety."[16]

Religion became more voluntary and individualistic at the turn of the nineteenth century, expanding and diversifying in a relationship of mutual benefit with the emergence of mass politics and the turn toward libertarian philosophies of civil government. As an expansive commercial economy based in real estate, cotton, and slavery gained dominance, impassioned appeals for repentance coincided with increasingly impassioned appeals for votes, with religious organizations providing law and order where government fell short. With growing detachment from civil authority, religion came to function less in its traditional role as a support for civil authority and common good and more in a compensatory role of managing problems ignored but often created or exacerbated by government policies. Religion's function as a safety net was certainly not unprecedented, nor was its traditional function as the pillar of civic rule demolished, but the libertarian ideology associated with Jefferson's election involved a new kind of symbiosis between religion and politics based on new ways of practicing both.

Religion figured significantly in the growth of partisan political debate. Men like Connecticut's Reverend Hawley upheld the connection between religion and government as essential to both and decried the rampant immorality they believed would result from separating the moral force of religion from government.[17] Supporters of Jefferson, on the other side, condemned the religion of their political opponents as a screen for tyrannical impulses and resisted the efforts of their opponents to link religion to civic responsibility. In Jefferson's camp, evangelicals who felt oppressed by state religions joined with democrats more or less indifferent to religion in a coalition challenging government authority to dictate the common good.

Inside religious groups, the meaning of religion was hotly contested as people defended beliefs and practices they considered to be "true religion" as distinct from beliefs and practices that violated their standard or fell short. Baptists condemned infant baptism, Calvinists railed against belief in universal salvation, and orthodox Presbyterians were not alone in viewing Methodists as disgraceful and possibly insane. Along with these insider debates over theology and religious practice, however, a more generic, political debate about religion moved forward focused on religion's relationship to state authority. Baptist hostility to state intervention in religion exerted a disproportionate influence in this debate, bolstered by partially similar conceptions of religion advanced by John Locke and many of his followers, that religion was a matter of opinion best left to individuals.

For Baptists, each church was "a garden enclosed" against "the open wilderness" of the world "where every beast of prey can range at pleasure."[18] Especially in the South and West, where law enforcement was lax and civil courts few and far between, tightly controlled Baptist communities provided refuge from the anarchy and violence of American life. Baptist membership soared in the first decade of the nineteenth century along with the vast expansion of US territory through the purchase of Louisiana, enthusiasm for the laissez-faire economic policy, and the emergence of a partisan political movement opposing federal government authority.

Methodist organizations grew at an even greater pace than Baptist churches after 1800, and their contribution to the new relationship between religion and politics was considerable. With their emphasis on religious experience and effective methods for stimulating it, Methodists played a major role in pushing religion toward more voluntary, emotional, and individualistic expression, which complemented the libertarian policies of Jeffersonian democracy. But in 1800, countervailing aspects of Methodist organization, not least its recent origins in the monarchical Church of England, occluded recognition of Methodism's potent synchronicity with Jeffersonian democracy. By contrast, Baptists were directly involved in political debates about religion, siding consistently with Jefferson in opposition to federal authority and publicly proclaiming their reasons for doing so.

While Baptists rejected the state's meddling in religion, weak federal government and freedom from government intervention enabled Baptist churches to operate almost like independent states on their own. Carefully guarding the boundary separating the church from profane society, Baptists excluded nonmembers from participation in rituals and disciplined members aggressively. Once a month, churches met for disciplinary hearings, moderated by the minister and conducted according to procedures approved by the church, which all church members were required to attend. Attendees were required to sit in their seats without interrupting or whispering until given leave to speak or retire. Decisions regarding membership and discipline required a two-thirds majority vote of male church members, and punishments were meted out of a wide range of offenses, from intoxication, gambling, swearing, gossip, and hypocrisy to spousal abuse, mistreatment of slaves, dishonesty in business, misrepresentation of land claims, and property destruction. Outside New England, where Baptists were a religious minority and courts of civil law were well established and maintained, Baptists churches might be the only social institutions, beyond families, with any impact on people's lives. Baptist discipline came to define civilized behavior where other forms of government were lacking and where other forms of church governance were less developed.[19]

Baptist demands for the right to worship without impediment enabled the success of Jeffersonian politics. In Virginia, harassment of Baptists by the established Anglican Church since colonial days contributed to popular support for the Virginia Statute of Religious Freedom drafted by Jefferson in 1779 and passed into law in 1786. In Massachusetts and the District of Maine, where Baptists had long been subjected to legal discrimination, Jefferson's Republican Party drew heaviest support from towns with strong Baptist churches. Despite his own materialistic philosophy, Jefferson made a practice of befriending Baptist ministers and other religious leaders whose churches had been marginalized by state religion. Jefferson drew some of his strongest support from these evangelicals, as well as from men with materialistic philosophies similar to his. As he remarked in 1800, "I have long labored to rally the Physicians & Dissenting Clergy who are generally friends of equal liberty."[20]

Baptists praised Jefferson's fiscal policies, as well as his role as a protector of religious liberty. In a July Fourth oration during Jefferson's second term, Baptist leader John Leland expressed gratitude to the president for lifting tax burdens imposed by the previous federal administration for repayment of national debt. Taking note that none of the Bible burnings or destruction of church buildings predicted by Federalists had come to pass during Jefferson's first administration, Leland thanked the president for his trust in the people and closed his sermon with "ten thousand times ten thousand more" thanks to Christ "for forgiving us all our debts, and opening the gates of heaven for all who love and obey him."[21]

As Leland's expression of gratitude suggested, Baptist engagement in politics centered on the protection of Baptist growth and liberty. While Baptist devotion to the practice of church government might have prepared men for leadership in secular politics, Baptist leaders focused instead on evangelizing people and bringing them under the governance of Baptist churches. When Baptists and other evangelicals did rise up in protest against Sunday mail delivery beginning in 1810, their failure to intervene successfully revealed the limit of their political influence.[22] Their most significant influence on politics lay in their support for religious voluntarism and the freedom of churches from state control.

As the American population soared from 3.9 to 7.2 million and four new states entered the union between 1790 and 1810, evangelicals participated enthusiastically in the inventiveness and expansion of the American society. While suspicious of threats to their authority, evangelicals channeled people's doubts about themselves and one another in a forward-looking direction; religious conversion and revivalism encouraged people to leave their mistakes behind, work hard, and redouble their commitment to the future. Evangelicals promoted the need for religion in the explosion of commercial and territorial growth, highlighting the corruption of life outside of Christ and proffering grand images of personal destiny and world renewal that galvanized enthusiasm for American expansion.

An effective coalition of pietists and rationalists enabled Jefferson's election and two-term presidency, abetting the shift toward libertarian policies in government as well as the growth of evangelical religion, especially in its Baptist and Methodist forms. The shift toward libertarian government and the growth of evangelical religion are both well known.[23] But the codependence of libertarian politics and evangelical religion in the formative era of American politics and religion has not received the attention it deserves.

Historians emphasize the importance of increasing investment in laissez-faire policies of economic growth in Jeffersonian America and the coincident unleashing of individual ambition, growing indifference to traditional patterns of collective morality, and erosion of deference toward political elites. Historians also recognize that evangelical religions flourished during this time in response to greater political inclusiveness and resentment of educated elites. But Nathan Hatch's influential interpretation of the growth of evangelicalism in his 1989 book, *The Democratization of Christianity*, constrained discussion of the relationship between religion and politics in a way that continues to affect the way history is taught. Written during Ronald Reagan's presidency and the rise of the religious right, Hatch's book overplayed the democratic aspects of evangelical religion and turned attention away from the larger political consequences of evangelical alignment with libertarian politics. Misrepresenting evangelicalism as antiauthoritarian and disregarding the connection between the growth of evangelicalism and the growth of slavery and invasion of Indian lands, Hatch did as much to mask the developing relationship between religion and politics as to reveal it.[24]

Though important corrections to Hatch's representation of religious authority in early nineteenth-century evangelicalism have since emerged,[25] his work continues to set the framework for discussion of religion and politics in this period.[26] Echoing the rhetoric of Baptists and Baptist spin-off groups in the early nineteenth century, Hatch's interpretation of evangelicalism as the liberation of Christianity from control by educated elites fails to pierce the evangelical cloaking, and exploitation, of doubt. Evangelical religion surged in the context of bitter partisan conflict, the growth of libertarian policies with respect to slavery and Indian rights, and profound ambivalence toward authority. Only by appreciating these dynamics—and the blinding mistrust of secular politics that evangelicals helped to fuel—can we make headway in understanding religion's powerful relation to American politics.

The mutually beneficial relationship established between evangelicalism and libertarian politics was not premeditated or entirely deliberate, but people did sense that they were living in the midst of contending forces of chaos and social control, that unsavory deals were being made all around them, and that the need for religious discipline coincided with abandonment of other restraints. In dynamic coalescence, commitment to religion's transcendence became more adamant as evangelical participation in libertarian politics became more reliable. As an insistent marker of religion's transcendence, supernatural experiences and claims proliferated, obscuring religion's relation to politics.

At the turn of the nineteenth century, aggressive defenders of religion blocked the critical inquiry into religion and politics that had developed in the 1790s. In that decade, rejection of monarchy as a religiopolitical institution stimulated criticism of the royalist authority of religion, challenging conceptions of God as a divine king and practices of humiliation and self-abnegation associated with belief in his absolute sovereignty. Bold inquiry into religion engaged a wide spectrum of people and made serious intellectual debate about the relation between religion and political power popular, exciting, and accessible. However, the forces of fear and authoritarianism roused to squelch this intellectual movement were overwhelming and their effects long lasting. With the increasing respectability of evangelicals, their growing cultural authority, and their success in managing religious doubt, critical inquiry into the mutually dependent relationship between libertarian politics and American evangelicalism was stifled.

Naive conceptions of reason also played a role in obstructing analysis of the politics of religion and in beating back the strong trend toward secularity that had developed in America in the course of the eighteenth century. The idealistic belief that reason was grounded in nature proved inadequate as a political philosophy, and anticipation that natural reason would liberate mankind from political and religious tyranny proved overly optimistic. In a world where violence, cheating, and unrest were common, appeals to the authority of the Bible and punishments for sin proved more effective means of discipline than appeals to the rational nature of mankind. In a young and divided nation beset by rising currents of mistrust that eroded many forms of social interaction, religious denominations grew apace with partisan political organizations, as organs of governance supplementary to a weak state.

Religion came to designate a diffuse realm, protected by the state, where people built communities, conceived relationships with God, and lamented the corruption of the state and of profane, mistrustful society. Religion's political aspect as a form of collective decision-making—much like politics in its focus on governance, election, and opinion—was no longer directly subject to the state and had to be respected, supplicated, or manipulated. By demonizing religious skepticism and stoking fears that sinister forces threatening religion were always poised for attack on innocent Americans, evangelicals kept dispassionate analysis of the coextensive terrain between religion and politics off limits.

By developing techniques for managing doubt, evangelicals turned that eroding force to their advantage. Subverting religious doubt, evangelicals made admission of it a step in conversion that could be revisited to rekindle belief whenever trust in God faltered. The ritual practice of managing and manipulating doubt spilled into larger questions about American identity and the direction of American government, providing a strategy for managing concerns about America and linking idealism about America to evangelical religion. With doubt the cultural sickness that religion nursed, religion thrived as a way to interpret, relieve, and feed it.

CHAPTER ONE

Faith in Reason and the
Problem of Skepticism

Jailed in Paris in 1793 for criticizing the terrorist regime controlling the French Revolution, Thomas Paine worked on a book to expose terrorist regimes in the Bible. Published in two parts in 1794 and 1795, *The Age of Reason* intended to unmask the Bible as "a history of wickedness that has served to corrupt and brutalize mankind." Although he acknowledged that the Old Testament contained some "elevated sentiment reverentially expressed of the power and benignity of the Almighty," Paine argued that on the whole, "the obscene stories, the voluptuous debaucheries, the cruel and torturous executions, the unrelenting vindictiveness, with which more than half the Bible is filled," were more characteristic of "the word of a demon than the Word of God." As for the New Testament, he maintained that the gospels were unreliable hearsay and that the miracles ascribed to Jesus ought not to be taken seriously. With "every mark of fraud and imposition stamped on the face of it," Paine insisted, accounts of the birth and resurrection of Jesus had been fabricated by "Christian Mythologists." Doctrines of damnation and salvation, which had proved so lucrative to the Catholic Church over the centuries, had been contrived by priests who manipulated fear in the service of political tyrants.[1]

By demolishing the authority of biblical revelation, Paine hoped to expose God's "TRUE REVELATION," the rational order of nature. Although clouded over by ignorance, superstition, and predatory priests, God's true revelation could be seen in the material world: "THE WORD OF GOD IS THE CREATION WE BEHOLD," Paine proclaimed, "and it is in *this word*, which no human invention can counterfeit or alter, that God speaketh universally to man." Thus Paine the true believer exposed tyrants who preyed on people's fears while pretending to be their saintly defenders. With Catholicism his first target but not stopping there, Paine sought to expose the whole "Christian system of faith" as a form of Jacobinism, calling Christianity "a species of Atheism—a sort of religious denial of God" that "professes to believe in a man rather than in God." Interpreting efforts to divinize Jesus as a stratagem priests used to dominate other men, Paine called people to rely on their own reason instead.[2]

Paine's *Age of Reason* fused two meanings of reason—objective order and skeptical criticism—into one politically charged package.[3] He was not alone in holding these competing and potentially conflicting notions of reason together, or in directing them against established religious and political authority; Thomas Jefferson and other celebrants of reason thought along similar lines. But Paine's skeptical criticism of biblical authority became popular among working people, igniting a firestorm of fear and controversy at all levels of society. This firestorm resulted in effective efforts to block political skepticism from undermining respect for biblical authority.

The catalyst of a significant shift in public opinion at a moment of formative development in American politics and religion, reaction against Paine's *Age of Reason* contributed to new understanding of the relationship between religion and politics. Against Paine's effort to link the two by attacking unwarranted authority in both, evangelicals elevated religion above politics and censored religious skepticism. Combined with permissive attitudes toward skepticism typical of partisan political attacks, the squelching of religious skepticism forged a new kind of cultural consensus about the difference between religion and politics.

Paine's different usages of the term reason expedited this process and facilitated attacks against him. At one level, he celebrated reason as the organizing principle of nature embedded by the Creator in man and in the material world. Manifest in nature, Paine believed, reason was an objective expression of the moral order and integrity of the universe. This sense of reason as natural order, plainly evident for everyone to see, lay behind Paine's objection to mysticism and hearsay in the Bible, and his demand that "A thing which everybody is required to believe requires that the proof and evidence of it should be equal to all, and universal."[4]

At another level, Paine understood reason as an activity of mind, building on and making use of things. Paine's own flair for inventing things—most notably, an iron bridge to expedite commerce and travel—animated his sense of reason as an activity that expanded upon the rational order of nature for human benefit.[5] This constructive activity of reason was complemented by its deconstructive work of discerning faulty constructions, exploring fallibility and corruption in government, and unmasking tyranny and fraud, which Paine regarded as violations of the moral integrity of material things and the natural order of reason. In his political and religious writings, Paine's bold attempts at unmasking tyranny and fraud generated most attention. As John Adams commented with regard to one of Paine's earlier writings, he "has a better hand at pulling down than building."[6]

Paine's *Age of Reason* tied these meanings of reason together in a political attack on Christianity and biblical revelation. Willingness to accept the fabulous stories in the Bible "on hearsay" exemplified the disregard for the natural order reason that weakened human character and allowed dictators to seize power. The man who went along with such "moral mischief," Paine asserted, "prostituted the chastity of his mind"—and with far-reaching consequences; once a man professed to believe "things he does not believe he has prepared himself for the commission of every other crime." Paine looked forward to the day when people recovered their ability to activate natural reason—"The most formidable weapon against errors of every kind." Once people were really free to wield that weapon, the religious supports propping up tyranny would be exposed and a "revolution in the system of government would be followed by a revolution in the system of religion."[7]

Paine's denunciation of biblical revelation fell on fertile soil. American printers turned out tens of thousands of copies of *The Age of Reason* in eighteen editions, and the inexpensive pamphlet—twenty cents for the second American edition, about the cost of a pound of pork, a pound of raisins, or a pound of tallow[8]—circulated widely. As Lyman Beecher recalled New England in the 1790s, "That was the day of the infidelity of the Tom Paine school." Even boys "that dressed flax in the barn," Beecher recalled, "read Tom Paine and believed him."[9] Kentucky Presbyterian Robert Stuart remembered how Paine's book was "extensively circulated, and his principles imbibed by the youth particularly, with avidity; so that Infidelity, with all its concomitant evils, like a mighty tide, was desolating the land."[10]

Though hardly the first to doubt biblical revelation, Paine popularized and politicized it, making skepticism of biblical revelation a natural extension of challenging oppressive taxes and other forms of tyranny, as well as a means of striking back at wealthy elites and institutional authorities who benefited from people's fear and submission. The connection Paine drew between democratic republicanism and freedom from Christianity brought new cadence to the popular drumbeat against political authority in the 1790s, and made assault on biblical revelation popular among many Americans inclined toward democracy. While various forms and degrees of religious skepticism already existed in America—including doubts about the divinity of Jesus and the miracles described in the Bible—Paine made those doubts politically volatile.

Paine's political critique of religion also sharpened the division in public opinion over the meaning of democracy. Those who defined democracy as the antithesis of political order decried Paine's *Age of Reason* as evidence of the destruction of everything sacred that ensued when rabble-rousers attempted to overthrow the legitimate authority of government. On the other hand, many of those who defined democracy as the people's direct control of government through their exercise of natural reason took delight in reading *The Age of Reason* or in hearing excerpts read aloud in taverns or around trees where the pamphlet was posted. Eager to throw off all forms of human oppression, proponents of reason as the basis of human equality embraced Paine's argument that religion should not be taken on authority any more than politics.[11]

Paine's *Age of Reason* may have enjoyed greatest popularity in Kentucky and the Mississippi Valley. When General Anthony Wayne's soldiers defeated Indians along the Miami River in the summer of 1794 and treaties that fall opened Kentucky's bloody ground to a dramatic increase in the flow of people passing through Lexington, Paine's *Age of Reason* came with them. Bibles were still relatively rare and expensive in the 1790s, although they would not be so for long, and Paine's "cheap pamphlet," complained a nineteenth-century historian, "was used instead of the Bible" and could be found virtually everywhere east of the Mississippi, "in the cabin of the farmer, on the bench of the tailor, in the shops of the smith and the carpenter, on the table of the lawyer, and at the desk of the physician."[12]

In Kentucky, where Baptists had established a significant presence in the 1780s, with forty-two churches by 1790, their proportional representation in the state eroded dramatically over the next decade, from one in twenty-three Kentuckians to one in forty-three in 1800. In 1795, leaders of Kentucky's Baptist Association referred to the "common calamity" of Christianity's decline and tried to sustain morale by enumerating "the duties incumbent on us in this lamentable time." By 1800, many of Kentucky's leading citizens were skeptically inclined; deism prevailed among lawyers and politicians, and the state's first governor, James Garrard, originally a Baptist preacher, became a Unitarian.[13]

Chafing at taxes imposed by the federal government and at various federal restrictions, including navigation rights on the Mississippi and occupation of Indian lands, Americans in the West invoked Paine as an opponent of overweening federal control. In 1796, the *Kentucky Herald* published excerpts of a letter "from the celebrated Thomas Paine" protesting the growing gap between the democratic sentiments of the American people and the repressive character of their federal government. The *Herald* agreed with Paine's observation that "[t]he American character is so much sunk in Europe, that it is necessary to distinguish between the government and the country."[14]

Then the tide began to turn. Denunciations of Paine's *Age of Reason* escalated on both sides of the political divide over democracy, and perceptions about Paine took on a life of their own, sometimes in conflict with what he actually wrote. Though Paine extolled the wisdom of God and the moral virtue of reason, opponents of democracy condemned *The Age of Reason* as atheistic and immoral. Forced to defend themselves against charges attached to Paine, advocates of democracy distanced themselves from him and his manifesto on religion. Denounced as a symptom of the extremist folly of the French Revolution, *The Age of Reason* came to represent a dangerous assault on religion that Americans on both sides of the partisan political conflict over democracy opposed.

Through its effect on both politics and religion, rejection of Paine's *Age of Reason* contributed to a new kind of symbiosis between the two. Longstanding disdain for Paine as a low-class, rotten revolutionary—"culled from [the] garbage," one newspaper wrote[15]—acquired new force as a result of his assault on the Bible, adding to the weight of political opinion against the democratic reforms Paine advocated, not least of which was the abolition of slavery. At the same time, reaction against Paine helped to secure religion's privileged place in American society, making respect for the authority of biblical revelation a greater and more predominating force in American society and contributing to a general consensus that religious skepticism should be treated as a species of immorality. Paine came to be perceived as the embodiment of fears that the United States might succumb to the violence of the French Revolution, that unconditional faith in reason led to atheism, and that all vestiges of social order would crumble if religious skepticism spread further among ordinary people.

The divorce between reason and skepticism, precipitated in the reaction against Thomas Paine, shaped the cultural matrix in which American political and religious organizations developed. To fully appreciate the effects of this divorce on American political and religious institutions, the marriage Paine represented between faith in reason and willingness to doubt and dismantle institutions of political and religious authority requires further discussion.

Though never a stable partnership, the wedding of belief that human reason was objectively grounded in the natural order of things with zeal for exposing the tyrannies that prevented men from exercising natural reason was a powerful combination. Thomas Paine was not alone in joining the two; his friend Thomas Jefferson did so, along with many others caught up in revolutionary movements in the Atlantic world. Paine merits particular attention because of the popularity of his writings and their political and religious effect in the early republic. Paine's opinions, as well as the history of their reception in the United States, provide a context for understanding a variety of problems in the early republic, including Jefferson's reputation for duplicity and his failures as president.

Paine's own faith in reason was partly rooted in his Quaker background. Reverberations of Quaker belief in human equality abound in Paine's writings, as do echoes of Quaker rejection of ecclesiastical hierarchy and Quaker lore about persecution by Catholics during the English Reformation. Born in 1737 to a Quaker father and an Anglican mother in Norfolk, England, Paine encountered Quaker practice as a child, and this early religious influence fed his belief in the importance of "doing justice, loving mercy, and endeavoring to making our fellow creatures happy." While Paine's faith in reason led him to reject the divinity of Christ that Quakers embraced, the Quaker practice of relying on the inner light of Christ initiated Paine's belief in the light of reason, epitomized in his famous assertion: "My own mind is my own church."[16] If rich men considered devotion to reason to be something only they could afford, Paine celebrated nature's gift in every man. He thought no institution, political or religious, should interfere with the free expression of reason's universal light.

Angry resentment of British government colored Paine's democratic faith. Forced to leave school at thirteen to apprentice with his father in the manufacture of whalebone corsets, a job demanding physical strength as well as ease with women, both of which he may have lacked, Paine found intermittent work as a tax collector in the 1760s and early 1770s. That job brought him into repeated contact with the misery caused by British taxes and prompted him to speak out against the system of government taxation that enforced poverty. When his marriage to the daughter of a prominent shop owner failed along with his financial and political endeavors, Paine escaped to America in 1774 at the age of thirty-seven, with personal resentment of British life in tow, along with faith in reason, desire for a new world, and an extraordinary talent for straightforward, passionate prose. With the support of Benjamin Franklin and Benjamin Rush in Philadelphia, Paine launched a career as a pamphleteer that galvanized popular enthusiasm for American independence and hatred of British monarchy.[17]

Paine's first American pamphlet, *Common Sense*, published in Philadelphia in January 1776, had twenty-six printings in 1776. Paine's claim that over one hundred thousand copies sold that year may have been an exaggeration, but nothing was more widely read, circulated, or heard that year except the Declaration of Independence, issued six months later. *Common Sense* escalated desire for revolution with its rousing claims that "[t]he cause of America is in a great measure the cause of all mankind" and "[t]he sun never shined on a cause of greater worth."[18] When people speculated that John Adams might be the author of the pamphlet's anonymous first edition, Adams confessed to his wife that "I could never have written any Thing in so manly and striking a style." Adams "flattered" himself, though, that he would have done much better as an "Architect" of government than "the Writer" of *Common Sense*. Even before he knew it was Paine, Adams thought the authors had "very inadequate Ideas of what is proper and necessary to be done, in order to form Constitutions for single colonies, as well as a great Model of Union for the whole."[19]

Reaction to the pamphlet was divided in the Continental Congress, especially when Paine's authorship was discovered; many in the Congress disdained Paine as low class and politically dangerous. Nevertheless, the passionate reasoning of *Common Sense* had a powerful effect on public opinion, which broke the stalled political debate in the Congress over whether to declare independence. George Washington credited the pamphlet with "working a powerful change there in the Minds of many Men."[20] Writing as this change was taking shape, Washington declared, "the sound doctrine and unanswerable reasoning contained in the pamphlet *Common Sense*," combined with the "flaming arguments" of British violence on American ports, "will not leave members [of Congress] at a loss to decide upon the propriety of separation."[21]

With its stirring use of the terms "America" and "Americans," *Common Sense* evoked a collective sense of political identity that united American patriots across class and region. In that pamphlet and in his *American Crisis*, which Washington ordered read aloud to soldiers in the Continental Army before they crossed the Delaware River on Christmas eve in 1777, Paine's muscular, vernacular language roused fervor for American independence. No one did more to evoke a sense of national identity or to popularize the idea of civil government without monarchy.[22]

Common Sense presented a critique of the British monarchy and its claims over people based on the principle that God was the only sovereign to whom people owed their lives and allegiance. "For all men being originally equals," Paine declared, "no *one* by *birth* could have a right to set up his own family in perpetual preference to all others for ever." Compounding that violation of basic human equality, "Men who look upon themselves born to reign, and others to obey, soon grow insolent," Paine argued, "and the world they act in differs so materially from the world at large, that they have but little opportunity of knowing its true interests." Enumerating the heinous acts committed by George III and his minions against British subjects in America, Paine argued that the weight of these misdeeds compelled Americans to free themselves from vassalage at once. The law of nature by which God created men equal had been egregiously violated by the British monarchy's vicious assaults on individual dignity and "degradation and lessening of ourselves," Paine argued. Declaring independence was the only course of moral action left.[23]

With the evils of Catholicism taken for granted, *Common Sense* emphasized the analogous relationship between monarchy and the religious tyranny of the Rome: "monarchy in every instance," Paine argued, "is the Popery of government." The Catholic Church had long been the great obstacle to human happiness, Paine believed, and protestant denunciation of Catholic authority played a crucial role in the liberation of natural reason. Not by accident did rebellion against the Catholic Church coincide with opportunities to build a new world apart from Europe. "The reformation was preceded by the discovery of America," Paine explained, "as if the Almighty graciously meant to open a sanctuary to the persecuted in future years, when home should afford neither friendship nor safety." The geographical placement of America was also providential: "Even the distance at which the Almighty hath placed England and America, is a strong and natural proof," he wrote, "that the authority of the one, over the other, was never the design of Heaven."[24]

Like his appeal to multiple meanings of "reason" two decades later in *The Age of Reason*, Paine joined two different meanings of "common sense" in one potent political message. Taking common sense in its most familiar form to mean that which everyone could see and agree on, Paine interlaced it with a second understanding of common sense as the ability to penetrate deception. With no indication, and perhaps no awareness, of their incompatibility, Paine joined an essentially conservative notion of common sense that could be used to support social convention and collective prejudices to a more radical notion—similar to the *bon sens* of methodic doubt associated with René

Descartes, Pierre Bayle, and David Hume—that challenged social convention and prejudice. In an exciting deployment of the both meanings of the term at once, Paine yoked the more conservative claim that support for republican government was a matter of popular consensus to a more radical iconoclasm driven by skeptical criticism of convention and authority.[25]

With the success of the American Revolution appearing to support his loaded view of common sense, Paine participated in debates about the Pennsylvania Constitution and the US Constitution, then returned to England in 1787 filled with admiration for American independence, and eager to promote egalitarian social policies in his native land. His next major work, *The Rights of Man*, published in 1791, recast the ideas of *Common Sense* for a British audience and contributed to a wave of popular enthusiasm for British political reform. After that publication, appeals to "the rights of man" became a staple of democratic expression throughout the Atlantic world.[26] In the United States, Fourth of July celebrants often drank to "the rights of man," and no one except the president of the United States was toasted more often between 1791 and 1795 than Thomas Paine.[27]

A frequent visitor to France after 1787, Paine was an early supporter of the French Revolution and was elected to the French National Convention in 1792. After the coup d'état by the Jacobin Club, so called for their meeting place in a confiscated Dominican convent on the Rue St. Jacques, Paine was imprisoned for condemning the execution of Louis XVI and criticizing the Jacobin purge of moderate revolutionaries. He published *The Age of Reason* to salvage devotion to the rational order of nature that moderate revolutionaries espoused from the more thoroughgoing destructiveness into which the French Revolution descended. "The people of France were running headlong into *Atheism*," Paine later explained, and he wrote *Age of Reason* "to stop them in that career."[28]

The downward trajectory of Paine's reputation in the United States was bound up with American recoil against the Revolution in France. The egalitarianism of Paine's political philosophy lost support as detractors equated his skepticism of biblical revelation with Jacobin violence and atheism. At a crucial moment of political and religious formation in the early republic, the backlash against Paine contributed to efforts already underway to strengthen religion in the early republic and give it a new kind of autonomy in relation to politics that, like religion, was becoming more responsive to popular opinion, but also more conservative with respect to the rights of women and blacks.[29]

As religious and political institutions developed, skepticism about biblical authority and its antidemocratic effects became a cultural no-man's land. In a circular process of cause and effect, attacks on Paine expedited that process. The author of *Common Sense* may have lost touch with popular opinion in America, but that was partly because political and religious activists were using his writings and reputation to reshape popular opinion. A variety of different American writers made Paine's attack on religion an opportunity to draw a line across which reason dared not go. Paine's downfall from patriotic hero to pariah was an accelerating vehicle of popular opinion that helped ostracize religious skepticism and guard the authority of biblical revelation against political criticism.

The rise and fall of Paine's reputation marked a trajectory of popular opinion that other proponents of reason such as Thomas Jefferson and the brilliant freethinker Aaron Burr had to negotiate. The shadow cast by the fall of Thomas Paine fell on Jefferson, Burr, and others associated with them, limiting the confidence in reason that had brightened the revolutionary era to a space restricted by adherence to biblical revelation. A few enthusiastic proponents of the rational order of nature joined deist groups like the Theophilanthropists associated with Paine, but outright skepticism of biblical revelation doomed organizations that challenged the growing national worship of biblical authority. The force of the reaction against Paine strengthened the link between reason and revelation and drove a wedge between reason and skepticism, making faith in biblical authority the basis of common sense reasoning and casting suspicion on any form of rational inquiry that did not affirm biblical authority and the institutions supporting it.

An example of the politics involved in defeating religious skepticism, Connecticut's North Haven pastor Benjamin Trumbull prepared a series of lectures aimed at redirecting democratic impulses among ordinary people toward willing submission to religious authority. Claiming massive evidence in support of biblical revelation, Trumbull outlined the dangers of infidelity with respect to both individual morality and social order. In response to demand from ministers, the Adams administration supported publication of Trumbull's lectures in 1799 through an act of Congress. Aiming to stop "The uncommon growth of infidelity and licentiousness" and "the increase and spread of books, fraught with misrepresentation, bitterness, and blasphemy against the eternal and almighty SAVIOUR, and his holy religion," Trumbull was particularly concerned that religious skepticism had made its way to "the common people," who of course were ignorant of the decisive arguments against religious skepticism familiar to the educated class. Endeavoring to reach a broad audience, Trumbull "attempted to make the language" of his lectures "familiar, and the arguments clear and striking, that they might be understood and felt, even by persons of an ordinary capacity." Trying to locate the vernacular where Thomas Paine thrived, Trumbull bowed stiffly in the direction of popular opinion. "I have suffered myself to be more diffuse than is necessary for the learned," he pontificated, "to enliven the language" so that neither language nor argument would be "dull and unentertaining."[30]

Efforts by religious leaders to halt the spread of skepticism not only reflected the politics of class but also the increasingly partisan political organization of American public life. Federalists—as supporters of the federal government and its moral authority came to be called—blamed the rise in popular skepticism toward revealed religion on Jefferson and his followers and endeavored to tie Jefferson's political philosophy to Paine's attack on biblical revelation. Jeffersonians defended against that attack by distancing themselves from Paine and asserting their commitment to Christian morality. Meanwhile, Paine tried to redirect criticism of his religious view back to the politics: "all this war whoop of the pulpit has some concealed object," Paine asserted in 1802. "Religion is not the cause" of the animosity unleashed against his attack on the Bible, Paine insisted, "but is the stalking horse" for "the leaders of the Federalists" to "conceal themselves behind."[31]

Jefferson's opponents were not the only ones attacking Paine's religious skepticism; one of Jefferson's most prominent defenders in New England, the popular revolutionary leader hero Samuel Adams, strove to divide Paine's virtuous writings from his dreadful excursion into criticism of biblical authority. In 1776, Adams recalled, Paine's pamphlets in support of the American Revolution had inspired many patriots; there was no champion of political independence more influential. "Your *Common Sense*, and your *Crisis*," Adams recalled in an open letter to Paine, "unquestionably awakened the public mind, and led the people loudly to call for a Declaration of our national Independence." In those halcyon days, Adams remembered, he thought Paine would always be remembered as a hero—"I therefore esteemed you as a warm friend to the liberty, and lasting welfare of the human race." But Paine's recent treatment of Christianity caused Adams to change his mind: "when I heard, that you had turned your mind to a defense of Infidelity, I felt myself much astonished, and more grieved." Adams assured Paine that while some may have followed him into infidelity, the good people of New England "are fast returning to their first love." In that region if not across the whole country, loyalty to the Christian religion was stronger and more enduring than any infatuation with skepticism. "Do you think that *your pen*," Adams demanded caustically, "can unchristianize the mass of our citizens?"[32]

Citing rumors of a new edition of Paine's *Age of Reason*, Adams berated Paine for the political damage his polemic against Christianity had caused Thomas Jefferson: "Our friend, the present President of the United States, has been calumniated for his liberal sentiments, by men who have attributed that liberality to a latent design to promote the cause of infidelity." Adams interpreted Paine's attack on biblical revelation as an attack on the social harmony he hoped Americans were beginning to enjoy after the stresses of war. "Will you excite among them, the spirit of angry controversy," Adams asked angrily, "at a time, when they are hastening to unity and peace?" Concerned that skepticism toward authority had spread from politics to religion, Adams asserted that religion and liberty were not opponents, as Paine would suggest, but rather twin pillars of the social order jeopardized by the divisiveness of Paine's skepticism. "Neither Religion, nor Liberty," Adams asserted, "can long subsist in the tumult of altercation, and amidst the noise and violence of Faction" that Paine wanted to stir up.[33]

Baptists stepped vigorously into the furor over Paine, with some Baptist leaders perceiving that the only way to avoid Paine's critique was by situating religion in a realm entirely removed from politics. One of the most influential Baptists, John Leland, thought that Paine's imputation of tyranny to religion "held good, against every system of church government," except those based on the autonomy and unique privileges of biblical revelation. With regard to Paine's argument that religion and politics were coextensive, with irrationality in one the counterpart to tyranny in the other, Leland acknowledged the challenge that Paine posed for any group that did not insist on complete separation of church and state. "Long have I waited; but in vain," Leland wrote, "To see somebody handle Paine." Admitting the truth of Paine's argument that religion and politics were often coextensive, Leland wanted to sequester religion in a safe zone outside the political realm. Only then would Christians find "an argumentative prison / Which should confine the Age of Reason / With bar, and bolt, so strong and stout, / That it should ne'er again break out."[34]

Leland played an important role in Paine's defeat. Like Paine, Leland respected working people and addressed them vigorously, without condescension. Like Paine, he embraced the American Revolution as a turning point in world history, and like Paine, he believed that liberty assisted moral virtue. Paine himself would have agreed with Leland's assessment of the "American revolution, constitution, and new government, as things designed by divine Providence to open the way for the emancipation of the true church." For

Leland, of course, America promised to emancipate the true religion of biblical revelation "from anti-Christian darkness and tyranny," whereas for Paine, reason would liberate humanity from the Bible's darkness and tyranny.[35]

Facing attacks from evangelical supporters of Jefferson, as well as from Federalists who sought to preserve the traditional linkage between religion and government, Paine continued to defend his faith in reason. Amidst the din of partisan rancor and mistrust, Paine's idealism about natural reason seemed increasingly naive and even pathetic. Applauding devotion to the universal light of reason as the highest form of religion, Paine sung paeans to the God whose implantation of reason in nature and humanity was evident for all to see. Perhaps in response to the diminishing idealism about human reason occurring all around him, Paine's faith in the rational order of nature became more overtly and insistently religious.

While in France, Paine joined the Society of Theophilanthropy, a new religion created by members of the republican Directory that governed France between 1795 and 1799. Presenting Theophilanthropy as an alternative to both Jacobin atheism and the Catholic Church, society members conducted religious services in Paris and outlying cities in buildings formerly owned by the Church, singing hymns to the God of nature and proclaiming God's existence, the soul's immortality, nature's wonders, and the golden rule.[36] Similar societies sprung up in New York and Philadelphia. While Napoleon banned the society in France after he assumed power in 1799, the small American societies received a temporary boost after Jefferson's inauguration in 1801. But the low state of Paine's reputation made any society associated with him suspect. The evangelical revivals coinciding with Jefferson's election marginalized them even further.

Theophilanthropy derived as much from English deism as from French republicanism. Deism developed in England in the late seventeenth century through writings by John Toland, Matthew Tindal, and others critical of superstition and belief in miracles but eager to uphold belief in the divine Creator of nature and reason. Numerous defenders of biblical revelation rose up to attack deism, and it declined in England by the mid-eighteenth century as a result of the barrage of religious criticism. Primarily through the influence of Thomas Paine, deism was reinvigorated in America and became popular among laboring people as a corollary of revolutionary ideology and democratic politics.[37]

The New York Deistical Society, formed in 1795, drew its members from the New York Tammany Society, the political club founded in 1789 to advance democratic republicanism. Tammany clubs, named after the legendary Lenape leader Tamanend, the Indian friend of early colonists in Pennsylvania, met in "wigwams" in Philadelphia, Annapolis, Savannah, and other American cities during the revolutionary era. Under the leadership of Aaron Burr, the New York club developed into a powerful political machine during the late 1790s.[38]

In 1795, the New York Tammany Society faced a crisis when President Washington blamed the revolt by Pennsylvania farmers against federal taxes imposed on whiskey on "certain self-created societies," whom he accused of spreading "an ignorance or perversion of facts, suspicions, jealousies and accusation of the whole government." Members of the New York Tammany Society who did not want to be confused with the perpetrators of that so-called Whiskey Rebellion proposed a resolution in support of Washington and the federal government. That resolution was defeated, prompting its supporters to resign, leaving Tammany in the hands of democratic members who resented Washington's speech and demanded a more perfect world in which men like themselves would take charge. The blind deist Elihu Palmer lectured to the Tammany Society that year, recruiting members for the formation of an adjunct society dedicated to "the promotion of moral science and the religion of nature." Founded on the belief "[t]hat the universe proclaims the existence of one supreme Deity, worthy the adoration of intelligent beings," Palmer's New York Deistical Society adopted an evangelical mission, requiring "[e]very member . . . to promote the cause of nature and moral truth, in opposition to all schemes of superstition and fanaticism, claiming divine origin."[39]

Bolstered by the upsurge in partisan activity around Jefferson's election, Palmer established a newspaper, the *Temple of Reason*, and hired the political radical and former Irish priest Dennis Driscol to serve as editor. Published for four months in New York from November 1800 through February of the following year, the paper advertised Palmer's Sunday evening lectures and printed writings by Paine and other deists, including Paine's lecture to Theophilanthropists in Paris, which opened with the claim that "RELIGION has two enemies, Fanaticism and Infidelity, or that which is called Atheism. The first requires to be combated by reason and morality, the second by natural philosophy."[40]

Support fell away after a pamphlet written by the antidemocratic John Wood linked the society to the notorious Illuminati of Bavaria. Wood's pamphlet also accused New York Governor Dewitt Clinton and members his family of being affiliated with the Deistical Society. The Federalist press picked up on the allegation and sharpened their attacks on Clinton by linking him to Paine and Palmer. "This Society of Deists," claimed the *Trenton Federalist*, "formed in New-York for the purpose of undermining the Christian Religion, is composed of the Democratic Party, especially the Clintonians—Its members correspond with Tom Paine and Mr. Jefferson—They swear an oath of secrecy when admitted to the Society, and also of enmity to Christianity."[41]

When subscriptions to the *Temple of Reason* declined in New York, Driscol relocated to Philadelphia in 1801, where a sister society of Theophilanthropists had formed. From Philadelphia, Driscoll attacked John Wood as "a wooden-headed bigoted Presbyterian, calculating from the meridian of Scotland" who apparently believed, "that nothing more is necessary to making people universally hated than to call out, *infidel* and *atheist*." With this despicable tactic, Wood attempted to demean "the respectable family of Clinton" for their support of "a religious society of theists in New-York, whose object is to promote the cause of moral science and general improvement, in opposition to all schemes of religious and political imposture."[42]

The *Temple of Reason* failed in Philadelphia, sputtering to an end in February 1803 with hope of its resuscitation in Baltimore, where Driscol moved, unrealized. Palmer continued his Sunday lectures in New York but they became more sporadic and appear to have ended in the summer of 1804. The *Prospect*, a new paper founded by Palmer that summer ceased publication the following spring, unable to survive because of "opposing itself constantly to the current of public opinion." Dewitt Clinton severed any association he might have had with religious skepticism, moving on to become a prominent Presbyterian and vice president of the American Bible Society.[43] As opponents of Federalism like Clinton drew increasing support from evangelicals and idealism about natural reason apart from Christianity became increasingly unpopular, support for a free-standing religion based purely on nature and reason dwindled and societies devoted to it declined.

One deistically inclined organization—Freemasonry—did maintain a strong presence after 1800 by emphasizing its compatibility with Christian belief and practice. Though Calvinists found its optimism about natural reason wrongheaded, and opponents of democracy distrusted its egalitarian elements, Freemasonry flourished in many American towns in Jeffersonian America, and membership was a sign of respectability. Membership in Masonic fraternities did not require church affiliation—prominent Jews in Charleston found Masonry a means of establishing themselves in the city's business and professional circles—but the organization had a Protestant ambiance and often drew church members, even ministers, who perceived little if any conflict between it and liberal Christianity. In many Lodges, deistical opinions about God and nature combined easily with Jeffersonian political rhetoric. As Dewitt Clinton declared at his installation as Grand Master of the Grand Lodge of New York, Masonry "inculcates the natural equality of mankind: it declares that all brethren *are upon a level*," he asserted with reference to the builder's tool symbolic of the mason's emulation of the Divine Architect, and "it admits of no rank except the priority of merit, and its only aristocracy is the nobility of virtue."[44]

A broadside printed in Portsmouth, New Hampshire, in 1801 captured the deist character of Masonic thought as well as its compatibility with biblical imagery and Christian sentiment. "E'er time's great machine was in motion, Or light had emitted a ray," the Masonic ode began, "Enwomb'd in the bowels of Chaos, All nature in embryo lay." Echoing the biblical book of Genesis, "the word of the great Architector Bid matter approach to the birth: Then his hand spread th' etherial blue curtain And moulded the solid, round earth." Freemasons were virtually predestined, much like Christian saints: "From the chaos of mankind selected, A qualified, fraternal band, By affection and honour cemented, The Masonic Order shall stand."[45]

In Massachusetts, the gregarious pastor of Salem's East Church, William Bentley, admired Thomas Paine's genius until it crossed the line into an assault on Christianity. An avid practitioner of Masonic rites, Bentley seemed equally pleased with the new decorations in his Masonic Lodge as with the delightful organs newly installed in several Boston churches. "Master & Wardens have ea[ch] a pedestal, & the Master a Canopy," he wrote describing new additions to his Lodge in December, 1800, not least of which was a fine new Bible: "The bible is large with Silver Emblems & w/ an handsome damask Cushing." At a meeting of the Marine Society that Bentley attended the next summer, he and his fellow ministers dined on turtle from Havana, prepared by one of the city's best-known Masons. "Our chief Cook was Prince Hall, an African, & a person of great influence upon his Colour in Boston, being Master of the African Lodge," Bentley noted approvingly in his diary, adding that "Masonic Negroes are evidently many grades above the common blacks of Boston."[46]

The increasingly partisan character of American life at the turn of the century worked to erode some of the acceptance Masons enjoyed. In New England, Federalist ministers suspected a nefarious link between the secret rites of Masons and the fabled Illuminati of Bavaria, freethinkers alleged to have devised plans for overthrowing Christianity and ruling the world. The New England Calvinist Jedidiah Morse targeted Reverend Bentley, whose Jeffersonian politics, rationalist theology, and devotion to Masonry he could not abide, as the agent in a sinister conspiracy rooted in Europe: "Morse, at last,"

Bentley wrote in his diary in 1798, "to create hatred rather than refute, has insinuated that I might be one of the Illuminati."[47]

In earlier decades, deistical tendencies pervaded the religious lives of many educated Americans, coexisting more or less happily with Christianity until partisan warfare politicized them and made them more difficult to defend. In the 1780s, most of the men involved in constructing government in the United States had deistical tendencies; while respectful of Christian morality and mildly observant of Christian rituals, Washington, Franklin, Adams, Jefferson, Madison, and others respected Jesus as an exemplar of moral virtue and tended toward belief in a unitary God of nature who instilled men with reason. Washington's fairly regular appearance at church, but avoidance of services where participants were expected to demonstrate their belief in the miraculous saving power of Christ was typical.[48] While deistical tendencies prevailed in many elite churches, Paine's more radical and sarcastic skepticism caught fire among less affluent and educated Americans, alarming many whose mild deism was not coupled, as Paine's was, with democracy.

In Boston and other commercial towns in eastern Massachusetts, educated men often drifted toward Unitarianism. Harvard's appointment of Henry Ware as Hollis Professor of Divinity in 1805 underscored this general trend in eastern New England, as well as Harvard's pointed departure from its Calvinist origins. In their commitment to free will, emphasis on Jesus as an example of moral virtue and their eagerness to downplay the miracles described in the Bible, religious liberals in Massachusetts staked out ground distinct from that of either democratic skeptics like Paine on one hand or spiritual descendants of Jonathan Edwards on the other who were gathering their forces in western Massachusetts and Connecticut, holding out for rigorous biblicism and Calvinist submission to the absolute sovereignty of God. Religious liberals in eastern Massachusetts might have opinions about God similar to Paine's while staunchly defending Christianity against Paine's attack at least partly on the grounds that Paine's skepticism was low class and too democratic. Jeremy Belknap, a minister of Boston's elite Federal Church otherwise known for his enthusiasm for free scientific inquiry, condemned *Age of Reason* in 1795 as a "species of vulgar infidelity, founded partly in pedantry, partly in debauchery, and partly in ill manners."[49]

Presiding over congregants with strong commercial interests and ties to British trade, many theologically liberal clergymen supported the Federalist party. There were exceptions, however, the most notable being Salem's cosmopolitan William Bentley. An avowed Unitarian and Jeffersonian, Bentley irritated Federalists who wanted to discredit his democratic sentiments by linking them to Paine. He admired Paine's talents and regretted "the preju- dices of the time" that led the Quakers of New York to refuse Paine's request to be buried in their cemetery. When Paine died in 1809, Bentley was kind: "Mr. Paine possessed all the vigor of intellect with all the power of expression." He was also astute in assessing Paine's ability to speak directly to ordinary people: "No man had greater ability in assisting the public mind whenever he favoured its inclinations. When he dared openly to insult it, it trembled, it felt, it was silent, it was shaken." Of course, Bentley thought Paine had gone too far in denying biblical revelation, calling *The Age of Reason* a "contemptible publication."[50]

Other theologically liberal clergymen agreed. Ministers willing to ques- tion miracles and the divinity of Jesus were nevertheless unwilling to sup- port Paine's democratic challenge to biblical revelation. Entering students at Unitarian-leaning Harvard received copies of the *Apology for the Bible* written by English bishop and Cambridge professor Richard Watson, which offered a point-by-point refutation of the "vulgar and illiberal sarcasm" of Paine's pamphlet. Noting that skepticism of revealed religion had previously been confined to the "great and opulent," Watson accused Paine of "endeavoring to spread its poison through all the classes of the community."[51] Those in charge at Harvard intended to enlist their young men to serve as antidotes to the widespread contagion of that democratic poison.

Precisely because of its democratic aspect and significant popular appeal, Paine's *Age of Reason* precipitated skepticism's retreat from religion in the United States. The more Federalists condemned religious skepticism as an indicator of the pernicious effect of democracy on public morality, the more Jeffersonians became cautious about expressing skepticism of the Bible. As an agent of partisan politics for many Americans, religion became increasingly invulnerable as those skeptical of supernatural intervention became branded as infidels and atheists.

While Paine's popularity in America derived from his ability to join com- mon sense realism with *bon sens* criticism of social convention, his descent into ignominy coincided with the rupture of that combination. With the vio- lence of the French Revolution held up as the prime exhibit of what French skepticism caused, the more conservative understanding of common sense as popular wisdom took over, bolstered by efforts to equate common sense with acceptance of the authority of biblical revelation.

Paine's choice of *Common Sense* as the title for his Revolutionary pamphlet of 1776 came at the recommendation of the Scottish émigré, physician, and so- cial reformer Benjamin Rush who promoted a form of common sense realism developed by Presbyterians in his homeland. In the mid-eighteenth century, Scottish Presbyterians challenged the argument advanced by the Scottish philosopher David Hume that ideas about the world were not grounded in the order of nature but instead were social conventions. In reaction to Hume's skepticism, the 1764 work by the Scottish theologian Thomas Reid, *Inquiry into the Human Mind on the Principles of Common Sense*, posited a straightforward correspondence between nature and reason enabling the mind's direct knowledge of the world. While Paine's belief in the straightforward manifestation of reason in nature was similar, his skepticism of conventional deference toward biblical authority was radically different. Reid and his followers positioned common sense in direct opposition to skepticism of miracles and other aspects of biblical revelation, arguing in circular fashion that the authority of the Bible was good evidence for the truth of what it revealed.[52]

In New Jersey, the Scotland-born Presbyterian John Witherspoon taught a variant of common sense realism while president of Princeton from 1768 to 1794. Indebted to Reid's philosophic predecessor Frances Hutcheson, Witherspoon promoted the idea that moral sentiment was at once built into human nature and entirely compatible with biblical revelation. Suspicious of Paine's antiauthoritarianism long before *The Age of Reason* denounced this connection, Witherspoon taught many future lawyers, politicians, and religious leaders that adherence to protestant Christianity made common sense.[53]

Beginning in the late 1790s, Timothy Dwight, president of Yale College, encouraged ministers trained at his institution to study Scottish common sense philosophy as part of a concerted effort among New England ministers to eradicate Painite skepticism of biblical revelation. The combined influences of Witherspoon and Dwight played a major role in stifling the subversive aspect of Paine's understanding of reason. By 1807, when the new Andover Divinity School opened in Massachusetts to provide theological education and train American foreign missionaries, Scottish common sense realism had become a bulwark of American protestant defense against skepticism of biblical revelation.[54]

The dangers of infidelity became an easy excuse for partisan attack as both religion and partisan politics became more prominent in American life. With his involvement in the French Revolution compounding his reputation for dissolute behavior, Paine was the obvious target. But Paine was not the only one to become associated with the poison. The leading partisan of the early republic, Thomas Jefferson, was continually attacked for his religious skepticism, as well as for his association with Paine.

Jefferson's 1787 work, *Notes on the State of Virginia*, contained the infamous assertion, "it does me no injury for my neighbour to say there are twenty gods, or no god. It neither picks my pocket nor breaks my leg." Jefferson's opponents repeatedly condemned this cavalier claim as tantamount to acceptance of atheism. The *Daily Advertiser* in New York advanced a common interpretation: "the question is not what injury an atheistical wretch may do to his neighbor; but the destruction that must ensue, from the propagation of atheism to the whole community." Clearly, Jefferson's insouciance with respect to religion was "a principle" upon which "no government can exist."[55]

In a caricature of Jefferson's alleged effort to supplant the authority of the Bible with that of French reason, Hartford's *Connecticut Courant* represented Jefferson as "Lord Philip" of Sodom calling men to "Throw down the Altars" in "the pure spirit of Democracy." As the *Courant*'s parody unfolded, the people "swear unto him by the gods of the Democrats, even *twenty gods.*" Philip's scribe Abraham, apparently a stand-in for Thomas Paine, stepped forth to offer his book for sale. The people of Sodom agreed to the purchase, accepting "a book of knowledge for ourselves, and for our households and for our kinsfolk." This marvelous book, the "true unction of Democracy," Abraham promised, "will awaken you from your *Delusion*. It will *illuminate* you and make you as gods knowing good and evil."[56]

In real life, Jefferson admired Paine but also tried to keep his distance. He praised Paine's contributions to American independence, corresponded with Paine about events in France and Paine's numerous inventions, including a wheel turned by gunpowder explosions, improvements for carriages and wheelbarrows, and a method for calculating the timber in trees before they were cut. He supported Paine's ingenious plans for building an iron bridge, approved his passage back to America aboard a government ship in 1801, and met with him privately in the White House in 1802.[57] At the same time, Jefferson attempted to keep his sympathy for Paine from public view and expressed annoyance in 1791 that a personal note he wrote expressing pleasure about the forthcoming reprinting of *The Rights of Man* appeared in that pamphlet. Aware that many of his strongest supporters were Baptists, Methodists, and New-Light Presbyterians, Jefferson took pains to keep his personal views about religion private and sought distance from Paine. In 1824, thirteen years after leaving public office, Jefferson absolutely refused a request to publish one of his letters to Paine. "No, my dear sir, not for this world," he responded, "Into what a hornet's nest it would thrust my head!"[58]

Fear of being attacked for religious skepticism was not the only thing that separated Jefferson from Paine. While Paine spent much of his life in cities, and his idealism about human progress dovetailed with his respect for urban energy and ingenuity, Jefferson's idealism was essentially agrarian. He shared a love of mechanical arts with Paine, but his nostalgic commitments to land and property were essentially conservative and rooted in the past.[59] His depictions of the rational order of nature were less dynamic than Paine's and reflected the investment in stability inherent in his upper-class education. Jefferson's agrarian conservatism only exacerbated the tension between his own self-interest as a gentleman farmer and his egalitarian rhetoric. While Paine and his naiveté about natural reason came to seem foolish, Jefferson became president of the United States. His appeals to reason came to seem duplicitous.

One source of Jefferson's reputation for duplicity was the tension within his philosophy of reason between skepticism and affirmation of natural order. Another source was the tension between the egalitarian aspect of his philosophy and his own prejudices. Both tensions are evident in his *Notes on the State of Virginia*, a book often cited by his detractors. In that book, which he compiled in 1781 in response to the French government's request for information, Jefferson rehearsed arguments about fixity in nature advanced by the Swedish naturalist Carolus Linnaeus and the French naturalist George Louis LeClerc, Comte de Buffon. "Every race of animals seems to have received from their Maker certain laws of extension at the time of their formation," Jefferson wrote. Not only sizes of animals but also the variety was fixed: "Such is the economy of nature," Jefferson explained, "that no instance can be produced of her having permitted any one race of her animals to become extinct; of her having formed any link in her great work so weak as to be broken."[60]

Some of the disparities between this presupposed order and what investigators at the time had actually found could be dismissed as gaps between what certainly existed in nature and what had been discovered so far. Although wooly mammoths had not yet been sighted in America, Jefferson believed that the existence of wooly mammoth skeletons meant that live animals of the species still roamed somewhere on the continent.[61] Other disparities were more difficult to explain, especially those involving the human race. In the Linnaean scheme of species unity to which Jefferson subscribed, differences in human beings produced by climate and other environmental factors yielded a variety of secondary features such as a skin color, but the integrity of the species brought into being by the Creator remained inviolate. The essential commonality of each member of the species with respect to every other member followed logically from this position and from the complementary belief, to which Jefferson subscribed, that all human beings had descended from a single set of parents.[62]

Jefferson's medical friend in Philadelphia, Benjamin Rush, ventured that leprosy was the cause of black skin and that it passed by heredity and was difficult to eradicate, though he hoped science would produce a cure. For the abolitionist Rush, the point of this argument was clear: "That all the claims of superiority of the whites over the blacks, on account of their color, are founded alike in ignorance and inhumanity." Reason called for benevolence as well as an end to black enslavement: "If the color of the negroes be the effect of a disease, instead of inviting us to tyrannise over them, it should entitle them to a double portion of our humanity, for disease all over the world," Rush added idealistically, "has always been the signal for immediate and universal compassion." A Unitarian raised a Quaker with adult ties to the Presbyterian and Episcopal Churches, Rush was an enthusiast for the world-transforming power of Christian sentiment.[63]

Jefferson's very different understanding of the natural history of negroes revealed the extent to which his commitment to white supremacy and entanglements in the slave system led him to complicate the Linnaean principle of species integrity and question the idea that human beings were descended from a single set of parents. Jefferson's argument for the fixity of black and white difference made natural order an argument for social conservatism with respect to racial equality; whatever "secretion" black skin color derived from, Jefferson asserted, "the difference is fixed in nature, and is as real as if its seat and cause were better known to us." Seeking to explain this fixed difference, he proposed two explanations, that blacks had fallen from full membership in the human species over time, or in the explanation he seemed to prefer, that God gave them a degraded form of human nature to start with. Any suggestion that the original order of nature had been violated "must be hazarded with great diffidence," Jefferson warned: "our conclusion would degrade a whole race of men from the rank in the scale of beings which their Creator may perhaps have given them." Jefferson's cautious framing of these remarks made his potential contribution to Linnaean theory seem well considered but ominous. "I advance it therefore as a suspicion only," he wrote, "that the blacks, whether originally a distinct race, or made distinct by time and circumstances, are inferior to the whites in the endowments of both mind and body."[64]

If Jefferson's suspicions about black inferiority reveal the conflict between his conservative understanding of the rational order of nature and the more democratic aspects of his philosophy, his attitude toward Native Americans reveal another kind of discrepancy, one that exposed the weakness of Jeffersonian reason as a viable philosophy of government. Jefferson viewed Indians as essentially the same as whites, but more primitive in their advance toward civilization. In *Notes on the State of Virginia*, he contrasted the cheery ruddiness of Indians and the compatibility between their redness and whiteness with the brooding dullness of blacks. "Are not the fine mixtures of red and white, the expressions of every passion by greater or less suffusions of colour in the one," he asked, "preferable to that eternal monotony, which reigns in the countenances, that immoveable veil of black which covers all the emotions of the other race?" Jefferson placed the dignity of red men in the context of the natural virtues of the American continent, which he was proud to extol. To refute theories advanced by Comte de Buffon and others that "there is something in the soil, climate and other circumstances of America, which occasions animal nature to degenerate, not excepting even the man, native or adoptive, physical or moral," Jefferson pointed to the bravery, loyalty, and eloquence of American Indians as compelling evidence that the natural environment of the North American continent was not inferior to that of Europe.[65]

Jefferson's celebration of Indians' rightful place in the natural environment of North America was a perfect expression of his rational view of nature. While highly paternalistic and Anglo-centered, Jefferson's ascription of the primitive state of Indian culture to environmental factors reflected his idealism about nature and his belief that Indians could become Americans through the acquisition of civilized arts reflected the apparent harmony between this idealism and his democratic philosophy. In addition to the problems involved in trying to foist this vision onto Indians, Jefferson worked aggressively to undermine the very idealism about Indians that he promoted. His two-faced operations in dealings with them epitomized the duplicity that opponents often perceived in Jefferson's character. Whatever it said about his personal failings, Jefferson's inability to translate his proclaimed faith in natural reason into government policy, even to the point of sabotage, revealed the untenable and unrealistic nature of that faith.

Jefferson's vision of Indians and their place and future in North America could not explain or hold up to the lust for Indian land that drove his Indian policy as president and that played a major role in the demands for western expansion fundamental to Jeffersonian politics. Through the unacknowledged disparities between reason on one hand and political and economic interest on the other, Jefferson's rhetoric of benevolent paternalism came to operate as a cover for ruthless efforts to make Indians east of the Mississippi dependent on the US government, forcing them to sell their lands and move farther west.

With acquisition of Indian land his ultimate end, Jefferson assembled a team of soldiers and diplomats led by Secretary of War Henry Dearborn, Superintendent of Indian Affairs William Henry Harrison, and Indian expert Benjamin Hawkins, charging them with responsibility for maintaining control of the territories where Indians hunted, American settlers intruded, and agents of England, Spain, and France recruited Indian allies. While publicly proclaiming friendship, respect for Indian rights, and commitment to Indian well-being, Jefferson's confidential letter to Dearborn in December 1802 set a different agenda. Pushing Indians into European habits of farming and husbandry would reduce them to economic dependency, he told Dearborn, and induce them to sell land for the cash they need to acquire (or pay off debts for) farm animals, tools, and household goods acquired from the US government.[66]

While strengthening US forts with the ostensible aim of protecting Indians from violence, Jefferson's team of frontier diplomats and military men worked to acquire strategic pieces of Indian land that better isolated Indian groups from one another and facilitated the western expansion of American settlement through Indian land. Soon after taking office as president in 1801, Jefferson instructed Dearborn to organize a commission to buy land from the Cherokees and work out agreements with the Cherokees, Chickasaws, and Choctaws to begin building a road through their lands from Nashville to Natchez on the Mississippi. In July 1801, Dearborn sent a letter with Jefferson's instructions to the commission emphasizing that "[a]ll fair and proper means should be exerted to evince to them a really friendly disposition on the part of the Government of the United States." In an attachment responding to news of Cherokee resistance to more land sales, Dearborn instructed the commission further. "You will impress upon them the belief, that the United States have no desire to purchase any of their land unless they are quite willing to sell; that we are not in want of lands," he explained disingenuously, "but only wish to be accommodated with such roads as are necessary to keep up a communication with all parts of the United States, without trespassing on the lands of the red people."[67]

In 1802, Jefferson instructed Hawkins to pressure the Creeks for sale of the fertile land in the fork of the Oconee and Ocmulgee rivers that Americans in Georgia were already invading. That sale split the Creeks into factions supportive and opposed to assimilation.

The Cherokee faced similar pressures and divisions. In 1805, American agent Return Jonathan Meigs gave Doublehead's party a choice between losing annuities promised by the US government to the Cherokee people or selling ten million acres above the Tennessee River and accepting the existence of roads built through Cherokee lands without Cherokee permission. After he accepted the deal, Doublehead was murdered, the Cherokee became more factionalized, and many removed to Arkansas.[68]

Around the Great Lakes and Ohio River Valley, Indians opposing federal annuities and Jefferson's arguments for assimilation broke off from those more willing to accept annuities and promises of assimilation. In December 1808, after setting plans in motion, unbeknownst to them, for the acquisition of their land on the Wabash River in the Treaty of Fort Wayne, Jefferson promised a delegation of Miami and Delaware Indians that "we shall all be Americans. You will mix with us by marriage. Your blood will run in our veins, and will spread with us over this great island."[69] Agreed to by chiefs rewarded by the US government, the treaty included the sale of more than two and a half million acres for about two cents an acre.

Whatever capacity Jefferson had for compartmentalizing his activities to avoid internal conflict,[70] his rhetoric about Indians depended on a philosophy of nature inadequate for managing US-Indian relations. Philosophic commitment to the assimilation of red and white people had little meaning for white settlers who hated Indians and wanted them out of the way. As a cover for Jefferson's underlying strategy of land acquisition, proclamations of fair play and brotherhood illustrate the dishonesty inherent in Jefferson's Indian policy. They also illustrate the superficiality of a political philosophy predicated on natural reason that diverted attention from genuine debate and installed a backdrop of political idealism that could be promoted as if it were real or, alternatively, exposed as fundamentally dishonest.

Thomas Jefferson and Thomas Paine, each in his own way, promoted faith in natural reason as a revolutionary political philosophy aimed at freeing men from the injustices associated with political tyranny and slavish deference to authority. In addition to facing resistance from opponents of democracy, both men were encumbered by a belief in the rational order of nature that, ironically, was more religious than rational. Accused by their detractors as skeptics eager to destroy religion, neither man's skepticism was as thoroughgoing as their critics alleged.

There were some in the early republic who ventured further into open-ended critical inquiry, not only doubting the legitimacy of inherited political authority, miracles, and the authority of biblical revelation, but also the idea that reason was the driving force in nature and human history. Though not a philosopher preoccupied by the problem of natural reason, Aaron Burr operated in a political world shaped by the idealisms of Jefferson and Paine without being an idealist himself. Combining skepticism about the natural goodness of reason and the rationality of nature derived from his study of

Calvinist theology with commitment to the freedom of mind and expansion of political and territorial ambition associated with American independence, Burr avoided Paine's naiveté and the gap between idealism and intention that beset Jefferson.

No one more exemplified the new latitude for ambition derived from free-thinking or the suspicion it came to engender than Aaron Burr, the grandson of the great Calvinist theologian Jonathan Edwards. Vice president of the United States during Jefferson's first term, Burr killed Alexander Hamilton, the chief architect of federal policy during Washington's administration, in a duel in 1804 and stood trial for treason three years later for alleged plans to seize US territory to establish a new empire of Mexico. His reputation was profoundly affected by Hamilton's hatred, which dogged him before the fatal duel and long after Hamilton's death, and his character was often the subject of vicious attack. Burr's intelligence, ambition, and freedom from ideological restraint made him seem cynical to Hamilton and many others, while those closest to him perceived him as honest, sincere, charming, and brilliantly realistic.[71]

A hard-driving student whose father Aaron Burr, a minister, hoped his son would follow in his path, Burr the son excelled in the early 1770s at Princeton under the tutelage of John Witherspoon, where his father had served as the school's first president and his grandfather Jonathan Edwards had spent his last days. He took a postgraduate year in Bethlehem, Connecticut, mentored by one of his grandfather's most prominent disciples, Joseph Bellamy, whose approach to theological instruction focused on the refutation of religious skepticism. Bellamy supplied students with many opportunities to hone their skills; when his library became available for purchase at his death, prospective buyers were surprised to discover that it consisted mainly of skeptical works. Burr may have elected to spend the year with Bellamy in order to read these works, having already decided not to enter the ministry, or he may have come to that decision as a result of spending time in Bellamy's library. In any event, exposure to the collection did not operate as Bellamy intended; in agreement with skeptical arguments against the authority of biblical revelation and ecclesiastical judgment, Burr wrote that spring of 1774, "I came to the conclusion that the road to Heaven was open to all alike." Politely dismissing the need for religion, Burr moved on to the library of his brother-in-law Tappan Reeve, where he read military history and constitutional law, and then joined the Continental Army during the American Revolution, rising to the rank of colonel.[72]

As vice president of the United States, Burr received a letter of moral warning from Jonathan Edwards's most influential disciple, Samuel Hopkins of Newport, Rhode Island. Hopkins recalled Burr's grandmother, the legendary Sarah Pierrepont Edwards, who had visited Hopkins on the way to help her daughter care for baby Aaron. Hopkins also recalled Burr's mother and father, both of whom died before Burr's third birthday, and especially his mother, Esther Edwards Burr, whose "pious exercises respecting you," Hopkins wrote, "when you was a fatherless infant, and sick unto death as was feared; but mercifully recovered in answer to fervent prayer." Writing to Burr now might be "futile," Hopkins acknowledged, for "[i]t is reported, and it is believed by a number, that you do not believe in divine revelation, and discard Christianity as not worthy of credit." Were this so, he wanted Burr to know that "[i]t would be very grievous to me, and I know it would be inexpressibly so to your pious and worthy ancestors, were they now in this world." As "an infidel," Hopkins did not hesitate to tell the vice president of the United States, a man "cannot be so useful as mischievous, nor can he be happy but miserable, in his life; and dying so will be inconceivably miserable forever."[73]

Burr's upbringing within New England's archest form of Calvinism may have inured him against the naiveté of faith in natural reason, but it also exposed him to repeated threats of the horrible effects of exclusion from God's grace, not least of which included estrangement from God's people and, most dangerously, from the sovereign power of God holding the universe together. In opting for belief in universal salvation, Burr brushed aside Calvinist threats of damnation and hellfire with aplomb, but the shadow of Calvinist estrangement hung around him like a wraith, following him everywhere, adding to suspicions that he was an orphan from Christian society.

The Calvinism Burr opted out of was not simply an extension of ideas and practices received from the sixteenth-century reformer John Calvin; it was also an eighteenth-century religious movement aimed at defeating modern skepticism and far more strenuous in its rejection of natural reason than Scottish common sense realism. Directed against theologians who tried to make Christianity compatible with liberal rationality and free will, Edwardsian religion sought to destroy even the mildest forms of religious skepticism. In their stand against confidence in natural reason, proponents of this movement denied that individuals had any ability to think or act virtuously until God enabled them to do so by intervening supernaturally to free them from their imprisonment in self-love. For Burr's Calvinist mentor Joseph Bellamy, the "Self-Supremacy and Independency" of a man who trusted his own resources was despicable, a rejection of God's control over everything and nothing less than hatred; he "can't bear that God should be so great and so sovereign, and himself so vile, so little, so absolutely at Mercy." If such a man failed to receive the *"all-conquering irresistible* Grace" that enabled him to beg for forgiveness for his rebellion from the God, then he isolated himself from Christian society in the most provocative and ultimately self-destructive way.[74]

While Bellamy assumed that no one could live cheerfully after attending to all the arguments proving that "it is horrid Pride and Insolence for us to pretend to know better,"[75] Burr seems to have done precisely that. While Calvinists became increasingly strident in the 1790s, insisting that infidelity be defined to include skepticism in all its forms, and that when reason had no predetermined end in God it was immoral,[76] Burr threw his lot in with the open-ended future.

As an engaging and canny attorney, a US senator from New York from 1791 to 1797, and the political organizer credited with bringing the New York State Assembly into Jefferson's camp prior to the presidential election of 1800, Burr was the most charming and sophisticated campaign operative in the country. During the presidential election of 1800, he forged an alliance among competing democratic factions in New York, managed a disciplined corps of young activists who brought unprecedented numbers of New York artisans and shopkeepers to the polls, and turned his house into party headquarters where the young men under his management could find coffee, levity, and bedding at almost any hour. At a time when most candidates for public office, including Thomas Jefferson, avoided the immodesty of direct campaigning, the dapper Mr. Burr approached people directly for their votes, spoke at campaign rallies, and even contemplated plans for a "spontaneous" outpouring of popular enthusiasm in his honor.[77]

Burr's boldness in forging ahead with a modern approach to politics and a modern style of self-presentation made him stand apart from others. Though a master of partisan activity, he remained skeptical of political as well as religious ideology; the Federalists who supported him in his run-off against Jefferson in the Electoral College understood that his primary loyalty was to his own honor rather than to Jefferson. In his furor against Burr's insouciance, Alexander Hamilton explained that he had "a religious duty to oppose" Burr, whom he called "the haughtiest of men" and one who craved "Supreme power in his own person."[78] On the second anniversary of Burr's mortal wounding of Hamilton, Hamilton's friend William Coleman described Burr as an "isolated being," driven by "systematic selfishness" and "unprincipled ambition." For Coleman as for Hamilton, Burr was "an *artificial* man."[79] However much animosity colored this perception, Coleman sensed the extraordinary degree of intellectual independence and self-calculation in Burr that derived, at least in part, from his freedom from religion.

Burr seems to have assimilated the skepticism of David Hume, or come to a sense of the malleability of human perceptions similar to Hume's. Those who read beyond Hume's *History of England* to encounter his less-known *Treatise of Human Nature* found Hume's argument that ideas were feelings imposed on things and that perceptions of cause-and-effect relationships were artificial interpretations of events driven by social convention and other forms of preconception.[80] This challenge to natural reason disturbed the idealisms about American independence promoted by many supporters of Jefferson and Paine; for the otherwise liberal philosopher and patriot Joseph Priestly, skepticism of intelligent causation in nature was "unquestionably atheism." As Priestly explained in 1803, "For if one part of the system of nature does not require an intelligent cause, neither does any other part, or the whole." Whatever his understanding of intelligent causation, Burr maintained polite respect for the social conventions associated with religion, such as his daughter's marriage in a Dutch Reformed Church in Albany in 1801. But he acted in the world with extraordinary freedom. His freedom from ideology, both religious and political, made him an independent man.

Burr may have been an "isolated being" with respect to his attitude toward systems of belief and his estrangement from most members of the extended Edwards clan which, as his cousin Timothy Dwight reminded him, *"cousin'd it to the tenth degree,"*[81] but he was also a sociable, personable man. He enjoyed public life and intimate company, and people in both circumstances enjoyed him; in Richmond during his trial for treason, friends supplied him with oranges, butter, ice, and good clothes to replace the torn leggings and blanket coat he was wearing when arrested. His jailer treated him with great civility, accommodating his habit of staying up late, burning candles long after the nine o'clock curfew.[82]

Burr's twenty-four-year-old daughter Theodosia sat by him at the trial, believing in her father's greatness and shaped by his outlook on the world. She had been a precocious child, able to write intelligible letters to her father when she was only five. At ten, she studied Gibbon's *Decline and Fall of the Roman Empire* and read French and Latin. She took up Greek at twelve and studied with the best tutors in piano, dance, geography, and Italian. A strong advocate of female education, Burr organized his daughter's education on the principle that girls' intelligence was equal to boys' and that, to assume their rightful positions in the world, women had to be educated as equals.[83] Burr's dedication to his daughter's education reflected his skepticism toward the conventional prejudice that women were, by nature, the intellectual inferiors of men. It also reflected a moral commitment to women's equality that skepticism had yielded.

Writing to his wife on February 8, 1793, from Philadelphia, Burr explained how their daughter, by means of an education equal to that of the most promising young man, might inspire others: "I yet hope, by her, to convince the world what neither sex appear to believe—that women have souls!" A week later, he acquired Mary Wollstonecraft's *Vindication of the Rights of Women* and stayed up most of the night reading it. In a letter to his wife the day after, he called the book a "work of genius" and expressed dismay that none of his acquaintances was ready to accept its argument. "Is it owing to ignorance or prejudice," he asked his wife in a letter from Philadelphia in 1793, "that I have not yet met a single person who had discovered or would allow the merit of this work?"[84]

In her *Vindication*, Wollstonecraft argued that belief in women's natural inferiority to men was a vicious assumption that operated against the betterment of humanity: "There must be more equality in society or morality will never gain ground," she argued, "and this equality will not rest firmly even if founded on a rock, if one half of mankind are chained to its bottom by fate, for they will be continually undermining it through ignorance or pride." The path to women's social equality was education: "if women be allowed to have an immortal soul, she must have, as the employment of life, an understanding to improve."[85] Burr agreed. He also enjoyed his daughter's intelligence, as he had her mother's: "The happiness of my life depends on your exertions," he wrote his daughter five years after her mother's death, encouraging her continued study, "for what else, for whom else do I live?"[86]

Theodosia was the central figure in Burr's life after her mother's death in 1794, when Theodosia was eleven. Father and daughter corresponded regularly when apart and his letters reveal their close camaraderie. In 1801, he confided happily to Theodosia that he "had a most amiable overture from a lady" and that, "If I should meet her, and she should challenge me, I should probably strike at once." A letter two years later showed how the lightheartedness they shared extended to religion: "I am now going to smoke a segar and pray for you," he promised.[87] Theodosia was her father's closest friend and the embodiment of educated womanhood who represented, more than anything, his happiness and optimism about the world.

In 1801, a few months before her eighteenth birthday, Theodosia married Joseph Alston, son of one of South Carolina's richest men. While not her intellectual equal, he was passionately in love with her and she was receptive. She could hardly have been unaware of the advantages of wealth, or of the disparity between the lifestyle she and her father enjoyed and their strained financial resources. With a huge rice plantation as a wedding gift from his father, Joseph became busy growing wealth, acquiring slaves, and making his way in South Carolina politics. Theodosia was isolated. While she enjoyed a cordial welcome as daughter of the vice president of the United States and new member of one of South Carolina's most prominent families, she found no one of her intellectual caliber or skeptical disposition to befriend and never thought of South Carolina or her husband's plantation as home. After the birth of a son in 1802, a uterine infection took hold and she spent much of the next several years in debilitating pain, as well as intellectual solitude. When her son died in June 1812, just after his tenth birthday, she wondered how she could continue to live. Her spirits revived at the news of her father's return from Europe, where he had repaired after the trial for treason. Despite her husband's concern that she was too sick to travel, Theodosia set off to meet her father in New York that December, bringing with her the tins containing letters and papers that Burr had left with her for safekeeping. On December 31, she sailed off from Georgetown, South Carolina, on *The Patriot* and was, like everyone else on that schooner, never seen again.[88]

Theodosia's isolation as a freethinking intellectual did not cause her disappearance at sea. But her isolation, early death, and failure to contribute much to society, despite considerable promise, are apt metaphors for the history of skepticism in the United States during the early nineteenth century. The charge of treason against Aaron Burr is an equally compelling symbol of skepticism's fate. His freewheeling approach to life and politics made him a suspicious character to fearful, jealous men, especially Alexander Hamilton, whose branding of Burr with the name of the Roman conspirator Cataline, long before the trial for treason, Burr was never able to shake. When Burr began to gather a private army to seize lands west of US territory from Spain, rumors circulated that he was plotting to create an empire of his own. Those rumors became fodder for partisan speculation; Federalists took them as evidence that former supporters of Jefferson in the West wanted to secede from the United States and that Hamilton had been right to accuse Burr of being a political conspirator. Fearful that Burr might be building a third political party in the West allied with Britain, Jefferson turned completely against him. In his effort to discredit Burr, Jefferson persuaded Henry Clay, the young lawyer and "Western Star" from Kentucky who defended Burr from treason, that he had been wrong to believe in Burr's innocence. While Burr had friends and supporters, his independence with respect to partisan ideology made him vulnerable, and his reputation as an honest man, which he cared deeply about, disappeared from public view in a blizzard of partisan mistrust.[89]

At the trial in Richmond in 1807, Burr was acquitted of the charge of treason on the basis of no evidence being found of any treasonous act. But his political career was finished. As the Richmond *Enquirer* announced during the trial, "*his* intellectual resources, astonishing as they are, can never hereafter endanger his country." By virtue of being charged for treason, "A. Burr has set like Lucifer never to rise again." Burr was the most brilliant American skeptic of his time, so his isolation would be complete. As the *Enquirer* promised, "his society will be spurned like the plague, because like the plague, it will be suspected of contagion."[90]

Burr stood apart not only from those Americans who believed that biblical revelation and supernatural grace were essential to moral virtue but also from men like Jefferson and Paine whose religious belief in the rational order of nature undergirded their belief in human liberty and equality. Their optimistically rational materialism may have seemed for a time more stable and comprehensive than Burr's open-ended pursuit of "understanding" and mental "improvement," but it proved too naive to support the expectations of brotherhood and social harmony it generated and not strong enough to withstand the attractions of biblical authority. While Calvinists lumped Jefferson and Paine with Burr as skeptics and therefore as infidels and even atheists, the skepticism in which Paine and Jefferson indulged was limited to particular targets—monarchy, miracles, and the repression of human liberty and equality. Their skepticism was less a habit of mind than a means to polemic in the case of Paine or, in the case of Jefferson, a means of ruling out options deemed unworthy of consideration. Burr's skepticism was a habit of mind—except, apparently, when it came to his own political ambitions. The rarity of that habit of mind meant that he was denied the friendly criticism that might have made him more politically successful.

The optimistically rational materialism of Jefferson and Paine had enormous influence in America in the late eighteenth century and drove effective arguments for American independence from Britain.[91] But after the Revolution, partisan activists exploited rising tides of suspicion, and defenders of biblical revelation discredited nature and reason as sufficient guides in themselves. No less important, the supporting principles underlying this optimistic faith, namely, that nature was rational and that human beings, once freed from monarchy and belief in miracles, were naturally virtuous, became increasingly problematic as a basis for political policy. The duplicity involved in making political interest appear to conform to preconceived ideas of rational order contributed to the insecurity that evangelicals stepped in to repair.

Skepticism soured as it flowed through channels of partisan activity and became confused with mistrust. As newspapers, public orations, and political toasts directed skepticism toward mistrust of government authority, supporters of the federal government dropped their reluctance to engage in partisan activity; resentful of the need to defend themselves, garner support, and appeal to a broad audience, Federalists oscillated between satire and shrill outrage as they associated Jefferson and his followers with hypocrisy, atheism, immorality, and even terrorism. Churned into the politics of mistrust, optimistic faith in human reason receded, and skepticism was increasingly represented as a symptom of decadence rather than a salutary habit of mind.

By the end of October 1802, when he returned to America, Paine's reputation had plummeted, and his arrival as a reprobate associated with the excesses of the French Revolution made sensational news. Hundreds of newspaper notices spread word of his return, and papers recirculated accounts of his arrogant and dissolute behavior. One paper suggested that his arrival in America should be greeted with the pealing of church bells.[92] Others ridiculed his "laughable conduct" at Fulton's tavern, where he repaired upon arrival, drank a good deal of brandy, and told the crowd assembled around him that he had come back to America "by the express invitation of his pupil Jefferson."[93] An anti-Jefferson paper in New York reported that Paine, "now a hoary and palsied libertine, divides his hours between blasphemy and intoxication" and that if he had his way in the engineering experiments that both he and Jefferson enjoyed, Americans "will have a government like a mouse-trap, to let all in, and none out; because, forsooth, their President has made such of old time in his nick-nackery."[94] Another New York writer, referring to Jefferson's passion for agriculture, "was inclined to think that it was in one of his meditations on manure that the idea of sending for Tom Paine first occurred to him." A Boston paper was practically hysterical on the topic of Paine's return, making him out to be "a lying, drunken, brutal infidel, who rejoices in the opportunity of basking and wallowing in the confusion, devastation, bloodshed, rapine and murder, in which his soul delights."[95]

Boston's *Republican Gazetteer* rose to defend Jefferson for "allowing" (not the same as inviting) Paine back in the country: "what if Mr. Paine should arrive in this land of free and equal liberty, must he be persecuted and hunted to death?" Paine's presence might even turn out to be a good thing for revealed religion, a holy cause to which the writer certainly lent his support, "by exciting more vigilance in christians" and "by bringing forward many able divines to preach and write against infidelity, who have devoted too much of their time, to the study of politics."[96] New York's *American Citizen* stepped forward with a one-sentence notice to "congratulate the friends of republican government on the arrival of Mr. Thomas Paine in the United States,"[97] but the notice may have provoked more snorts than nods. The *Morning Chronicle* sought high ground: "As the federal prints are teeming with attacks on Mr. Thomas Paine," the editors thought it fair to remind readers of the man's "past services."[98]

When Thomas Paine died in New York in November 1809, impoverished, alcoholic, and almost friendless, about a dozen people came to his funeral—these included two free black men, the Quaker Willet Hicks, the French feminist Margaret Bonneville who cared for Paine in his decline, and two of her sons. Most US newspapers failed to give the once-famous champion of the American Revolution even a simple death notice.[99] Two New York papers did reprint a British editorial acknowledging that "[t]he death of Thomas Paine may possibly attract the philosopher's attention for an instant," because "his "contentious and troubled spirit" had been "admired for a time." But now, "the dead calm of contempt" had superseded his "tempestuous hour of popularity." Such "moral vermin draw but ephemeral life," the writer concluded, calling the revolutionary's death an "admonitory event." Endeavoring "to bequeath a legacy of confusion to posterity," Paine's attack on Anglo-protestant culture had failed: "British liberty yet survives the enmity and the existence of the first of its modern calumniators."[100]

CHAPTER TWO

Partisan Mistrust

Although it proved the nation's ability to withstand a transition in power from one political party to another, Thomas Jefferson's election in 1800 institutionalized as many problems as it solved. The rancor involved in his square off with the embittered Federalist incumbent John Adams concentrated the atmosphere of mistrust that had been building through the 1790s. The political divide between Jeffersonians and Federalists grew as people from different backgrounds, walks of life, and regions of the country drew into a kind of ritual combat with each other, with partisan division channeling mistrust into increasingly well-organized grooves.

Organized mistrust in the form of partisan politics had far-reaching consequences, not the least of which involved religion. Partisan mistrust affected the social and intellectual climates in which religion developed, creating a thirst for higher authority and opening the throttle for religious enthusiasms to rush in to allay mistrust. Partisan mistrust also abetted the circular reasoning that defenders of biblical revelation insisted on—reasoning that invoked the Bible's authority as evidence of the truth of its contents, and diverted open-ended inquiry into endless loops of repentance for doubting God's truth and authority. The circular reasoning of political rhetoric only encouraged circular reasoning in religion, with presuppositions about political opponents operating as evidence of their dastardly intentions much as presuppositions about infidelity operated as evidence of immorality. To provide background for the argument that mistrust enabled the growth of evangelical religion and suppression of open-ended inquiry, this chapter surveys the atmosphere of mistrust in which evangelicalism began to flourish.

Jefferson's election signaled an important shift in the policies and philosophy of federal government. Opposing the centralization of federal power championed most ardently and effectively by Washington's Secretary of State Alexander Hamilton, Jefferson supported decreases in taxes, military spending, and federal monetary control. Against those who believed that government should operate as a moral construct sustaining social order, Jefferson and his allies formed an opposition movement protesting the restraints the federal government imposed on individual freedom and on state and local governments. With diverging interpretations of the meaning of "republican," this conflict divided those like Washington, Hamilton, and Adams who upheld the elitist republics of ancient Greece and Rome as models of public virtue from more democratically inclined proponents of representative government, like Jefferson and Thomas Paine, who minimized distinctions between the people and their government that Washington, Hamilton, and Adams upheld.[1] As they grew from an opposition movement into a successful political organization, the democratic-leaning Republicans behind Jefferson claimed the Republican brand for themselves.

Looking back, Jefferson called his election "the revolution of 1800," hailing it as a "peaceful" overthrow of paternalistic government that finally realized the principle of citizen liberty latent in the Revolution of 1776.[2] Jefferson's opponents took a much dimmer view, but agreed that his presidency would force a tremendous change in what Americans could expect from their government. The summer before Jefferson's election, in an article "addressing those who . . . are not yet prepared to part with their Bible, their morals, or their God," Hartford's *Connecticut Courant* warned that Jefferson "dislikes all government, which is capable of affording protection and security to those who live under it."[3]

Connecticut was Federalist territory, where supporters of strong government linked the unrestrained liberty they associated with democracy to immorality and atheism, and where belief in the government's responsibility for "affording protection and security to those who live under it" created fierce opposition to Jefferson. But not even Connecticut was immune to the libertarian democracy of Jeffersonian philosophy, as dissenters from the state's established Congregational Church established pockets of support for Jefferson prior to his election. State-supported clergy viewed these dissenters as "disorganizers" who threatened to rend the moral fabric of society. For state-supported Calvinists, as most Connecticut clergy were, strong government oversight of human enterprise was an asset to individuals, as well as a service to the common good; unrestrained ambition was a disease of human nature and not to be unleashed. Thus Jefferson was a disaster for the popular young Connecticut preacher Thomas Robbins. On July 4, 1800, the pious Mr. Robbins was happy to hear a rumor that Jefferson had died: "In the morning we had news of the death of Mr. Jefferson. It is to be hoped that it is true." When Jefferson lived to win, Robbins mourned: "I think it is clearly a great frown of Providence."[4]

During the administrations of George Washington and John Adams, an expanding public sphere for expressing political feeling on local, regional, national, and international issues enabled disparate groups to forge alliances with each other and together build mistrust against the common foe of oppressive government.[5] With newspapers enlarging the public spaces of debate and turning up the volume on public dissent, politics during Adams's term took on a new kind of life in taverns where men read newspapers aloud, and in streets and town halls where celebrations of the Fourth of July and Washington's birthday became partisan events. In many towns, critics of the antidemocratic interpretations of republicanism associated with Washington, Adams, and Hamilton formed Democratic-Republican societies. As precursors of partisan political organization, these societies enabled mistrust of Federalist authority to coalesce around support for Jefferson's election, contributing to a loose and otherwise unlikely alliance between elite slave holders in Virginia, Kentucky, and the Carolinas on one hand, and poor farmers, urban artisans, and religious minorities in every state on the other.

Before 1800, supporters of the federal government did not consider themselves to be a "party," but rather the rightful heirs of the American Revolution. Ensconced in commercial centers and well-established towns, Federalists were a more homogeneous group than Republicans, with common interests that included social stability, commitment to strong government and strong ties between government and religion, investment in their own cultural and economic enterprises, and worry about the divisive effects of party spirit. Only when democratic-leaning Republicans challenged these interests—and to some extent misrepresented and misunderstood them—did Federalists join in the fray and begin to conduct themselves as a beleaguered "party," thereby contributing to the enlargement of the public politicking they decried. Thus, in June 1800, the South Carolina Federalist Robert Goodloe Harper warned his constituents that Republicans sought to ruin the country. "If they mean to destroy all that has heretofore been done," Harper wrote, "It can do no good to the public, although it may gratify their lust of power, their animosity against opponents, or their party spirit." Since Republicans apparently intended "to repeal all the laws they have opposed, and to throw everything into confusion," Federalists should stand firm in opposition: "they will do infinite mischief, and ought to be kept out."[6]

Among the most important sources of cynicism coalescing into partisan politics, monetary policies benefiting creditors, speculators, and national defense crippled small farmers and artisans who launched numerous protests in the 1780s and 1790s. State and federal officials faced several armed rebellions during these decades, the most famous of which involved farmers in central and western Massachusetts led by the former Revolutionary War officer Daniel Shays. In arms against credit laws that forced and kept them in debt, many of the rebels were also opposed to the religious establishment in Massachusetts, which they perceived to be tied to commercial elites in the eastern part of the state. In 1786, several thousand men, about one-quarter of the adult male population, many with green pine sprigs representing liberty in their hats, raided the federal armory in Springfield, mobbed sheriffs, and closed county courthouses to halt foreclosures. Massachusetts Governor James Bowdoin called up an army, financed privately by his supporters, to overpower the rebels.[7]

Mistrust between small farmers and the federal government escalated during George Washington's two-term administration, breeding popular resentment against the government's high-handed policies that would spill, with help from Thomas Paine, into animosity toward Federalist religion. In 1794, the commander in chief sent federal militia to suppress a major revolt in western Pennsylvania, where as many as five thousand men, outraged at a new federal tax on whiskey devised by Treasury Secretary Hamilton, stood ready to attack the armory at Pittsburgh. Small farmers in every state suffered the effects of an increasingly commercial economy and often resented federal monetary politics aimed at developing that economy. In western Pennsylvania, where whiskey was the farmers' principal source of commercial revenue and means of getting out of debt, farmers rebelled against a tax that singled them out for punishment.

While generally sympathetic to farmers, John Adams was shocked by the Shays's and Whiskey rebellions, calling them acts of "terrorism" and "treason." When he succeeded Washington as president in 1796, he reacted strongly against further attempts to challenge federal authority.[8] Supporters of Washington and Adams pointed to Shays's and the Whiskey rebellions as examples of the horrors of democracy. One poem widely reprinted from *The New Haven Gazette* even depicted Daniel Shays as the devil. "Behold the reign of anarchy," the poet exclaimed, "From hell's dark caverns discord sounds alarms, / Blows her loud trump, and calls my *Shays* to arms."[9]

While the insurrections of 1786 and 1794 were armed attacks against the law, Fries's Rebellion in 1798 appealed to the US Constitution as a call to arms, a striking expression of the direct engagement in politics coming to infuse American popular culture. When the federal government, again with Hamilton's devising, instituted a direct tax on property in 1798 and sent tax assessors to count the number of doors and windows in people's houses as a way of computing taxes owed, German farmers in eastern Pennsylvania organized to halt what they rejected as unconstitutional actions by the federal government. While Daniel Shays had sought a new state constitution in Massachusetts and participants in the Pennsylvania Whiskey Rebellion had threatened secession, the farmers led by John Fries considered themselves to be operating under the aegis of the US Constitution. In response to a federal marshal's arrest of fellow leaders on charges of sedition, which he regarded as unconstitutional, Fries assembled a militia to prevent the prisoners being moved to federal court in Philadelphia. Federal agents apprehended Fries and others and brought them to trial on charges of treason and "levying war against the United States." In a last minute stay of execution in the spring of 1800 in the heat of the presidential election campaign, Adams pardoned Fries and his neighbors. Hamilton, the arch Federalist, was disgusted at Adams's failure of will: "[I]t is by temporizings like these," he complained, "that in times of fermentation and commotion, Governments are prostrated, which might easily have been upheld by an *erect and imposing attitude*."[10]

While farmers mounted political claims against federal authority, cynicism developed along partisan lines in many of the nation's growing cities where Democratic-Republican societies formed. Initially, these clubs were centers of idealistic faith in natural reason where men gathered to enjoy fellowship, celebrate the end of tyranny, and enthuse about the rise of political liberty in the Atlantic world. Thus in October 1792, the Tammany Society convened at its Great Wigwam in New York City to toast the French nation, Paine's *Rights of Man*, the abolition of slavery, and the apostle of liberty, Thomas Paine. The first toast celebrated democracy's future in the Americas: "May the new world never experience the vices and Miseries of the Olde, and May it be an Happy Asylum for the oppressed of all Nations and Religions."[11]

Turning from enjoyment of the prospects of universal liberty to concern over the US government's pro-British policies and unconstitutional restrictions on citizens' rights, Democratic-Republican societies became the cutting edge of organized political division in the United States. Thus in Charleston in 1794, the Republican Society of South Carolina met at "citizen Harris's hotel" to draft a resolution against the arraignment of Alexander Moultrie and

Stephen Drayton on charges of abetting the French minister, "Citizen Genêt," who recently had arrived in Charleston for the purpose of establishing a Franco-American alliance. According to the society's resolution, the constitutional rights of Drayton and Moultrie had "been grossly and flagrantly violated." The resolution insisted that the "attempt made by the representatives of the people in their legislative capacity, to accuse, try, convict, and condemn any citizen for any imaginary crime, is unjust, arbitrary, and in direct violation of the constitution of this state."[12]

Forerunners of the party system that brought Jefferson to power, these Democratic-Republican societies developed as vehicles for supporting candidates for public office at local, state, and federal levels. Taverns became headquarters for a new breed of political organizers who planned public events, worked to recruit voters, and relied on anti-Federalist newspapers to criticize government policies. While international events continued to provide a context for debate, attention shifted away from celebrations of revolutionary brotherhood throughout the Atlantic world toward increasingly pointed political disagreements with US foreign and domestic policy.

Rising tension between the administration of John Adams and the French government during the so-called Quasi-War with France in 1798 widened the rift between supporters of the pro-British policies of the federal government who thought the federal government deserved religious respect and those of Francophile Republicans. "Politics and party hatreds destroy the happiness of every being here," Thomas Jefferson wrote to his daughter Martha from Washington in 1798. Progovernment outrage at the political dissent fomented by Democratic-Republican societies inspired the Alien and Sedition Acts of 1798, which legalized the deportation of French and Irish immigrants agitating for transatlantic democracy and criminalized "False, scandalous, and malicious" writing against the president, Congress, and federal government.[13] While the Alien and Sedition Acts cracked down on political dissent and especially on newspaper editors sympathetic with democracy, they had the unintended effect of fueling the dissent they sought to repress, inviting complaints that Federalists were violators of the principles for which the American Revolution had been fought. The Alien and Sedition Acts ignited the upsurge of popular resentment against Adams and his Federalist allies that propelled Jefferson to victory.

Adams's particularly hated foe, Benjamin Bache, editor of Philadelphia's widely read and excerpted Republican *Aurora*, was nearly beaten to death for his editorials in 1797 and then arrested the following year for libel and obliged to pay an enormous bail of $4,000. Such efforts to suppress antigovernment

speech challenged the Federalist tendency to invoke the Constitution in support of government authority, enabling Republicans to take up the cause of
defending the Constitution, as John Fries had in denying the authority of
federal agents in Pennsylvania. Thus as the ban on antigovernment speech
moved through Congress in July 1798, the *Aurora* invoked the First Amendment, demanding "*Tar and Feathers*, to all those who attack freedom of the
press."[14]

Protests against the Alien and Sedition Acts challenged the moral authority of the federal government and the aura of religious self-righteousness in
which Federalists often enveloped themselves. In August, shortly after Adams
signed the Sedition Bill into law on July 23, the *Aurora* published a provocative and probably fictitious letter to its recently freed and impoverished editor,
"Friend Bache." The author, who signed his name OBIDIAH, explained that
passage of the Sedition Bill caused him to relinquish his previous allegiance
to Federalist doctrine. After learning "that there was to be but one standard
of opinion, and that all men's minds were to be governed by that standard,"
Obidiah wrote, he "began to doubt the uprightness of the creed, and to believe that persecution for political opinions might terminate in persecution
for religious ones that would lead all men to worship God in the presidential
manner."[15]

In Kentucky, State Assemblyman John Breckinridge introduced Resolutions in 1798, declaring the Alien and Sedition Acts "altogether void, and of
no force." The United States were not "united on the principle of unlimited
submission to their general government," the Kentucky Resolutions declared,
and Congress had no power "to create, define, and punish" crimes beyond
those specified in the US Constitution. Jealous protection of "the rights and
liberties of co-States" kept the "General Government" from usurping the
power of the States and the rights and liberties of individual men from which
all legitimate power derived.[16]

Implications for religion followed from such assertions of political liberty.
Argument against the suppression of political speech developed along the
same lines as opposition to religious freedom, with refusal of "unlimited submission" to government the driving force behind each, and with insistence
on freedom of political speech imbued with elements of religious force. Just
as "the states and the people" had, by ratification of the US Constitution,
"guarded against all abridgment by the United States of the freedom of religious opinions and exercises," so the federal government was prohibited
from interference in political speech. According to the Kentucky Resolutions,
"freedom of religion, of speech, and of the press" were essentially one: "inso-

much, that whatever violated either, throws down the sanctuary which covers the others." To maintain that sanctuary over freedom, "arid that libels, falsehood, and defamation, equally with heresy and false religion, are withheld from the cognizance of federal tribunals."[17]

Although he did not acknowledge his authorship at the time, the nation's foremost champion of religious freedom, Thomas Jefferson, had drafted the Resolutions that Breckinridge put forward in Kentucky. He was planning to send the Resolutions to political allies in North Carolina when Breckinridge convinced him that passage in Kentucky was more likely. James Madison presented similar Resolutions in Virginia, after shortening and toning down the draft Jefferson gave Breckinridge and omitting the explicit threat of states rights nullification that Jefferson had included. Breckinridge also omitted the term "nullification" in the Kentucky Resolutions of 1798 but reinserted it in 1799 when efforts to overturn the Alien and Sedition Acts failed in Congress.[18]

Focused more on undermining the credibility of the opposition than fair-minded analysis of issues, each side strove to cast doubt on the other side's ability to govern. While Federalist newspapers in every state accused Jeffersonians of being deceitful predators whose political designs threatened government stability and the security of the people, pro-Jefferson newspapers scorned Federalists as corrupt tyrants willing to violate "freedom of religion, of speech, and of the press." Typical of the pro-Jefferson papers, Pennsylvania's *Herald of Liberty* attacked the unscrupulous behavior of Federalist elites: "Does it warrant them to be wallowing in luxury and ease, whilst the laborious farmer and hardy mechanic are paying enormous & heavy taxes . . . and more wanted to support them in their dissipation[?]" Clearly not: "Our sacred regard for the people's interests, sanctions our publishing to the world this stupendous fabric of corruption & speculation."[19] Federalist newspapers threw down their gauntlet in return, casting aside previous hesitations about engaging in party spirit. Philadelphia's *Gazette of the United States*, whose name bespoke its claim to established authority, demanded "WHAT IS A DEMOCRAT?" and then summarily replied, "*A despot in power, and an insurgent out of power.*"[20]

While newspaper campaigns running up to the election of 1800 enflamed partisan mistrust, the electoral process cast doubt on government's ability to conduct an election. Following separate procedures mandated by each of the sixteen states, eligible voters chose electors over the course of several months from April to October of 1800. In December, the Electoral College met to cast separate votes for president and vice president according to rules stipulating that the candidate with the most votes would become president and the runner-up, vice president. This procedure, and the possibility of a tie between Jefferson and Adams worried people, but few if any expected a tie between Jefferson and his running-mate Aaron Burr, much less that such a tie would prove hard to break. When the House of Representatives met in February to resolve that tie, some members cast their votes for Burr instead, presumably as an interim president until a new election could be held. Rumors of a Federalist coup, a new Constitutional Convention, and even civil war flew as a stalemate in the House persisted, vote after vote. When word reached Washington that Republican militias in Pennsylvania and Virginia had begun organizing to forestall a Federalist takeover of US arsenals, the Federalist representative from Delaware, James A. Bayard, brokered a deal. On the thirty-sixth vote, the House elected Jefferson by a slim margin.[21]

The long stalemate in the House showed how entrenched political division had become. Party organization was still rudimentary in 1800, but voter turnout was on the upswing, and partisan organization of mistrust and cynicism through newspapers and campaign events had become a defining feature of American public life. Federalists lost the high ground of nonpartisanship while their opponents raced ahead in political organizing and made increasing inroads into Federalist territory, even in Connecticut, where sizable crowds in several towns commemorated Jefferson's inauguration on March 4. The partisan festival in New Haven commemorating Jefferson's second anniversary in office attracted more than a thousand attendees,[22] and in New Lebanon, celebrants drank the first of seventeen toasts to "The ever memorable 4th of March 1801—When propitious heaven snatched us from the very brink of tyranny and oppression." The twelfth toast in New Lebanon went out to "The Republican presses of the United States—May they spread the truth, in the dark and benighted regions of Federalism."[23]

If these toasts equated Federalism with religious corruption by innuendo, the fifteenth pulled no punches: "May true and undefiled religion pervade the whole earth, and that monster superstition become extinct." As that toast revealed, partisan hatred of Federalist authority carried a strong religious component. In their last toast, Jefferson's supporters in New Lebanon celebrated their commitment to defend the republic against the forces of royalist elitism they associated with Federalism, drinking to "The union of the States—May the links which form the chain be made of pure republican Gold so that the rust of aristocracy may not corrode and destroy it."[24] The Federalist clergy were distressed by the boldness of this insurgency against New England order. As the alarmed Reverend Thomas Robbins noted in his diary, "Democracy is now making its most violent efforts in this State. May the God of our fathers preserve us."[25]

Expedited by the expansion of partisan newspapers, the channeling of religious resentment into political dissent contributed to new levels of engagement in political life; partisan mistrust opened up politics as a public sport in which growing numbers of people participated. Republican cynicism about Federalist authority and Federalist cynicism about Republican democracy drew people into political debate through barbecues, dances, parades, and other campaign activities. Political caucuses became more important, and more subject to popular opinion, and voter turnout increased. In South Carolina, backcountry farmers teamed up with artisans and Francophile elites in Charleston to defeat old guard Federalists at the polls, and similar alliances also emerged in other states, propelled by civic feasts and festivals organized by Republicans.[26] Chipping away at traditional habits of decorum and expectations of deference, political candidates began to work for popularity and even campaign for votes, if only discretely, and behind the scenes.

Democratic-Republicans invoked the revolutionary spirit of 1776 as a precedent for their attacks against Federalists, but the translation of that precedent into a cause for political campaigning and voter turnout involved wresting the mantle of the American Revolution away from supporters of the federal administration. Ruling elites in every state belonged to small networks of interrelated families that included Revolutionary War heroes, and these elites often appealed to the unbroken line from the Revolution they represented as reason for their public authority. Opposed to "party spirit," these government leaders and their supporters viewed George Washington's transition from Revolutionary War general to president of the United States as the embodiment of the reconstituted social order that followed American independence. In asserting their bona fides with respect to the American Revolution, Federalists resisted interpretation of that event as an endorsement of mass politics and government by popular opinion.[27]

Washington's death on December 14, 1799, marked an important moment in this political process. Church bells pealed and shops closed their doors as news of the death spread from town to town. Black-bordered newspapers printed eulogies and notices of funeral parades and public speeches. People draped black cloth on buildings and wore black armbands and ribbons. The entire US Congress dressed in mourning for the duration of their session and First Lady Abigail Adams instructed ladies invited to her levees to do likewise. Given the escalating partisanship heading into the election of 1800, Federalists might have hoped that the public outpouring of grief over Washington's death would shame Republican challengers into silence. To the surprise and outrage of some, Republicans joined eagerly in public expressions of sorrow and made great efforts to appropriate Washington's legacy. The two Republican governors of Pennsylvania and Virginia called for days of public mourning with no less alacrity than their fourteen Federalist counterparts. This political maneuvering appeared to some Federalists as the height of hypocrisy. As one recalled angrily, Republicans "publicly and pathetically lamented and extolled" Washington at his death despite having opposed him while he was president. And no Republican was more infuriating in his "inconsolable" expression of grief at losing Washington than that "illustrious modern mourner," Thomas Jefferson.[28]

In life, President Washington was admired by many but distrusted by others disturbed by his willingness to act like a monarch. As democratic-leaning Republicans liked to point out, the formalities allowed by George and Martha Washington emulated the performances of British royals. While president, Washington received invited guests at formal receptions each week in the White House dining room, flanked by his cabinet at the fireplace. When the doors opened at three o'clock on Tuesdays, each visitor waited to hear his name announced and then proceeded to make his bows to the president and his cabinet, eschewing the new and more democratic custom of shaking hands. Martha Washington's levees took place on Fridays, when the First Lady, attired in white, sat on an elevated platform in the dining room with the wives of her husband's cabinet ministers arranged around her in order of descending importance. As each visitor heard her name called, she received the arm of a male escort up to the dais to make a curtsy. Jefferson scorned these levees with a republican nose for religious pretense, characterizing Martha Washington's popularity among the elites of Washington City with the disdainful remark, "They burn incense to her."[29]

While Jefferson's election showed that the nation could survive a transition in power from one "party" to another, it also ritualized political dissent and suspicion. Jefferson embodied a new order of cynicism in his disregard for pretentious authority and calculated stratagems of democratic informality. As an artful emblem of the common man, Jefferson arrived at his inauguration in a rustic American-made suit of brown and green and opened the White House afterwards to the people, some of whom made their entry through the windows. When farmers in Berkshire County, Massachusetts, sent a four-foot wide, twelve hundred pound cheese to the White House for the president's first New Year's celebration in office, Jefferson received the smelly gift in person and appeared delighted with the inscription, "THE GREATEST CHEESE IN AMERICA—FOR THE GREATEST MAN IN AMERICA."[30]

For dinner parties, Jefferson installed a round dining table to better aid conversation and abandoned the practice of seating guests hierarchically; the first guests to enter the dining room were those who happened to be standing by the door when dinner was announced. Deliberate informality was the hallmark of these events. The dumbwaiters Jefferson installed to keep servants out of the room, his hands-on approach to serving food, and invitations to help yourself, put guests at their ease. But Jefferson's *pêle-mêle* approach to hospitality was not a simple expression of fellow feeling. Branded "Epicurean artifices" by one contemporary, Jefferson's excellent food and wines, and guest lists crafted with an eye to upcoming political debates, all worked to expedite deal making.[31]

When the wealthy British ambassador James Merry and his wife (famous for her diamonds and splendid attire) arrived for their first official meeting with President Jefferson, the ambassador wore a velvet-trimmed and gold-braided coat, a plume in his hat, and a sword at his side. Jefferson made a tardy appearance in worn-down slippers and twirled a slipper on his toe during their meeting. In other deliberate acts of transgression against hierarchical formality, Jefferson opened the front door of the White House to visitors on occasion and made himself comfortable in a lounging robe. In his self-presentation, Jefferson celebrated the ethos of dissent against aristocratic authority and sanctimony that had brought him to power.[32]

The element of disguised art in Jefferson's deliberate informality infuriated his enemies, and some could barely contain themselves with outrage at his politically charged pretensions of innocent simplicity. Ambassador Merry took affront at the slippers as well as the "pantaloons, coat, and underclothes indicative of utter slovenliness and indifference to appearances and in a state of negligence actually studied."[33] James Madison used a theatrical term for the political posturing of both Jefferson and the Merrys, calling the blowup around the diplomatic visit a "farce." Alexander Hamilton despised Jefferson's manipulative character and derided his less-than-straightforward exercise of power as "feminine."[34] The *New York Evening Post*, sponsored by Hamilton, took Jefferson to task early on in his presidency for "a public address" against federal taxation made entirely "without sincerity" in order to "secure *his popularity*."[35] Even a friendly spectator at Jefferson's first inauguration saw political costume in Jefferson's grey wool stockings and breeches dyed green, the color actors wore to play the part of an unsophisticated coun-try person: "Everyone knew of course, that he had a fine French wardrobe of damask waistcoats, frilled shirts, and silk stockings."[36]

While the American system of partisan mistrust took hold in the election of 1800, partly through the persona of Thomas Jefferson, it hardly sprung into being through his devices alone. Jefferson was only the most powerful of modern provocateurs. While Jefferson's election involved the ritualized channeling of suspicion into partisan politics, reservoirs of suspicion outside the political sphere made that kind of political organization possible. The social turmoil associated with increasing diversity, population growth, geo-graphic expansion, and social mobility fed the reservoirs of mistrust upon which political activists drew. The breakdown (or escape from) tightly knit communities where people knew their neighbors and personal identity was an extension of one's community of birth, gave enterprising individuals new opportunities to remold themselves, and make use of others. The prolifera-tion of chameleon-like characters taking advantage of the relative anonymity of America's growing cities and new roadways contributed to the growing wariness that infested the early republic.

The con man Stephen Burroughs exemplified the new culture of indi-vidual liberty and personal ambition, as well as the predatory willingness to exploit innocence that bred mistrust. A connoisseur of artful self-presenta-tion with much less self-restraint than Jefferson, Burroughs's ability to shape his persona to advantage reflected the slipperiness associated with the strate-gic manipulation of public opinion that Jefferson exemplified so powerfully. The mischievous and only son of a Presbyterian minister in Hanover, New Hampshire, Burroughs invoked partisan politics to justify his failure to inherit any "merit" from his father: "But I am so far a republican, that I consider a man's merit, to rest entirely with himself, without any regard to family, blood, or connection." Fun-loving Stephen spent a short time at Dartmouth in the 1770s where, pursuant to his father's wishes, he roomed with a religiously enthusiastic tutor, "A man of small stature, and yet smaller mental abilities" who "assailed my ears," Burroughs recalled in his memoir, with "a perpetual stream of petulent criminations." Soon at odds with the religious men at Dart-mouth, Burroughs sailed off on a privateer during the Revolution, represent-ing himself as a physician. Excommunicated upon his return to New Hamp-shire, he found himself on his own with few resources besides a familiarity with the Calvinism for which he had previously found little use. "A stranger—moneyless—and friendless—There is one thing for Contrivance, which you may do," the young opportunist decided, no doubt enjoying a joke at the expense of his religious persecutors, "Preach!!" Taking the name "Davis" and equipped with sermon notes stolen from his father, Burroughs applied for the office of clergyman in Ludlow, Connecticut, where he made it through a trial sermon without incident other than "universal surprize, at my gay dress," which consisted of a "light grey coat, with silver plated buttons, green vest, and red velvet breeches." The parishioners of Ludlow sent him on his way, but "Reverend Davis" soon found success with a Presbyterian congregation in Pelham, Massachusetts, where he preached four Sundays for twenty dollars, which he used to buy an outfit more suitable for a clergyman.[37]

Hired on for an additional three months in Pelham, the ingenious imposter took advantage of the high incidence of misfortune in childbirth to collect additional fees during the week for funeral sermons in neighboring towns. When the Pelhamites began to wonder "how I could be prepared for preaching so constantly, and on so short notice, being as yet, only nineteen years of age," they demanded an "impromptu" sermon on John 9:5, "old shoes and clouted on their feet." Recalling that he "truly felt somewhat blanked" at this test of integrity, he nevertheless forged ahead "determined to do the best," and managed to carry it off, although some listeners did take offense at his application of "clouted on their feet" to them, implying that Pelham Presbyterians were jealous people displeasing to God.[38]

When a former classmate from Dartmouth exposed Burroughs's true identity, a posse of irate Presbyterians chased him into a barn in Rutland, where he held them off on a hay mow with a scythe. In the "sermon" he later claimed to have delivered on the hay mow, Burroughs delighted in the irony of deceiving religious people he viewed as hypocrites. In a parody of biblical prophecy, he wrote, "Then said the Lord, 'I will give them a Minister like to themselves, full of all deceit, hypocrisy and duplicity.'"[39]

Around the same time that suspicions began to be raised about his preaching, Burroughs fell into trouble as a result of his acquaintance with an alchemist in New Salem, an "adroit deceiver," who first duped him into believing that silver could be manufactured from copper and soon inspired Burroughs's next career move—into counterfeiting. Burroughs fled to Attleboro near Providence, where he recommenced preaching and trading in counterfeit coin. Arrested for attempting to pass false silver to an apothecary in Springfield in 1785, he was confined for three years (interrupted by a dramatic boat escape) in Boston Harbor's Castle Island Prison. From there, he taught school in number of different towns including Charleston and Savannah, married a Catholic woman, went to prison again, and got into the business of printing paper money. In 1799, to evade US authorities, Burroughs bought a farm in

Stanstead, Canada, just across the Vermont border, which became headquarters for a counterfeiting ring that operated in New England, New York, and
Pennsylvania. In 1809, according to the appendix to his memoir, he could
often be found in his *"picture shop"* in Quebec, where he "keeps for sale bills
of most of the banks of the United States, ready for signing." Meanwhile, his
daughter "supports herself in stile and elegance by the simple business of
signing the bills, in which art she has arrived to great perfection."[40]

Much as Burroughs viewed his impersonations of a Presbyterian minister
as no worse than the hypocritical self-righteousness that Presbyterians themselves displayed, so counterfeiting was part of larger culture of currency production. Many kinds of bank bills floated around in the early republic, and the
line between authorized and unauthorized bills was not always clear or useful. Despite the stipulation in the US Constitution that only the federal government could print money, individual states issued authorizations to print
money to numerous banks, some of which failed. A shortage of specie and
a distrust of Hamilton's national bank contributed to the states' willingness
to empower smaller banks and, in this unpredictable situation, a counterfeit
bill might serve its user better than legal tender printed by a failed bank. The
ethos of mistrust surrounding money went further, as Shays's Rebellion and
other rural rebellions testified. Mistrust extended to bankers who grew rich
on the credit extended to small farmers and artisans, fueled by the resentment
many people felt about interest rates that drove them into debt and about the
need to deal in cash to make ends meet in an increasingly commercial and
impersonal economy.[41]

Increasing reliance on cash—the apparent equivalent of value—epitomized
the problem of mistrust at a deeper level still. Like partisan exaggeration in
newspapers and political posturing in public, truth was hidden and possibly
nonexistent in securities backing cash. Like the unleashing of ambition in the
early republic, the flow of cash was unmanageable, easily exploited, and not
always valuable.

If stories about the counterfeiter Stephen Burroughs amused those who
appreciated his outlaw spirit, stories about people who fell into ruin by trust-
ing predators attracted a broad and empathic audience. While Burroughs got
rich gaming a system many thought was rotten, other people fell into poverty
and disgrace as a result of forces they could not manage, and several popular
novels recounted stories of such personal downfall. By far the most widely
read of these was *Charlotte Temple*, which sold forty thousand copies and
captured the imagination of the reading public on a scale comparable to the
most popular works of Thomas Paine. Much as Paine's writing unified feel-

ings of resentment, rebellion, and independence already in play, and made them clearer and more inspiring, *Charlotte Temple* represented feelings of remorse about the new political culture of independence, feelings with which many Americans identified.[42]

Charlotte Temple depicts a young woman's victimization by three forces—an unscrupulous teacher, an irresponsible soldier charmed by her beauty, and "the deceitfulness of her own heart." According to the author Susanna Rowson, also famous as an actress and playwright, the story was based on real incidents, with the names of people and places changed and "a slight veil of fiction" cast "over the whole." The purpose of the book was to warn young women that their own feelings could not be trusted and ought to be guarded against. "Oh my dear girls . . . for to such only am I writing . . . no woman can be run away with contrary to her own inclination."[43] The extent to which readers identified with the unfortunate "Charlotte" is evidenced not only by the book's frequent reprinting but also by a headstone marked with her name over an empty tomb in the graveyard of Trinity Church on Wall Street in Manhattan and by the pilgrimages many readers, touched by the story, made to the grave of this virtual heroine.[44]

Brought up to trust others, Charlotte allows her teacher Madame La Rue to persuade her to sneak away from school for an outing with a couple of soldiers. That small act of treason set in motion a train of catastrophes: "Charlotte had taken one step in the ways of imprudence; and when that is once done, there are always innumerable obstacles to prevent the erring person returning to the path of rectitude." Despite loving parents and a virtuous childhood, Charlotte is easy prey for Montraville, who quits the British Army to seek his fortune in New York, with Charlotte along as a mistress who thinks she is a fiancée until he abandons her in New York. A mirror for America herself, Charlotte laments her independence: "would not the poor sailor, tost on a tempestuous ocean, threatened every moment with death, gladly return to the shore he had left to trust to its deceitful calmness?"[45]

Left without money to pay for her decent rooms, Charlotte is helpless in resisting poverty and declining perceptions of her worth. Like others in the early republic caught in a spiral of debt, there is little Charlotte can do to save herself from destitution. "When once the petrifying aspect of distress and penury appear," observed Rowson, those "qualities, like Medusa's head, can change to stone all that look upon it." Her status as a woman and, as it turns out, a pregnant one, only narrows her options further. Her father arrives from England to find an "emaciated" Charlotte "[o]n a wretched bed . . . poorly supplied with covering" in a washerwoman's hut. Having lost all hope for her own life, she prepares to meet her maker with "humble confidence in the mercy of him who died to save the world." Her father's rescue of her infant daughter does little to mitigate the sad image of Charlotte's coffin carried from the washerwoman's hut to the grave.[46] La Rue's life also spirals downward: she spends her last years "in riot, dissipation and vice, till overtaken by poverty and sickness, she had been reduced to part with every valuable, and thought only of ending her life in prison." La Rue recovers just enough to beg forgiveness before sinking finally to death.

The popularity of *Charlotte Temple* says much about the consequences of American independence and the ambivalence Americans felt about going it on their own, not only as a nation independent of Britain but also as individuals whose ties to family, place, and tradition were often broken.[47] *Charlotte Temple*'s popularity is also an indication of how profoundly the problem of mistrust affected American women. With its emphasis on the deceitfulness of even the most innocent of female hearts, *Charlotte Temple* suggested diminishing confidence in human nature, and perhaps in women especially, and the need for religion as salvation from the world of deceit in which women were especially vulnerable.

Along with being a cautionary tale about a young woman victimized by a web of treachery in a harsh and unforgiving world, *Charlotte Temple* argued for the complicity of victims in their own fates and intimated that innocence was a dangerous fantasy. If many young women were more resourceful in real life, Charlotte's weakness represented the truth of their disproportionate lack of power and their own vulnerability. Through the character of Madam La Rue, *Charlotte Temple* suggested further that women who did go it alone, especially those who sought pleasure, were sure to be the most vicious and contemptible creatures on earth. As a woman with a successful career as an entertainer, author Susanna Rowson had firsthand knowledge of such perceptions.

Charlotte Temple highlighted the enormous disparity in opportunities available to women compared to white men, and their profound dependency at a time when independence was a cherished principle and political engagement among white men was growing fast. The liberties of women narrowed in the United States in the late 1790s and early 1800s, in marked contrast to the expanding enfranchisement of white men, as well as in contrast to bolder assertions of female autonomy and greater cultural permissiveness with respect to women's activities in preceding decades. Contributing to narrowing views of women's place in society, memoirs of the recently deceased English feminist Mary Wollstonecraft, published by her husband William Godwin, appeared in 1798, revealing Wollstonecraft's sexual relationships outside of marriage and enabling critics to link her affirmation of women's rights to her debauched sensuality. As the preface to the first American edition concluded, "She had advanced too far in philosophy to be startled by adultery." Once "awakened," the preface went on snidely, "she was prepared to prostitute herself to the first man, whose person she might chance to like." The memoirs were sure to arouse "virtuous indignation" in the breasts of American women, who "will turn with horror from a detestable philosophy, which would degrade the sex to the lowest infamy."[48]

Condemnation of women's rights coincided with heightened mistrust of female sexuality and with new efforts to reform the behavior of women perceived to be licentious. These repressive efforts followed an era of freer intercourse between men and women and greater tolerance of adultery and prostitution, especially in America's growing cities. Philadelphia, America's most cosmopolitan city in the eighteenth century, had boasted a culture of gay sociability and tolerance of promiscuity where prostitution was rarely punished and, for some women at least, more of a temporary or intermittent activity than an identity. In the more repressive era after 1798, acceptance of women's sexual freedom declined and licentiousness became increasingly associated with poverty and loss of respectability. The ratio of children on city rolls born out of wedlock doubled in the decade after 1805, partly as a result of growing unwillingness on the part of husbands and fathers to accommodate all the children of their wives and daughters and partly as a result of the attentions of the Magdalen Society, incorporated in 1800, and its asylum for the reformation of prostitutes, which opened in 1807. By targeting and institutionalizing poor women, reform efforts may have alleviated suffering for some, but also contributed to perceived linkages between sexual freedom and low class and to women's retreat from aspirations to liberty and equality.[49]

While partisan activities made politics more inclusive, it entrenched new boundaries of power and status that excluded women. Even as they were drawn into the peripheries of partisan engagement, women participated in enactments of their own marginalization with respect to political engagement. Women were often spectators at partisan parades, listeners to political orations, and dance partners at partisan balls. They pinned emblems of party affiliation on their dresses and hats and occasionally got carried away; during the Quasi-War with France in 1798, one horrified congressman saw women "meet at the church door and violently pluck the badges from one another's bosoms."[50]

More often than occasioning such unladylike outbursts, partisan politics became a vehicle for establishing women's peripheral role in public life. The ritual eulogizing of female virtue on the part of both Republicans and Federalists masked a profound mistrust of women as candidates for citizenship and full participation in public life. Suspicion of women was hardly new. But partisan organization, as well as the enlargement of public participation in politics that partisan organization stimulated, orchestrated that suspicion in partisan performances that brought it into the open in a new way, often through rituals that appeared to dignify women's exclusion from equal participation.

When women did march in parades, they often did so as generic symbols of the republic rather than as active participants in political life or representatives of particular trades or ethnic constituencies. With emphasis on their pliant physicality and sameness, women were enlisted as symbols of the beauty of the American republic, the virtuous motherhood that men relied on for nurture, and the purity men swore to protect. In the Philadelphia suburb of North Farms, "one hundred young ladies dressed in white" marched in the Fourth of July parade in 1800, according to the Republican *Aurora*, but even there white dresses set them apart as symbols of unsullied virtue.[51]

Most often, women merely stood or sat in the audience as parades went by. On July 4, 1805, Boston's Committee of Arrangements of the Young Democratic Republicans put the following notice in *The Independent Chronicle*: "The Ladies are informed, that suitable seats will be allotted them, which will be pointed out by a person commissioned for that purpose." In 1807, the *Charleston Courier* placed a similar notice at the end of a description of fireworks to be displayed on the Fourth of July: "the Publick, & particularly the Ladies, are most respectfully notified that the lower suite of apartments of the Orphan-House, will be thrown open for their accommodation." Whether the ladies were meant to watch the fireworks from these apartments or retire to them before and after, their place in the proceedings was marginal but not therefore insignificant. Ladies had carefully scripted roles to play as approving supporters and embodiments of national virtue.[52]

While both Federalists and Republicans sought women's endorsement, Federalists engaged women more effectively in rituals that publicized their dual role as admirers of men and symbols of national purity elevated above the atmosphere of suspicion and mistrust. Always avoiding the provocative language of liberty, rights, and equality precisely because it led to what they perceived as an unmanageable extension of political privilege, Federalists called on women to exemplify the duty and sacrifice essential for a great republic.[53] In laying out duty and sacrifice as standards for female activity and making it clear that women were responsible for upholding moral virtue, Federalist politicians opened future pathways for women to follow as teachers and social reformers and for their amplified role in nineteenth-century America as arbiters and consumers of sentimental culture.[54] While Federalists counted on women to embody the commitment to duty and sacrifice that all Federalists—male and female—shared, the gender inequity of Republicans was more blatant. Federalists may have respected women more than their political opponents did or perhaps obscured their mistrust of women more effectively. The inconsistency of Republican rhetoric must have been painfully obvious to democratically inclined women who preferred the language of rights and equality to that of sacrifice and duty, and hoped for political inclusion.

The limits of women's enfranchisement became more clearly defined through partisan organization of public life. In the best-known instance of clear exclusion with respect to female suffrage, New Jersey passed a law in 1808 declaring women ineligible to vote; the law disenfranchised the few women qualified to vote according to provisions in the state constitution, which required voters to show they owned fifty pounds or the equivalent property. That requirement excluded married women from eligibility, since they were subject to the legal principle of coverture denying married women independent status and assigning any property brought to marriage to their husbands. Only a small minority of single women were worth fifty pounds, and they were likely to vote for candidates who adhered to Federalist policies supporting their wealth and status. In 1797, when the Federalist-dominated state legislature affirmed that women who met the property requirement were eligible to vote, Democratic-Republican newspapers hooted, scorned, and mocked. "Open wide your throats," one satirist demanded, "[a]nd welcome in the peaceful scene / Of Government in petticoats!" After men and boys dressed as women presented themselves at the polls in 1807, legislators agreed to a deal: Federalists would relinquish their support for women's suffrage in return for Republicans relinquishing their support for the suffrage of free blacks.[55]

In New Jersey and elsewhere, partisan political activities organized mistrust of both blacks and women in ways that affirmed their disqualification for political rights and ritually separated them from white men. While Democratic-Republican societies brought men of various European backgrounds—English, Irish, Scots, French, and German—together across ethnic, cultural, and linguistic differences and organized them to work effectively toward common political goals, women were ritually sidelined as supporters for whom white male actors often performed. Blacks, too, were increasingly ostracized and in increasingly blatant ways, despite numerous attempts of their own to participate. While partisan activists flattered women and took pains to disguise their mistrust of women as political actors, many had no compunction about exposing their lack of faith in the capability of blacks to become good citizens. Nothing reveals the poisonous nature of cynicism in the early republic more clearly than the escalating suspiciousness of blacks and the role of partisan activity in institutionalizing it.

In Orange County, Vermont, in October 1798, Federalists made public ridicule of blacks a means of shaming all proponents of democracy. According to the *Vermont Gazette*, "A number of Aristocrats in this vicinity, in order to burlesque the republican liberty poles, permitted their negroes (or rather commanded them) to raise a pole, with some satirical motto." Although in 1777, Vermont had been the first state to abolish slavery, this burlesque two decades later shows that some Vermonters took black inferiority and political ineligibility as a given. Apparently the Federalists who planned the event meant to make Democratic-Republicanism look ridiculous by showing black actors around a liberty pole. But the blacks subverted the satire by not going along simply as pawns. While the Federalist authors of the charade "were exulting in the anticipated mortification of the republicans," the blacks took the opportunity to make their own political statement: "these impudent fellows set about the rebellious employment called 'thinking' the result of which was this striking motto—FREEDOM TO AFRICANS." Without saying whether the motto was spoken aloud or written out, the Democratic *Gazette* concluded that the event had "recoiled" upon the Federalists, "and proved that those beings whom they treat as their horses, possessed a manly and rational sentiment which never warmed the breasts of those whom they are made to call their masters."[56]

Blacks resisted their exclusion from political life in a variety of ways, but the forces raised against them were overwhelming. Even as the population of free blacks increased dramatically in Philadelphia, New York, Boston, and other northern cities, the number of free blacks voting, never more than a tiny number, declined to zero, partly as a result of explicit legislation, as in New Jersey in 1808, but primarily as a result of general intimidation and inability to meet property requirements. In New York, a small community of black artisans found employment as bootmakers, carpenters, mechanics, barbers, caterers, and launderers in the early nineteenth century, but few if any of these owned property; by 1816 not a single black person was assessed for property in New York City, despite the fact that blacks counted for almost 9 percent of the city's free population.[57] There, as elsewhere, black workers faced increasing competition from Irish and German immigrants and also from black newcomers fleeing the South. They also faced escalating racial hostility from poor whites who resented black labor and from wealthier whites who rationalized their fear of black resentment by interpreting that resentment as savage depravity rather than in terms of thwarted aspirations to political legitimacy.

In southern states, mistrust of blacks pervaded white cultures as black populations soared, especially in the lower South. Beginning in the 1790s, the boom in cotton production brought enormous profits that fueled the expansion of slave plantations in the states and territories of North and South Carolina, Georgia, Alabama, Mississippi, and Louisiana. Cotton was the mainstay of swelling commerce of this region; by 1804, profits from foreign export reached $1.7 million and in 1807 they jumped to $4.3 million. The slave population tripled between 1790 and 1820, with most of that growth occurring in the lower South where the number of blacks in some areas exceeded the number of whites. In 1800, South Carolina Governor Jim Drayton expressed pride in the contribution that the slave economy made to the country, calling South Carolina's cotton industry a "matter of National Joy." A few years later, a visitor to Louisiana observed the fear underlying this expanding slave economy: "One can see how gnawing is the anxiety," the traveler reported, "which far from diminishing with time, is growing, because the colored population is growing faster than that of whites."

When Jefferson purchased Louisiana from Napoleon in 1803, free people of color in New Orleans hoped for United States citizenship. In a petition to Governor William C. C. Claiborne in January, 1804, fifty-four "free Citizens" of color expressed their "lively Joy" in the new political arrangement and their faith in American justice. Shortly after, US General James Wilkinson observed that free people of color "universally mounted an Eagle in their Hats" as a sign of their new patriotism and political engagement. But Louisiana's Black Code of 1806 removed the right of self-purchase that had previously enabled the growth of a prosperous free black community. The Black Code of 1806 also strengthened the caste distinction between slaves and free people by requiring free people of color to take responsibility for policing slaves. When Louisiana became a state in 1811, slaves lived under heavy surveillance, and state laws prohibited free people of color from any political participation. As the governor of the Mississippi Territory, Harvard alumnus Winthrop Sargent reminded General Wilkinson that year "[i]n Slave Countries the Danger of Insurrection always exists, and Inhabitants should be prepared to meet the event."[58]

The danger of insurrection was a powerful source of anxiety throughout the South as the number of slaves increased and refugees arrived in New Orleans, Charleston, Richmond, and Baltimore from St. Domingue in the 1790s, with news of the black revolution there. Whites fleeing that island reported on the horrors of bloodshed, property destruction, and starvation, while the slaves they brought with them knew that a successful revolution had been launched, and that black rights and a black republic, however weak, had been established in the Atlantic world. The revolution in St. Domingue ignited hope of black rights and explicitly linked that hope to the principles that had inspired the heroes of the American Revolution. Inspired by Patrick Henry's famous cry, "Give me Liberty, or Give Me Death," the revolutionary leader Toussaint Louverture made "Death or Liberty" his call to arms in St. Domingue. Louverture paid homage to the American Revolution while underscoring, in his revision of Henry's cry, his refusal to live as a slave.

In South Carolina, the revolution in St. Domingue struck terror into the hearts of wealthy low-country planters and commercial exporters at the heart of the growing slave economy in the 1790s; in 1794, when France liberated slaves in all her colonies in response to the turmoil in St. Domingue, members of the Huguenot church in Charleston fired their minister when he dared to incorporate French nationalist hymns in church services.[59] Fearing the spread of rebellion from St. Domingue, a police force patrolled the streets of Charleston and groups of more than seven blacks were outlawed after dark. In 1801, the city council imposed restrictions on blacks meeting during daylight hours. By 1807, blacks meeting for "dancing or merriment" were required to show a permit, and the fine for illegal meetings was raised tenfold to one hundred dollars. In Charleston's notorious Sugar House, blacks who could not pay the fine were flogged, and "whooping" and "hallooing" brought ten lashes until 1806, when the number of lashes for such offenses increased to twenty. Whites expected black resentment, and when fires broke out, they often suspected blacks of arson. The frequent outbreak of fires in Charleston on the anniversaries of the Fourth of July suggests that some blacks took the holiday as an occasion to express their feelings about American freedom.[60]

While Federalists took the danger of insurrection as reason to exert stronger restrictions on the slave trade, Republicans resisted such controls. Democratic-Republican societies developed in South Carolina to protest economic restraints imposed by Federalists, including any hindrance to the trade in slaves, which southern proponents of slave growth insisted on defining as property. Thus in 1795, in strenuous resolutions against the treaty that Secretary of State John Jay had negotiated with Britain two years earlier, the Republican Society of Pendleton County protested the rights extended to Britain to intervene in the trade between South Carolina and the West Indies. Not only did the Jay Treaty restrain Carolinians "from exporting in our own bottoms any articles of West-India produce, and even of *cotton*, an article of our own growth," the protesters complained, but, to satisfy the "claims of British creditors," southerners had to watch "the value of the Negroes and other property carried away."[61]

Democratic-Republican activists in the South Carolina low country forged a shrewd political alliance with independent farmers in the backcountry uplands where sentiment for the common white man, and resentment of wealthy elites, was strong. While low-country Federalists mistrusted backcountry farmers and their penchant for democracy, a new generation of Democratic-Republicans wrested political control of the state from Federalists by organizing backcountry farmers and promoting the growth of slavery and cotton among them. As backcountry Republicans became slave-owning cotton producers in their own right, they formed political organizations to extend the slave economy into Georgia, Alabama, Louisiana, and Mississippi.[62] Strong political support for the growth of slavery may have been the most significant and lasting effect of Democratic-Republican organizing.

As slave populations grew and free blacks faced growing discrimination and tightening restrictions, fear and frustration mounted. In Richmond, in the midst of the political campaign that swept Virginia's son Thomas Jefferson into the nation's highest office, frustration at black exclusion from political freedom fueled plans for a major slave rebellion. Home to many skilled black workers, Richmond was "the metropolis of *Negro-land*," according to a white observer, where free and enslaved blacks found employment in numerous industries and piloted boats along waterways. Blacks and whites mingled in taverns where Democratic-Republican societies gathered, and where people read political news aloud and drank to toasts printed in partisan newspapers.[63]

The enslaved blacksmith Gabriel planned a slave revolt in the shadows of Jefferson's election campaign of 1800. The conspiracy was an act of defiance against a political system that celebrated freedom but enslaved blacks and an organized effort to kill all whites perceived as enemies to black rights. Much as the conspiracy reflected black indignation at the hypocrisy of white politics, it also borrowed from the principles and procedures of the American political system; the slaves involved in the conspiracy held their own election in the summer of 1800, voting for Gabriel over Jack Ditcher to lead the rebellion. Thwarted by an August thunderstorm on the night of the rebellion, news of the conspiracy leaked. Governor James Monroe called up the state militia to arrest the conspirators, and Gabriel and several others were chased down, tried, and hanged. Concerned about the repercussions for Jefferson and fellow Republicans, whom Federalists constantly associated with incendiary democracy, Monroe tried to prevent newspaper coverage, but news of the rebellion spread by word of mouth, adding to the atmospheres of mistrust mounting at the time of Jefferson's election.[64]

In Philadelphia, home to the nation's most thriving population of free blacks, black professionals, artisans, and entrepreneurs maintained a foothold in the city's economy, even as they faced growing discrimination. Home ownership, never easy for blacks, became increasingly difficult in the first decade of the nineteenth century, and black unemployment rose as a result of growing competition for work and the instability of Philadelphia's commercial economy. Poor blacks, many of them immigrants from the South, sick from malnutrition, disease, and abuse, had a hard time surviving. Their increasing numbers contributed to white anxiety. An ugly scene in front of Independence Hall on July 4, 1805, marked this escalating mistrust. For decades, Philadelphians of all backgrounds had assembled on the square outside Independence Hall to mark the anniversary of the nation's birth with toasts and orations by civic leaders and general festivity. This tradition of patriotic inclusion ruptured in 1805 when dozens of angry white men accosted the blacks who had come to participate and ran them off, yelling curses.[65]

In Philadelphia as elsewhere, partisan activity served as a vehicle for ostracizing blacks from public life. Since the 1790s, Democratic-Republicans had used public celebrations of the Fourth of July as occasions to read the Declaration of Independence aloud and attract crowds sympathetic to the Declaration's principles of liberty and equality. (Federalists preferred to celebrate their patriotism on Washington's birthday in chilly February, when orators eulogized the first president's heroic exemplification of the chief hallmarks of good citizenship—duty and sacrifice.) With the Fourth of July celebration in Philadelphia in 1805 a magnet for partisans celebrating Jefferson's second term in office, the eviction of blacks from that celebration was one instance of a larger political process in which Democratic-Republican organizations became aligned with the interests of slave holders and firmer boundaries of black exclusion from public life were established. In earlier days, Democratic-Republican societies had followed Thomas Paine in calling for abolition and black political equality, but during Jefferson's presidency, party organizers joined the interests of slave-holding planters to those of small farmers and artisans opposed to Federalist trade and monetary policies.

Thus partisan organization of anxiety and mistrust worked most insidiously around the issue of black rights. In their efforts to challenge Federalist authority, Republicans backed away from support of black liberties, even though such support was a logical extension of their political philosophy, as old democratic stalwarts like Thomas Paine and Benjamin Rush continued to explain. As mistrust of blacks became a major galvanizing force within Jeffersonian politics, the inclusive logic of democratic equality was swept aside. Although the ostensible purpose of the partisan alliance between southern planters and poor white farmers and artisans was to unseat Federalist officials who resisted debt relief and the expansion of wealth, black exclusion from Democratic-Republican politics was the most significant effect of that alliance and the often-unacknowledged means to the expansion of white wealth.

Blacks protested these forces arrayed against them and submitted only under duress to the increasingly strict limitations imposed on their public activity. In Philadelphia the year before their eviction from the Fourth of July celebration in 1805, a group of young black men assembled in the southwest side of the city and, adhering to a tradition of forming black militias for security and community pride, organized "themselves into a company" to mark Independence Day. The group "appointed a captain, lieutenant, and ensign" and marched "without arms" through streets of Southwark in the early evening after the festivities at Independence Hall. Within an hour, the organized company began to grow into an unruly crowd as others, "armed with clubs, swords, &c," joined the march, and several whites were attacked. When some in the crowd "threatened to murder a Mr. Kane and family," according to the witness, "a Mr. Burchell, an American" intervened and the crowd dispersed. The following night, a group twice the size assembled—"from one to two hundred, armed as before"—and took over the streets of Southwark, "damning the whites, and saying they would show them *St. Domingo*."[66]

On the first night of the march, "[t]he constables were called out." On the second night, "the sheriff attended with a posse to subdue" the marchers. Within the week, other cities were alerted. On July 10, New York's *Evening Post* reprinted the warning sounded in Philadelphia: "It behooves our police to keep a strict watch, as several very serious reports respecting these riots are in circulation."[67] Conflicts over ownership of the streets and the rights of blacks to assemble in America's northern cities escalated as political life in those cities became increasingly inhospitable to blacks.

In earlier decades, life on the streets was less regulated, more fluid and unself-conscious, and more open to blacks. Pinkster celebrations in New York and New Jersey towns drew large boisterous crowds, open markets, and public parodies of white aristocracy. Held in late May or early June, these festivals, called "Pinkster" after the pink azalea blossoms that celebrants wore, derived from traditions associated with the Feast of Pentecost brought by Dutch settlers to New York and New Jersey that African Americans appropriated and revised to reflect their own ideas and traditions. In Boston in 1803, Pinkster celebrations drew "a motley group of thousands" that included "blacks and a certain class of whites." As mistrust of black assembly escalated, these celebrations dwindled and disappeared; thus in Albany in 1811, it became illegal "to march or parade, with or without any kind of music" on "the days commonly called Pinxter."[68]

In New England for much of the eighteenth century, blacks had gathered during the time of elections for music, food, dance, and parodies of public office. In more than a dozen New England towns during the season of spring elections, blacks selected a mock "ruler" who "reigned" for several days. These were political events only by indirection and implication; more straightforwardly, they belonged to the general revelry associated with elections, when few people voted, campaigning for office was unheard of, and people came to town and got drunk after listening to sermons about their duties to God and Christian rulers. On those spring afternoons when townsfolk and rural visitors saturated themselves with rum and cider, jibes at the ruling elite must have been part of the general amusement. In that respect at least, the street life of many whites on election days in New England may not have been too different from that of blacks.

Once partisan activists began organizing public life and once Democratic-Republicans began recruiting people into partisan alliances that politicized festivals, taverns, and street life, election days became much more serious events. Liquor flowed no less capaciously, but political organizers increasingly took control of its distribution. Toasts to liberty, equality, and Republican leaders, along with insults aimed at Federalist tyranny, polarized the process of political decision making at the same time that process expanded to include increasingly large numbers of independent white men. Fights broke out, as they did in earlier years, but brawls became more political in Jeffersonian America as people became more schooled in and driven by partisan ideology. Efforts to exclude blacks from public expressions of citizenship were part of this evolving process.

As president, Thomas Jefferson lamented the demoralizing effects of slavery, but resisted every Federalist attempt to abolish or curtail it. Acting out of both political expediency and profound mistrust of blacks, Jefferson continually opposed any extension of political rights to blacks. As Jefferson's predecessor in presidential office, John Adams had lent a hand to Toussaint Louverture, who hoped for US recognition of the black republic and for an end to the embargo on trade to St. Domingue imposed by France that was starving the island. Adams hosted Toussaint's emissary, Joseph Bunel, at a dinner in December, 1798, supported a bill containing a provision to lift the embargo of US ships to the island, and authorized an expedition of warships to guard the harbor at Cape François. Jefferson, then vice president and chair of the Senate, was highly displeased: "We may expect therefore blacks crews and ... missionaries" passing easily "into the Southern states," he warned as the bill moved through Congress. From Jefferson's perspective, the existence of black political rights in St. Domingue was a threat to social order in the United States: "If this combustion can be introduced among us under any veil whatever, we have to fear it." Once he became president, Jefferson quietly put an end to the supports that Adams had introduced. In 1802, Napoleon's soldiers captured Toussaint, who died in prison in France the following year. In December 1803, when Toussaint's successor Jean-Jacques Dessalines declared St. Domingue to be the independent Republic of Haiti, Jefferson simply failed to acknowledge that Haiti existed. As far as the US government was concerned, Haiti remained a nonentity until 1862.[69]

Although many Federalists supported the abolition of slavery, they were not proponents of black suffrage or equality. In objecting to the notorious three-fifths rule by which slaves were partially counted in determining the number of representatives a state could send to Congress, Federalists preferred that slaves not be counted at all. Federalist, as well as Republican, presumptions of black inferiority became more firmly entrenched as a result of growing mistrust of blacks, fear of black revolution, and rapidly expanding slave populations in the South. When overt references to Jefferson's relationship to Sally Hemings hit the newspapers in 1802, "dusky Sally" and her "sable arms" became Federalists clichés for Jefferson's moral degeneracy.[70]

Though many Federalists in New England and the middle states were distressed by the expansion of slavery and its evil effects on blacks and whites, their social instincts were often hierarchical and antidemocratic. Abigail Adams was exceptional in insisting that James Prince, whom she had taught to read and write, be allowed to attend an evening school for apprentices in Philadelphia in 1797: "The boy is a freeman as much as any of the young men," she insisted. Federalists often acknowledged the humanity of blacks and protested the inhumane treatment of slaves, but many presumed that blacks were innately inferior to whites and resisted egalitarian forms of social and political integration.[71]

In the partisan organization of American public life that took root in the election of 1800, critics of Federalist elitism ignored the humanitarian aspects of Federalism or dismissed them as arrogant attempts at social control. Federalist mistrust of democracy, and bitter defensiveness at being dragged into partisan battle, led to the decline and eventual disappearance of the Federalist Party. As support for the moral authority of government gave way to more libertarian policies, the civic humanitarianism of Federalism, which stressed the importance of education and social improvement, passed into religious missions designed to operate above politics.

Meanwhile, a coalition including promoters of unrestrained commerce, celebrants of natural reason, Baptists, and other evangelicals critical of federal authority, wielded sufficient political clout to enforce the establishment of secular government. Advocates of national expansion and unrestrained commerce drew increasing support from evangelicals, whose growth was also unrestrained and enhanced by the demonization of religious skepticism and by the decline of deist celebrants of natural reason, or their gravitation toward evangelical circles where reason and revelation were treated as coextensive. As their ranks swelled, evangelicals brought their investment in Christian reason and progress as well as their antipathy to open-ended, critical thought along with them to support, or at least not interrupt, the expansion of a national economy and political system that depended on the exploitation of blacks and consent of white women.

With increasing regularity, people joined religious groups in much the same voluntary spirit as they favored political parties, choosing the one most representative of their interests. In this respect as in so many others, religion in the early republic developed in symbiosis with new forms of political organization and within a context of cultural politicization unprecedented elsewhere. Only in the United States did the international struggle over the meaning of democracy at the turn of the nineteenth century become institutionalized in mass politics. Unknown in other countries before the last decades of the nineteenth century, partisan politics directed at "the people" emerged in 1800 as the principle means of organizing public life in the United States.[72]

Religion followed suit. Aggressive marketing of biblical authority and supernatural experience drove the expansion of competing religious groups and strengthened their autonomy as freewheeling enterprises aimed at a mass audience and based on freedom of choice.[73] Free to uphold superior standards of moral practice, condemn corruption in the profane world, and work to advance the progress of religion, religious people pursued their own interest and were more detached from obligations to support civic government than many of their predecessors had been. Even as religious groups operated as spheres of governance with their own internal politics, cynicism toward civic government and resentment of Federalist notions that government should operate as a moral construct in people's lives pushed religion and politics apart, with the effect of granting both religion and politics increased freedom and autonomy.

After the War of 1812, evangelicals gained enough popularity and public support to take up reform efforts directed toward the common good, or what they imagined it to be.[74] By that time, however, slavery and Indian removal were well established, as were libertarian policies with respect to the acquisition and development of property and other material resources. Preoccupied with their own operations and moral superiority, evangelicals specialized in shaping personal piety and providing rhetoric about the United States as a Christian nation where piety was free to grow.

The basic dynamic at work in the organization of public life in the early republic was mistrust of the other party, and this dynamic affected the development of religious organizations as well as the growth of political parties. Claimants to "religion" invoked opposing groups as foils against which to define themselves. As coalitions formed among like-minded religious groups, opposition to others brought coherence. When the growth of Catholic immigration accelerated, the anti-Catholic bias engrained in American notions of biblical revelation and common sense took on new life as evangelicals treated Catholics as religious enemies with loyalties to foreign government.[75]

Mistrust drove the growth of religious institutions at a deeper level still. Suspicion of skeptical reason stimulated insistence on religious authority and new strategies of religious defense, both of which stimulated religious growth. As the next chapter will argue, fear of free thought contributed to the vitality of religious growth, the moral and theological issues that evangelicals addressed, and the feelings and behaviors associated with religion, generating new and more effective means of managing doubt about the truth and purpose of religion.

CHAPTER THREE

Religion to the Rescue

Jane Talbot, published with little fanfare in 1801, was Charles Brockden Brown's last novel. Unlike his sensationally dramatic and more famous gothic novels—*Wieland* (1798), *Arthur Merwyn* (1799), and *Edgar Huntley* (1799)—*Jane Talbot* is a love story with a happy ending. Inside that conventional framework, however, Brown explored skepticism's reputation as an indicator of untrustworthy character and religion's triumph as the necessary arbiter of trust. Revealing the conditions that respectable young people were expected to adhere to in the increasingly straitlaced cities of Philadelphia and New York, where the sex-saturated pleasure culture of the late eighteenth century was fading into disrepute, the novel acknowledged that religion must be accepted and skepticism relinquished as a means to securing happiness, social approval, and respectable sex. Reflecting the cultural shift from skepticism to religion provoked by anxiety and cynicism, the title character reaffirms the Christian piety of her childhood, now "stronger than it ever was" after a flirtation with skepticism.

Providing close description of the moral refurbishment occurring in the fast growing cities of the mid-Atlantic states, *Jane Talbot* participated in an even larger process of social formation sweeping through different regions and among a variety of demographic groups in the early republic. Religious activity and membership rose sharply at the turn of the century, and in its several different iterations, strident campaigns against religious skepticism drove efforts to create new forms of community and restore the commitment to moral order supposed to characterize earlier times. In western regions, Presbyterians, Methodists, and Baptists staged mass demonstrations of supernatural power aimed at defeating unbelievers.[1] In southern states, members of the same religious groups nurtured influential pockets of religious governance against a sea of religious skepticism and indifference.[2] In New England, activists worked to inoculate impressionable youth against religious skepticism through public education and Sabbath observance,[3] and a new generation of young men and women found employment as teachers and moral guardians as publicly supported primary schools sprung up across the region.[4] In New York City, Philadelphia, and Baltimore, evangelicals attracted many, especially young women, who found refuge in religious societies that offered protection from moral corruption and from the religious skepticism believed to support it.[5]

In the cities Charles Brockden Brown knew best—Philadelphia and New York—skepticism enjoyed more sophisticated support than anywhere in the United States. In Philadelphia, the hub of philosophical activity in the early republic, city planners, medical philosophers, and abolitionists gathered around Benjamin Rush and Joseph Priestly, enlightenment thinkers known for their scientific interests, liberal religious ideas, and democratic politics.[6] In New York City, enlightenment liberalism did not exert the same degree of influence but rationalist cosmopolites found a home there nonetheless. The Friendly Club Brown frequented in New York during the 1790s conducted discussions of literature, philosophy, and current affairs animated by familiarity with skeptical writers like David Hume, William Godwin, and Mary Wollstonecraft; Brown's 1794 book, *Alcuin*, presented dialogues about women's rights stimulated by those discussions.[7]

Unlike taverns where politics were constantly aired and newspapers often read aloud, the Friendly Club excluded partisan political debate. Like religious groups seeking a supernatural plane of reality above the partisan fray, the Friendly Club sought rational discourse and fellowship where philosophy and art might be nurtured without divisiveness and deceit. Though most members were Federalists, and criticism of political partisanship was often a Federalist refrain, a few Republicans were involved, with the ban against partisan debate enabling their inclusion. But partisan differences proved too strong, and the Friendly Club stopped meeting in 1800 or 1801, around the time of Jefferson's election. Adding to members' discomfort, conspiracy theories about *Illuminati* cast suspicion on private intellectual gatherings unaffiliated with religion—like the Friendly Club.[8] In a fictional narrative about the anxiety entailed in skepticism's decline and religion's role in that process, *Jane Talbot* reflected the failure of nonpartisan intellectual life in the United States, and religion's ascendance as a normative social force.

Brown wrote *Jane Talbot* in the midst of a decidedly reactionary turn in the intellectual life and social activities of America's urban centers. Federalists were ramping up their efforts at organized benevolence and educational reforms in response to losing control of the US presidency and facing stiff competition from Republicans at state and local levels.[9] Prominent Federalist women, like Elizabeth Hamilton of New York, wife of the secretary of the US Treasury Alexander Hamilton, became active in programs of urban benevolence.[10] A Plan of Union enacted between Presbyterians and Congregationalists funneled plans for moral redemption hatched in Federalist Connecticut through Presbyterian assemblies meeting in Philadelphia, providing Connecticut clergy access to the Presbyterian system of missionary organization. Commitment to education and moral reform on the part of Federalist clergy spearheaded the backlash against Jeffersonian democracy, compelling many supporters of Jefferson to proclaim their commitment to religion or mute their skepticism. With strong support from women, moral reformers in Philadelphia, New York, and New England linked religious skepticism to sexual immorality and incorporated defeat of the former into their crusade against the latter. *Jane Talbot* reveals the dynamics of this crusade.

Jane Talbot loves Henry Colden, a young rationalist who emerges from a murky background as a free thinker to a point of moral clarity: "There is but one meagre and equivocal merit that belongs to me," he tells Jane, "I stick to the truth." In hindsight, it is easy to see Henry as a transitional character with one foot in enlightenment reason and the other in romantic self-dramatization. To contemporary readers, who could not have known how romanticism would develop in the United States, he would more likely have been seen as the shattered, burned-out wreck that skepticism leaves in its turbulent wake when its practitioners live devoid of principles anchored in religion. Immersed in ruthless self-analysis, Henry has low self-esteem, what he calls "my extreme contempt and distrust of myself," as well as hyperbolic regret. "I look back with humiliation and remorse," he tells Jane, confessing that sticking to the truth "is a virtue of late growth," and one that affords little relief from self-recrimination. But the absence of specific evidence of any real wrongdoing, copious regrets for what Jane calls "a thousand misdeeds (as you have thought them)," and a habit of bending over backwards for the sake of others, suggest that Henry's failings are more exaggerated than real.[11]

Henry's extreme moral scrupulousness has the ironic effect of creating suspicion, prompting Jane to question his faithfulness and allowing others to freely slander his character. When a gossip tells Jane that Henry has been visiting a Miss Secker, Jane deduces that he has been unfaithful, when in fact

Miss Secker is a decrepit washerwoman and Henry is simply too modest to reveal his charitable efforts in her behalf. Expressing remorse for her mistrust of him, Jane scolds Henry for his concealment of good deeds and for the "tissue of self-upbraidings" that obscured his true character as "a very excellent man."[12]

However revealing with respect to Henry's character, the misunderstanding regarding Miss Secker is trifling compared to the mistrust propelled by Jane's "mother," Mrs. Fielding. A blend of benevolent patronage and strict adherence to respectable morality, Mrs. Fielding represents Religion, especially religion of the elite Federalist type. Much as Religion herself adopts the defenseless, Mrs. Fielding is Jane's mother by adoption. She reviles Henry for the crime of religious skepticism and commits her considerable emotional and financial resources to expelling him from Jane's sight.

Jane veers toward helplessness despite contrary signs of strength and independence. Her natural mother died when she was five, and her father is a hopeless incompetent unable to check the ruinous behavior of Jane's brother, whose reckless speculations, habitual deceit, and arrogant treatment of everyone make a strong contrast to Henry Colden's assiduous, not to say masochistic, virtue. Jane draws on the largess of Mrs. Fielding, who urges Jane to marry the man betrothed to her as a child, a man whose "religion had produced all its practical effects, in honest, regular, sober, and consistent conduct," but who "never reasoned on the subject" or felt himself inclined toward "[a]ll those expansions of soul" that Jane finds so attractive in Henry.

Henry's "friend" Thompson betrays him, telling Mrs. Fielding that Henry had been brought up to respect the "sacred precepts" of religion "on which the happiness of men rests," but through exposure to William Godwin's *Political Justice* fell captive to "that pernicious philosophy which is now so much in vogue." Godwinian skepticism, Mrs. Fielding declared, delivered "the worst poison under the name of wholesome food" and concealed "all that is impious, or blasphemous, or licentious, under the guise and sanctions of virtue." In his tête-à-tête with Mrs. Fielding, Thompson maintains that he tried to counter "every horrid and immoral tenet" Henry advanced, but found Henry unstoppable in his "new faith." Henry's letters to Thompson revealed him to be, in Mrs. Fielding's appalled paraphrase, "the advocate of suicide; a scoffer at promises; the despiser of revelation, of Providence and a future state; an opponent of marriage, and as one who denied (shocking!) that any thing but mere habit and positive law stood in the way of . . . intercourse without marriage."[13]

Like the early republic itself, Henry and Jane have orphanlike qualities.

Removed from their families of birth, both are uneasy about independence and profoundly unsure of their capacities for self-reliance. Torn between her attachment to her religious mother and her love for the skeptical Henry, Jane has difficulty finding a way out of that conflict, or any escape from the tumultuous feelings that confront her at every turn. A move in the direction of independence from Mrs. Fielding, by declaring she would be happy to live in the humblest surroundings with Henry, prompts the punctilious Henry to back off from Jane for the sake of her welfare. Meanwhile, the gossip who previously interfered in their relationship forges a letter, leaving the impression that Henry and Jane spent an amorous night together and that Jane was delighted to be Henry's paramour. "I have got into a maze again," Jane tells Henry. Tangled in deceit and self-reproach and fearful that her reputation now reflects badly on Henry, Jane seeks her mother's love and turns Henry away. "My safety lies only in filling my ears with my mother's remonstrances and shutting them against your persuasive accents," she tells him. "I have therefore resigned myself wholly to my mother's government."[14]

Henry also comes back to God. Leaving Jane to the "government" of Mrs. Fielding, he embarks on a dangerous voyage to Japan via the Sandwich Islands and eventually lands in Hamburg as "a trusty agent" of the Dutch East India Company, gainfully employed for the first time in his life. "I have awakened from my dreams of doubt and misery," Henry writes Jane upon his return to America, "to the living and delightful consciousness, of every tie that can bind man to his Divine Parent and Judge." With Mrs. Fielding passed to her reward with forgiveness of Henry on her lips, Jane and Henry are free to marry and consummate their love.[15]

Like the redeemed character he created, Charles Brockden Brown engaged in acts of radical skepticism and fertile imagination that he gradually learned to restrain. Born in 1771 in Philadelphia to a Quaker family descended from shipmates of William Penn, Brown was full of "plans and scraps of Eutopias" as a young man, according to his "friend" and biographer William Dunlap, "by which to improve and secure human happiness." Such energetic idealism coincided with resistance to the authority of received opinion: "Ever fond of analysis, Charles, even in very early life, would take no opinion on trust." While "ostensibly studying law, but in reality indulging himself in every freak," according to the judgmental Dunlap, Brown lost his mooring. Immersed in radical philosophy and creative writing during the 1790s, "his reading at this time tended to bewilder rather than enlighten and to confirm his predisposition to skepticism." Indulgence of this sort led Brown to what Dunlap, who sounds much like Henry Colden's "friend" Thompson in *Jane Talbot*, called "plunging tenets and dangerous doctrines."[16]

Much to Dunlap's approval, Brown brought his flights of fancy to earth and his penchant for skeptical analysis under control: "From the regions of poetry and romance; from visionary schemes of Utopian systems of manners, Mr. Brown, like many others, became a sober recorder of things as they are."[17] Between 1803 and his last bout with consumption in the winter of 1809–10, Brown turned his talents as a writer to geography and politics, working to showcase the extraordinary resources of the North American continent and advance public debate about the dangers of foreign entanglement. In 1804, the same year *Jane Talbot* was published in England, Brown married Elizabeth Linn and returned from New York to live in Philadelphia. With his marriage, Dunlap reported with satisfaction, Brown began "enjoying in an uncommon degree that domestic happiness which had always appeared to him as the consummation of human felicity, and for which he was so eminently formed."[18]

Brown undertook the journey from religious skepticism to marriage that he imagined in *Jane Talbot*. Brown's turn away from radical philosophy coincided with his marriage to a woman whose father and brother were both well-known ministers. The wedding took place a few months after the death of Elizabeth's brother, John Blair Linn, D.D., the pastor at First Presbyterian Church with whom Elizabeth had lived and Charles had corresponded with warm affection. John Linn embodied the evangelical upsurge against skepticism coursing through the country, as revealed in his exchange of letters with the Unitarian philosopher Joseph Priestley. In response to Priestley's argument about the similarities between Jesus and Socrates, young Linn sought to correct the elderly Priestley on certain points of Calvinist Christology. Priestley would have none of that and chided Linn for treating disbelief in the divinity of Jesus as if it were a sign of moral degeneracy: "[H]ow can you say," Priestley demanded, recalling Linn's tone of pompous condescension, that "'I cannot but express a wish that our free intercourse of opinions which has passed may rather promote harmony than discord;' when if I be the person you describe, you would disgrace yourself by any harmony with me."[19]

Acceptance of religion's necessary place in society was the price Brown paid for intimacy with the Linns. While maintaining reticence with regard to its metaphysical claims, Brown expressed respect for religion as a means to social harmony, domestic happiness, and the quelling of inner turmoil. Thus he cherished the irenic habits of his Quaker upbringing while placing himself beyond the reach of theological discipline. "There are others who will pass me by as a visionary: and some, observing the city where I thus make my appearance, may think my pacific doctrine, my system of rational forbearance and forgiveness carried to a pitch of *Quaker* extravagance," he wrote in an essay near the end of his life. "The truth is, I am no better than an outcast of that unwarlike sect, but cannot rid myself of reverence for most of its practical and political maxims."[20] If Brown followed these maxims in abandoning fiction—an art that evangelicals often looked upon dubiously—*Jane Talbot* was his last effort to explore the subjective states that kept young people from getting down to business. Jane Talbot's frantic confusion and Henry Colden's isolation as an intellectual unwilling to bend to religious pressure were precisely what Brown moved beyond.

With Elizabeth and respect for religion settled, Brown's attention as a writer shifted away from the interior labyrinths of American psyches to the political dangers threatening the nation's future prosperity. But the concerns about honesty, deception, and religious destiny evident in *Jane Talbot* also persisted in Brown's political writings, as did traces of his sensitivity to the fact that these matters had something to do with sex. Focused on threats to American integrity from within and without, these political writings presented concerns similar to those *Jane Talbot* depicted in interpersonal, emotional terms.

With the enormity of the continent and its vast resources as the backdrop in his late writing, Brown envisioned the future America as a peaceable kingdom bound together by a healthy commerce that promoted mutual respect among different ethnic groups. Emerging as an advocate of American imperialism, Brown pointed to the positive effects that political empires of the past had in fostering peace among inhabitants of various ancestry. "One of the consequences of extended empire," he wrote in his last political essay, "is to pull down barriers which separate mankind from each other; to enlarge that circle which each man calls his country; to take away the grounds of dissension and rivalship; to create one nation out of many, to blend into one system of friendly, and especially commercial intercourse, tribes that formerly looked upon each other as natural and hereditary enemies." Brown had no trouble imagining an American empire that would surpass anything the world had known: "Curious examples of this *consolidation* are to be found in the history of Europe; one memorable one is afforded by the history of Asia, but the most magnificent of all will be given to posterity in the history of North America."[21]

Conspiring to prevent this rosy outcome, however, and despite all the benefits of nature working to promote it, were insidious forces of deception and manipulation. While not claiming to be a "prophet," Brown wrote in 1809 that he would "not be surprised" if the United States entered into war with England or divided itself into competing nations. War and disunion lay ahead if foreign and domestic politics were not managed in a more practical manner, with attention to commerce driving political decisions, rather than "groundless hatreds and insane attachments to foreign states." In an effort to transcend the mistrust generated by partisan crusades for power and ruthless efforts to demolish political opponents, Brown constructed an imperial point of view that transcended both Republican and Federalist platforms: "As I believe in the policy of justice and peace and unrestricted trade in our present circumstances, I can claim no kindred with one party," he wrote in 1806, meaning the Republican party that supported Jefferson's embargo on foreign trade. "I believe that the merits and demerits of Great Britain and France, in relation to us, are *exactly equal*," he went on, distancing himself from Anglophile Federalists as well as Francophile Republicans: "the conduct of *both*" England and France "is dictated by no principle but ambition, and measured by no rule but *power*." Given the enormous resources of the North American continent, all the US government needed to do to enable the development of an American empire was wait out the conflict consuming European powers during the Napoleonic Wars and focus on building domestic commerce.[22]

While Brown advanced these arguments about foreign and domestic policy apart from any explicit reference to religion or theology, his vision of a peaceable American kingdom complemented visions advanced by some of America's most ardent evangelicals. With the profound disharmony of political conflicts as background, millennial visions of the future acquired new popularity and political cachet at the turn of the nineteenth century. The more dangerous and intractable the political conflicts appeared, the more transcendent visions of social harmony appealed, and seemed to be the only answer. If partisan deviousness, unrestrained ambition, infidelity, and sexual license all stood in the way of social harmony, they were also foils against which visionaries imagined an ideal empire.

Though less partisan and more sympathetic to open-ended reason, Brown was no less outraged than Connecticut clergy were by the dishonesty rife in the early republic. Writing in 1806 in a pamphlet that distressed Thomas Jefferson sufficiently to cause him to block its publication in the United States, Brown pointed to the irony of Republicans, who supposedly despised monarchy, deferring to whatever their leaders said. He condemned them for misrepresenting every critic of Jefferson as a proponent of monarchy and for infecting "public sentiment" to such an extent that any proposal advanced by a Federalist was dismissed out of hand. Attentive to the circular reasoning typical in political invective, Brown exclaimed, "The measures that such men recommend are considered part of the system attributed to them."[23] He blamed Jefferson for "establishing a system of corruption" undermining the integrity of the federal government and "extending the web of intrigue to influence elections over the whole country." Likening the president to the "sly animal in the fable" who, wanting not to burn his paws, commissioned others to bring him warm chestnuts from the fire, Brown condemned Jefferson's practice of extending large favors to congressmen as a way of getting them to do his bidding. These manipulations weakened the presidency as well as the Congress, Brown believed, with consequences as distasteful as they were dangerous. "He has placed himself also in a state of dependence," Brown observed with obvious repugnance, "whereby he is driven to do unrighteous things, and which disables him from becoming useful, should any course of events restore to him the love of honest fame."[24]

Brown injected sexual innuendo into Jefferson's reputation as a skeptic. "When we first knew him," Brown wrote, "he was a youth of ingenuous temper whose ignorance of the world exposed him to become the prey of any sharper (of either sex) by whom he might be assailed." Lacking any "fixed principles," Brown explained, Jefferson inevitably fell into "a deep decline of character," with a noxious tendency to skepticism that left him unmoored from common sense: "Like others who had fallen into the idle habit of questioning established truth, his faculty of weighing evidence is impaired." Brown could have said much the same about the fictional Henry Colden or about his own youthful reasoning. The sign of Jefferson's departure from reality was his confidence in reason: "If any gentleman assume as a principle that mankind can be governed by reason," Brown wrote, "we would advise him to commence a course of experiments with his own family, and see how far reason will go." Of course, Brown would not stoop to mention Jefferson's own domestic arrangement, at least not directly: "If there be blemishes in his private character, we have nothing to do with them."[25]

Brown's characterization of Jefferson as a sly fox and his expressions of frustration at the partisan political manipulation of public sentiment echoed the plot of *Jane Talbot*, where manipulations by a scheming gossip wreaked havoc on the efforts of Henry and Jane to find a little peaceable kingdom of their own. The foreign entanglements of Jane's brother and his devious use of her inheritance to support his French mistress, "that prodigal jade, Mademoiselle Couteau,"[26] compromised Jane's independence and deepened the shadow of ill repute cast on the whole Talbot family, much as political entanglements with European powers (especially France) threatened American peace and security. In making the shift from analysis of interpersonal treachery in fiction to analysis of treachery in politics, Brown saw the kind of distasteful and dangerous intrigue he had explored in fiction operating at the highest level of government at the expense of American virtue and independence.

The almost miraculously happy ending of *Jane Talbot*, with the union of Jane and Henry under the aegis of religion, was Brown's future American empire in microcosm. Flourishing commerce among peaceful tribes in a vast American empire required fealty to the empire's government and obedience to her laws, much as individual impulses required respect for moral government. Henry Colden relinquished his religious skepticism and unwillingness to accept truth on authority; only then did he find social acceptance and relief from the mistrust that blackened him in everyone's eyes, including his own. Jane's path was more twisted. In accepting her obligation to Mrs. Fielding after an ineffectual attempt at independence, she gave up the opportunity for rational self-government, claiming to "be contented with the approbation of a pure and all-seeing Judge." Renewed financial security sweetened this submission, but honest assessment of that exchange, and of the power that flowed to Jane as an agent of religion, was not a feature of Jane's newfound equanimity. Repressing critical thought, Jane drew Henry into "the living and delightful consciousness, of every tie that can bind man to his Divine Parent and Judge." Her missionary endeavor to save Henry brought her a new confidence and authority as the agent of religion's reign, and means to Henry's surrender of independence.[27]

Between 1801 and 1804, the years between the publication of *Jane Talbot* and Brown's marriage to Elizabeth Linn, tens of thousands of Americans were reeling with religious feeling and engaging in practices aimed at rendering imagined worlds of heaven and hell palpable and compelling. Americans were also organizing themselves into religious groups and expanding religious operations to an unprecedented degree.[28] Brown settled down among the elite Presbyterians of Philadelphia at the same time Presbyterians were attempting to exercise greater control over the city through new forms of missionary effort. Brown's turn toward political writing and visions of American empire coincided with his new affiliation with evangelicals in the city and with the efforts of religious leaders in Philadelphia to extend their religious government over the city.

In 1802, Presbyterian activists solicited funds to hire a Presbyterian chaplain to oversee the city's jail and hospital and to create a Presbyterian Society that would orchestrate urban reform efforts in Philadelphia's three Presbyterian churches. Like the political union of the United States, the plan called for two hundred members drawn into a legal corporation with procedures for electing officers and replacing departing members. The corporation would welcome individuals from other denominations provided they submitted to the will of the Presbyterian majority. Maintaining a polite but firm distinction between Presbyterians and other evangelical groups who supported their ministers at far more modest levels, members were to pay annual dues of $5, enabling the society to start the new chaplain at an annual salary of $1,000, with a supplementary fund to support the growth of the mission and increases in the chaplain's salary.[29] (In 1800, a carpenter might earn $1 a day, about one-third of what the new chaplain would make.)[30]

The authors of the plan drew another polite but firm distinction between the "humane and charitable institutions" that already existed in the city and were "justly considered as constituting its prime ornament" on one hand and the need for an explicitly religious framework to envelop these social services in supernatural authority on the other. Appealing to the higher realm of the spirit upon which evangelicals rested their authority, the authors failed to understand how the citizens of Philadelphia could allow themselves to attend so effectively to the "temporal wants" of the poor while ignoring their even greater need for "the instructions and consolations of the gospel." To be sure, the city already allowed ministers from different denominations access to its public institutions, and some ministers did take occasional time away from their many obligations to attend to parishioners inhabiting these places, but such attentions were clearly inadequate. The time had come for Presbyterians to take the lead in attending to the desperate needs for spiritual guidance among inhabitants of Philadelphia's public institutions and, at the same time, help satisfy the powerful thirst for benevolence felt by the city's evangelicals. The authors of the plan understood the drive to benevolence as a matter of common sense. "When a person under the influence of genuine Christianity, considers how infinitely more valuable the soul is than the body, what must be his sensations," they asked, "when he observes that unspeakable pains are taken to relieve and accommodate the mortal part, while very little attention, comparatively, is given to that which is immortal?"[31]

The Presbyterian Plan resonated with notions of civic responsibility that Federalists often shared with an older generation of civic leaders like Benjamin Franklin. It also exuded the kind of patronizing religious elitism that annoyed democratic supporters of Jefferson, including those hostile to religious skepticism. But if the religious orientation of the Presbyterian Plan for civic improvement reflected the partisan political culture in which it emerged, it also foreshadowed the evangelical consensus that would take shape after the War of 1812 through concerted efforts to establish evangelical morality as the normative standard at home and abroad. Presbyterians and their Congregationalist allies in New England played the leading role in these missionary endeavors, compensating for the decline of Federalism as a political party. Missionary efforts to bring the United States and the world to Christ would bridge some of the political differences separating evangelicals in Jeffersonian America, even as other political differences, especially over slavery, divided them.

According to the Presbyterian Plan of 1802, the Presbyterian Society of Philadelphia would function as a missionary operation similar to societies recently organized in Europe to take the gospel to heathen lands and similar also to the rapidly expanding Presbyterian missions to the Indians of America, to which the General Assembly of Presbyterian ministers and elders meeting in Philadelphia in 1802 devoted much attention.[32] Advocates for Presbyterian influence over the poor heartily approved of far-flung missions, but thought the demand at home more pressing. As the authors of the Philadelphia Plan asked plaintively, "Is not the soul of a criminal in the jail of Philadelphia as great as that of an Indian on the banks of the Ohio?" Clearly, "preference" lay with the poor of Philadelphia, so close at hand. A Presbyterian chaplain would help them obtain consolation for their sufferings on earth and guide them along the path to heaven, while also improving life in the city for everyone and even benefiting the economy: "Without this instruction," children in the Betteringhouse "may become pests of society in this world, and candidates for misery in the world to come—Instruction and admonition may render them useful at present and happy hereafter."[33]

Such concern for the poor and their apparent disregard for religion was not without a sexual dimension. Philadelphia was home to open prostitution, with more than a dozen bawdy houses in 1799, and a culture of sexual pleasure associated with lusty songs, provocative dress, libidinous masquerades, extramarital arrangements, and many children born outside of wedlock. Many of those children were incorporated into the families of their mothers or fathers. For mothers and children in dire straits, the city's Guardians of the Poor ensured that some fathers paid financial support. As these arrangements suggest, extramarital sex was more or less accepted in Philadelphia before the rise of evangelicalism at the turn of the century.[34] That tolerance diminished in the onslaught of evangelical campaigns linking sexual permissiveness to infidelity.

The Magdalen Society incorporated in 1800 was part of a broad effort among religious groups in Philadelphia to reign in unrestrained sexual activity and the indifference to religion associated with it. Organized by the Episcopal bishop residing in Philadelphia and several other prominent men, the Magdalen Society was founded to rescue fallen women from penury, disease, and religious ignorance and restore them to society through religious instruction as domestic servants or wives of religious men. Had her author allowed her to slip further into poverty, skepticism, and impulsive behavior, Jane Talbot would have been just the sort of character the Magdalen Society would have liked to redeem; the society's first project, Elizabeth Ogden, received room, board, and religious instruction at the home of a pious family and went on to become a school teacher.

The iconography of urban renewal imposed class distinctions on sexual freedom, thereby casting an added dimension of social shame onto the religious skepticism alleged to be a primary cause of sexual license. After 1810, the impetus to restore fallen women to respectable society gave way to perceptions of prostitutes as low-class criminals who belonged to an altogether different society and whose likelihood of redemption from sin was no longer a compelling image of religious work in the city. In this respect, the primary effect of the Magdalen Society was not the number of women saved from prostitution—fewer than sixty by 1814, when the police had assumed control over prostitutes and the number of bawdy houses had increased to forty—but in the picture of moral order it offered. Images of prostitutes saved by religion linked social order to control over female sexuality and to the coinciding defeat of religious ignorance and indifference.[35]

In eighteenth-century Philadelphia, neither extramarital sexuality nor religious skepticism had been associated with lack of education, poverty, or low-class status; mild forms of religious skepticism were commonplace among the most prominent men of society, and sexual liaisons among affluent women and men did not carry the burden of disgrace they acquired in the early nineteenth century. Women were far more vulnerable to poverty as a result of sexual activity than men, and the relationship between pleasure and women's rights may not have been widely accepted. But only when arguments against biblical revelation and Christian authority became democratized and popular among working people in the 1790s did the dangers of unrestrained female sexuality become a rallying cry for religious reform. At that point, women's interest in pleasure came to seem increasingly dangerous and even repulsive. For evangelicals, religion was the solution to the sufferings of women and their vulnerability to poverty. Commitment to a canopy of religious government, constructed over a world rife with latent female sexuality would rid that world of poverty and rampant free thought.

Presbyterians had a job cut out for them in Philadelphia. With Virginia and Kentucky, Pennsylvania was one of the most democratically leaning and solidly Republican states in Jeffersonian America. The Democratic-Republican societies that developed in the 1790s to support the French Revolution were especially active in Philadelphia and developed there as an important base of support for the organization of an opposition party to the federal administration of John Adams; Thomas McKean's election as governor of Pennsylvania in 1799 spurred the momentum of enthusiasm for Republican policies that culminated in Jefferson's inauguration in 1801. Based in Philadelphia, Benjamin Bache's popular newspaper *The Aurora* disseminated a steady stream of religious skepticism and political invective against antidemocratic interests in the 1790s and early years of the nineteenth century,[36] printing nine notices of Thomas Paine's *Age of Reason* in the first two months of its publication in 1794, as well as a commencement address delivered by Miss Ann Harker in December of that year, in which she observed that "[i]n this age of reason . . . we are not to be surprised, if women have taken advantage of that small degree of liberty which they still possess, and converted their talents to the public utility." After a short tribute to the "amazonian courage" of women in western history, Miss Harker told the men in her audience, "You have your immortal Thomas Paine, we have our Wolstoncraft [sic]."[37]

Mary Wollstonecraft's argument for women's equality became counterproductive once her sexual freedom—the female embodiment of infidelity—became known, much as Paine's proclivity to drink came to be seen as evidence of skepticism's wretched effects. Emulating the rhetoric of ridicule and character assassination prevalent in partisan politics, religious groups across the country became increasingly fervent in their evangelical outreach and proclamations of the need for reform, pointing with growing unanimity to "infidelity" as the cause of American immorality and social dysfunction. The Federalist clergy of New England played an important role in the development of this politically charged evangelicalism, disseminating appeals for religious activism in print and preaching tours. The similarity between their evangelical push and new forms of organized political activity developing across the country was not lost on some observers. As one newspaper from eastern Massachusetts reported, "Complaints from Troy [New York] are that the missionaries sent from Connecticut . . . discover more of the designs of Party, than of promoting the Gospel of peace."[38]

Germinating American visions of the anti-Christ that later developed into fundamentalism,[39] Connecticut clergy used apocalyptic imagery from the book of Revelation to cast religious skepticism, as well as the sexual immorality and political villainy presumed to attend it, as part of a fantastic supernatural battle. One of the nation's most learned opponents of infidelity, the president of Yale College and grandson of Jonathan Edwards, Timothy Dwight, warned in his Fourth of July oration of 1798 that skeptics in America and France were already engaged in "[a]ll that the malice and atheism of the Dragon, the cruelty and rapacity of the Beast, and the fraud and deceit of the false prophet, can generate, or accomplish." In the face of Republican success in making the Fourth of July a partisan holiday, Dwight reframed democracy as an orgy of evil. "The world is already far advanced in the period of the sixth [vial]," he announced authoritatively, and "no impious sentiment, or action, against God has been spared" as the end of time drew near. The sexual license Dwight feared and the political leaders whom he hated were essential elements of his scenario: "Chastity and decency have alike been turned out of doors; and shame and pollution called out of their dens, to the hall of distinction, and the chair of state." Should Christians not arise and wrest control of the nation, "our churches may become temples of reason" and "we may change our holy worship into a dance of Jacobin frenzy." The implications of religious skepticism were almost too degrading to contemplate. Dwight warned, "[W]e may see our wives and daughters the victims of legal prostitution." If "our sons become the disciples of Voltaire," he predicted, "our daughters" might become "concubines of Illuminati."[40]

Eager to assert religious control over the rapidly growing nation through schools, Sabbath observance, religious literature, and home instruction, the evangelicalism promulgated by Federalist clergy in New England focused on the need for instruction that would not simply compete with skeptical reasoning, but crush it altogether. In a sermon published in 1801, Dwight reached again for biblical imagery to warn against educating young women into open-ended rational inquiry. All education must be bound and anchored in religion, Dwight believed. While strongly committed to the growth of public education and the growing corps of young female teachers, he warned that temptations to infidelity were like Satan's seduction of Eve and that reason in female guise was the very epitome of moral disorder. "Will you send your daughters abroad in the attire of a female Greek?" Dwight demanded angrily, summoning up an image of innocent but also provocative schoolgirls studying philosophy in togas. The inevitable effect of such indulgence would be moral disaster: "Will you make marriage the mockery of a register's office? Will you become the rulers of Sodom, and the people of Gomorrha?" The linkage of sex and reason was a potent marker of infidelity especially when associated with the power of a woman's body to expose male weakness: "Will you enthrone a Goddess of Reason before the table of Christ?"[41]

In the religious revivals spreading through New England towns and villages at the turn of the century, repentance for indulgence in the paired vices of skeptical reason and sexual pleasure emerged as the primary script for conversion, and the trope of obedience to divine government emerged as the marker of Christian life, in contrast to the misrule of ordinary life. According to numerous accounts written by ministers who supervised the process of conviction—the self-arraignment before the bar of God in which individuals declared themselves guilty of sin and rebellion against him—young people stopped dancing and visiting and started praying and convicting one another. As Reverend Edward D. Griffin wrote about the young people of New Hartford, "They were now wrapt up in admiration of the laws and absolute government of God, which had been the objects of so much cavil and disgust." One young woman, "having been brought up in gay life," was "insensible of the deceitfulness of her heart" until humbled by Griffin's ministrations. When the conviction process made her aware of being "totally sinful," she was "anxious" to tell her male friend that she was not the innocent girl she had claimed to be, since "she had discovered that she hated God with all her heart." When public school inspectors found a teacher ready to quit rather than accept the required Calvinist tenet that, "God hath foreordained whatsoever comes to pass," the inspectors "endeavored to convince him," and the young man suddenly found himself "seized by the convicting power of truth." In a change of heart that Griffith took as evidence of the power of God, the young man became "filled with admiration of a government planned by eternal wisdom, and administered by unerring rectitude."[42]

In Norfolk, Connecticut, according to Congregational minister Ammi Robbins, "younger people, and persons of information and influence, were fast verging towards infidelity," and "[s]everal had nearly or quite renounced their belief in the holy Scriptures." Naturally the result of such skepticism, "profaneness increased like a flood, and various species of wickedness prevailed" until the prayers of pious Christians, and word of revivals in other towns, heralded a change of heart in several "very popular" people, "some far advanced in deistical sentiments." The change caught fire and "marvelous displays of divine power and grace were conspicuous." Since this was steady Connecticut, converts "were by no means noisy or boisterous, but, in silent anguish, seemed to be cut to the heart."[43]

The preponderance of women to men among those accepted into full church membership during the New England revivals was significant: twenty-eight to seventeen in Torrington in 1799, ninety-four to fifty-nine in Norfolk, and "[a]lmost two-thirds" in Lenox, Massachusetts. In the Middlebury revival of 1799 and 1800, female converts outnumbered male converts twenty-four to seventeen. Killingworth was atypical in its even distribution: during the revival that lasted from 1801 to 1803, forty-five women and forty-six men joined the church.[44] Many young women accepted the government of religion in their life in a more thoroughgoing way than before, even to the point of being willing to judge every impulse to think, feel, or act independently of that government as evil. They became social luminaries as a result, attaining status and exerting personal influence through the medium of religion. With even the tiniest impulse to religious skepticism squelched in evangelical women, the skepticism in which many men more freely indulged could be brought to heel, with marital sex and domestic tranquility as rewards.[45]

Most of the Connecticut converts were young—in their teens and twenties—and female converts consistently outnumbered male converts and often led men through the ritual process. In Bristol, a young husband "inclining to infidelity" tried to stop his wife from getting caught up in the revival, "calling it delusion, enthusiasm and priestcraft." He contemplated abandoning her for a life at sea, but at the last minute went with her family to the meeting house instead, where the sermons "made a deep and powerful impression on his mind." After a period of despair, he entered the self-conviction process, convinced of "the madness and wickedness of his former conduct, in opposing and making light of divine things," and emerged with hope that he would be forgiven. Though still waiting for further evidence of Christian behavior, his minister credited the "change of heart" that had already occurred as evidence "of the power of God in favor of divine truth."[46]

In their ambitious efforts toward religious reform, Calvinist clergy in New England had everything to gain from the 1801 Plan of Union, which was created to further collaboration with Presbyterian and Reformed Calvinists who had built strong institutions in New York, New Jersey, and Pennsylvania. In addition to facilitating the merger of missionary efforts in Indiana and other western territories, where British agents were suspected of supporting Indian resistance against American settlements, the Plan of Union represented a new evangelical drive to bring moral order and religious community to Americans who had lapsed into skepticism and debauchery or, like Catholic immigrants whose numbers were rapidly growing, were presumed to be grossly deluded regarding religion's basic principles and expectations. As the Calvinist Committee from New England reminded their Presbyterian brothers at the meeting of the Presbyterian General Assembly in Philadelphia in 1801, "it is only a realizing sense of the universality of God's government, our obligations to obey his laws and the inflexibility of his justice, which can give security for good morals, and ensure personal and social happiness."[47]

The Calvinist evangelicals behind the Plan of Union also aimed to compete with the increasing popularity of Methodism, and progress in that competition demanded some relaxation of the rigid Calvinist insistence on predestination and the limited reach of free will, which people not raised in a demanding Calvinist system found cold and intimidating. Especially after being exposed to the inviting warmth of Methodist rituals, to Methodist offers of salvation free to the willing, and to the stimulating physical exercises Methodists allowed, newcomers to Calvinism had to be persuaded that Calvinist conversion made people happy.

Timothy Dwight was a leader in the endeavor to soften evangelical Calvinism, and make it more attractive. Aware of the enormous popularity and emotional power of song, which Methodists engaged in at every opportunity, Dwight visited the Presbyterian General Assembly in Philadelphia in 1802 to encourage acceptance of an updated version of the famous hymnal of psalms compiled by the early eighteenth-century English minister Isaac Watts, which some Presbyterians had been using for decades, while others clung to Scottish hymns, or even had reservations about singing any tunes in worship. With help from an oversight committee attentive to the preservation of orthodox doctrine, Dwight incorporated a small amount of new material into the standard collection of hymns "so as to accommodate them to the state of the American Churches," including a reference to "our nation," expunging references to England, and adding some "versifications" of his own. Though not requiring its use, the General Assembly "cheerfully" endorsed the revised English hymnal.[48]

Methodists went well beyond Presbyterian caution in their use of hymns. In addition to Charles Wesley's popular songs, written to elicit feelings for God untethered from biblical psalms, American Methodist preachers created songs that freed individuals from emotional restraint and invoked sensations of supernatural energy and power, breaking barriers and transgressing boundaries of decorum that other groups strove to maintain. Methodists relied on song for religious instruction; in many cases, Methodist preachers like the western itinerant Samuel Parker broke into song or elevated the intensity of their prayers and homilies to make them indistinguishable from song. As a fellow preacher recalled of Parker, "Many were attracted to the Church to listen to the divine strains which he would pour forth upon his enraptured and weeping audiences." Like others in the army of Methodist preachers, Parker commanded "an eloquence and power in the pulpit that were irresistible, and wherever he went wondering and weeping audiences crowded to hear him."[49] The New England itinerant William Beauchamp was equally enthralling: "when holding out the promises and the invitations of the gospel, there was a soft tenderness, a sweetness in his voice, produced frequently by gentle breaks." Witnesses described how "a gentle thrilling sensation appeared to move the listening multitude, all bending forward to catch every sentence." Beauchamp's power to slay skeptics was legendary: "when he became argumentative . . . his whole system became nerved and his voice assumed a deep hollow tone." In one case, an "antagonist" was attempting to exit but fell down, overwhelmed as Beauchamp's voice reached its "highest key, and fell like peals of thunder."[50]

Not everyone succumbed. In 1805, the Philadelphia Quaker Elizabeth Drinker recorded in her diary a scene witnessed by her son: he "heard, as he pass'd the Methodist meeting last evening a noise which induced him to go in." Once inside, the young man saw "there was 5 or 6 under conviction, as they term it, laying on the flour screaming, kicking and some groaning, numbers of the congregation were singing over them." Repelled by the uninhibited performance egged on by singers, "he left them in their extasies—he never saw the like before," the mother wrote, "nor have I."[51]

As a Philadelphia Quaker and Federalist sympathizer, Elizabeth Drinker was accustomed to a far more sedate religious practice. Although Quakers had a history of religious extroversion derived from attentiveness to the inner light of Christ, and Shakers who emerged out of that tradition were competing for converts with great animation in Kentucky, Ohio, and Indiana in the early nineteenth century, Quaker effervescence had settled down in America as befitting their financial success and social status. The English preacher Dorothy Ripley claimed to be a Quaker preacher but was unable to secure a permit to preach from any Quaker group. Traveling in the United States, she appeared in Washington in 1802 "weeping and wailing" in the streets, fitting more into the mold of the Methodists who had originally encouraged her preaching than into that of the Quakers she sought to represent.[52]

The individual self-control esteemed by well-established religious groups as a remedy for debauchery and outright skepticism was difficult to maintain, especially on the frontier, where emotional restraint smacked of elitism. In the Kentucky revivals, New Light Presbyterians joined openly with Methodists, holding open communions with each other in which Methodists encouraged New Lights to be even more expressive. Baptists participated in the calls for conviction and conversion but conducted separate communions and baptismal events. New Light Presbyterian preachers moving into the Cumberland region from North Carolina ignited the Great Revival of 1801, which shaped religious expectations throughout the West and in many parts of the South. In Cane Ridge, Kentucky, in August that year, thousands of participants—many of them newcomers to Christ—attended a mass rally, with eighteen Presbyterian ministers and at least equal numbers of Methodist and Baptist preachers on hand to guide and encourage extraordinary performances of religious enthusiasm.

The foremost leader of the Great Revival, New Light Presbyterian James McGready, launched a head-on attack against religious skepticism with powerful images of a supernatural world designed to reframe people's conceptions of reality and to get them involved in acting out compelling dramas of personal and cosmic salvation. In one of his sermons refuting the skepticism of miracles and biblical revelation ascribed to deism, McGready explained how "this despised book, the Bible, unveils the mystery and opens a door of hope to a lost world." Beyond that door, entered through belief in the ongoing, objective reality of events described in the Bible, "Jesus comes, leaping upon the mountains, skipping upon the hills, flying upon the wings of everlasting love . . . wrests the keys of hell from the hands of the devil, and liberates millions of captive souls from his galling servitude." In another sermon, McGready asked, "When Jesus meets with his people at his table, what appearance will he make?" Ready with the most vivid answers, McGready pictured Jesus "hanging on the cross, all drenched in blood and tears," promising that, "you will see that face, brighter than the light of ten thousand suns, spat upon, black and mangled, swelled with strokes and red with gore, and expressive of love and indescribable anguish." There would be exquisite triumph as well: "you shall see him riding upon the white horse of the everlasting gospel, clothed with a vesture dipped in blood, and a name written upon his vesture and on his thigh—KING OF KINGS, AND LORD OF LORDS . . . with millions of crowns—one for every pardoned and believing rebel."[53]

The supernaturalism proclaimed in the Great Revival got off the ground through the efforts of women and children. In 1799, McGready faced challenges from a "considerable party" working to stop the enthusiasm he was trying to generate. In a sacramental meeting on the Red River in Kentucky in 1800, a woman's "shouting and singing" began to break the logjam and, with the help of fervent exhortations from the Methodist preacher John McGee, "the people frantically, joyously, expectantly began to cry and shout." At a sacramental meeting later that summer in Kentucky on the Gaspar River,

McGready found "[t]wo pious women . . . conversing about their exercises" and saw how these women had commanded the attention of "some little children." Taking a cue from the women, McGready turned his attention to the children. One "little girl . . . lay across her mother's lap almost in despair," when McGready stepped in to counsel the child in her distress: "I was conversing with her when the first gleam of light broke in upon her mind—She started to her feet, and in an ecstasy of joy, she cried out . . . O what a beauty I see in him—O why was it that I never could believe?"[54]

The most dramatic challenge to skepticism to appear in the Great Revival was a new exercise aimed primarily at "the scoffing, the blasphemous, the profane," known as "the jerks." In amazing performances interpreted as evidence of the existence of supernatural forces and their power to overwhelm skepticism, "[s]coffers, doubters, deniers, men who came to ridicule and sneer at the supernatural agency, were taken up in the air, whirled over upon their heads, coiled up so as to spin about like cartwheels, catching hold, meantime, of saplings, endeavoring to clasp the trunks of trees in their arms, but still going headlong and helplessly on."[55]

Accounts of other amazing events made it clear that participants linked the revivals, as well as the manifestations of supernatural power perceived to rain down in those events, to the defeat of religious skepticism. Stories about determined skeptics slain by the power of God poured out of Kentucky. In one report "[a] man rode into what was called the 'Ring Circle,' where five hundred people were standing in a ring, and another set inside. Those inside were on their knees, crying, shouting, praying, all mixed up in heterogeneous style." In the midst of what must have been an extraordinary emotional event, "[t]his man comes riding up at the top of his speed, yelling like a demon, cursing and blaspheming." Suddenly, "seized with some agency which he could not define," the unbeliever fell off his horse into a thirty-hour coma.[56]

The legend of the pious slave Cuff, a precursor to Harriet Beecher Stowe's Uncle Tom, circulated in the early nineteenth century as a narrative depicting the banishment of skepticism in the South and the sentimental and feminized portrait of Christianity that resulted. When Cuff's infidel master whipped him for praying, his mistress found herself "chained to the spot" in her garden where the black man endured his Gethsemane. With Cuff's bleeding body drawing the infidel and his wife to the body of Christ, Cuff "was freed," according to one account, "and employed by his master as a chaplain at a good salary."[57] Victory over religious skepticism was a distinguishing feature of stories like these about black piety and its impact on popular culture, both in the North and the South. Everything depended on cultural respect for supernaturalism and on silencing the skepticism about revealed religion that, prior to the first decade of the nineteenth century, was as pervasive in the South as it was elsewhere in the early republic.

Although in every region of the country, women played decisive roles in the expansion of evangelical authority and defeat of skepticism, stories about supernatural power at the turn of the nineteenth century highlighted the conversion of infidel men. Often taking female piety for granted, promotional accounts of revivals in cities and on the frontier focused on dramatic accounts of male conversion, leaving the impression that winning men over from skepticism was the top priority of evangelicals.[58]

In the avalanche of religious feeling that swept through the Cumberland region, witnesses described how skeptical men were smote down by the power of God and left with little choice but to go along with the religious feelings of women. For example, "one Miller fell who was telling his daughters lying in distress that if they would come again to such meetings he would beat them well. He fell with these words in his mouth."[59] Though written to show evidence of the supernatural power of God, this little story also exposed the culture of physical violence over which women sought control. In a similar story, one husband, a physician, attempted to stop his wife from attending a religious meeting first by refusing to let her ride her horse and then by applying a painful plaster "to bring her to her senses." Acting as if free from pain, she "arose from her seat and purposely brushed by him, when he staggered" under the power of God. He relented in his opposition to his wife's attendance at the meeting, dressed the blister created by his plaster, telling his wife, "I expect if you would join these people you would feel better." His own conversion soon resulted.[60]

Many testimonies to the presence of supernatural power in revivals described the "slaying" of unbelievers like soldiers vanquished in war; whatever their factual accuracy, these testimonies reveal the pivotal role that religious skepticism played in the narratives that evangelicals constructed about themselves, the society they intended to conquer, and the kind of public expression they aimed to silence. By 1811, when the Methodist preacher James Finley boasted after one revival in Ohio that "[m]any hardened sinners fell, before the power of God, like those slain in battle," images of skeptics forced to ground had become routine. Finley was almost happy to find one skeptic who remained standing, a "great champion of whiskey and infidelity" who "seemed to be at a loss to know what to do," while everyone around had fallen into heaps. Though "enraged" when Finley moved to embrace him, "[p]resently he began to tremble from head to foot, like an aspen leaf" and, to

Finley's great satisfaction, "screamed out with all his might and fell his whole length upon the floor." With the impact of a monster crashing to its death, the "noise might have been heard a mile."[61]

Finley's own story exemplified the narrative about the defeat of men's skepticism sweeping through the early republic from cosmopolitan Philadelphia to frontier Ohio. As a twenty-year-old at the Cane Ridge revival in 1801, he ran for the woods to resist falling down as people all around him collapsed. Raised a Presbyterian, he rebelled against Calvinist theology and gravitated to Universalism, a democratic movement that denied punishment after death and proclaimed Christ's love for all. He loved dancing even after marrying the pious Methodist Hannah Strane and once found himself "beguiled by Satan" in the form of another "young lady" who led him out to the dance floor. His wife's anguish—Satan made her dance as well—left him with "a desolate heart," which was restored to grace some time later with the help of his wife's ministrations, after a night he spent kneeling in the snow. Finley went on to half a century of work as a Methodist preacher, exhorting thousands in the West along the path of salvation.[62]

Though united in their opposition to religious skepticism, revivalists divided over matters of correct belief and practice. Methodists participated aggressively in the Great Revival launched by New Light Presbyterians, and the "camp meetings" that emerged through that revival became vehicles for the evangelical expansion in the West that enabled Methodists to outpace Presbyterians. Faced with considerable pressure from orthodox Presbyterians to separate from the Arminian theology and emotional extravagance that Methodists allowed, New Light Presbyterians splintered. Radical New Lights like Barton Stone, who believed that men had "rational faculties capable of knowing and enjoying God," broke with proponents of Presbyterian orthodoxy committed to the innate sinfulness of humanity. In response to growing apprehension among Presbyterians over New Light "irregularities," McGready returned to the orthodox fold. Other New Lights left the Presbyterian Church to join the Methodists, Shakers, Stone's new "Christian Church, or the independent Cumberland Presbyterian Church.[63]

In contrast to Methodists, Presbyterians conducted worship primarily through prepared sermons delivered by educated ministers intent on communicating orthodox doctrine. Like evangelical Calvinists in New England, Presbyterians promoted the upwelling of emotion in worship through participants' submission to ministerial control, which downplayed free will and cast suspicion on exhibitionists. The sacramental meetings conducted by

Presbyterians called for cathartic soul-searching culminating in communion. These meetings played a central role in the Great Revival and were precursors of the camp meetings that Methodists made a feature of their explosive growth after 1800. But conformity to clear behavioral and theological norms characterized Presbyterian worship during most sacramental seasons as ministers supervised the initiation of members into an organized experience of corporate unity in the body of Christ after extended periods of systematic catechetical instruction.[64] The sacramental meetings in the Cumberland region in the summer of 1801 breached those norms in a popular movement that Methodist leaders greeted with joy and worked to exploit and Presbyterian leaders in the East sought to restrain.

While Presbyterians and Congregationalists emphasized the importance of religious education in the battle against skepticism, Methodists hired passionate, often barely literate young preachers at subsistence wages to fan out across the country in itinerant circuits serving fledgling religious communities composed mostly of women. With an effective blend of hierarchical supervision and democratic outreach that no other organization could match, with the possible exception of the nascent Republican party, Methodism became a powerhouse of popular culture. From fewer than one thousand members in 1770, with marginal status after the American Revolution as a British-based organization suspected of Tory sympathies, Methodist membership reached a quarter million by 1820. The fastest rate of growth occurred between 1798 and 1812, when evangelicals collaborated and competed to defeat religious skepticism. While Calvinist-leaning evangelicals tried to badger and shame skeptics into submission, Methodists pleaded with them to release pent-up emotion, a practice that often released torrents of feeling interpreted as the power of God.[65]

Prior to the revivals that made skepticism anathema, Methodists were often mocked by admirers of Thomas Paine as well as by Presbyterians, Congregationalists, and Baptists who thought they were crazy people, or witches, out to dishonor the gospel. In the 1790s, James Finley recalled how ditties printed in almanacs caricatured the sect: "Methodism was a thing of contempt, and a Methodist preacher was considered as a special object of ridicule."[66] Rising from ignominy, Methodists became the fastest growing religious group in the nation, creating an "empire of the spirit"[67] that complemented Thomas Jefferson's "empire of liberty," as well as the empire of commercial enterprise championed by Charles Brockden Brown. With more unrestrained fervor than others, Methodists enjoyed extraordinary success in recruiting female performers, thanks to a system for religious growth that combined top-down management with a tireless crew of itinerant preachers and grassroots communities maintained by women.

Methodist success was not limited to the frontier. In Philadelphia, the number of members attending the city's four Methodist chapels almost doubled from 622 in 1799 to 1,117 in 1801, with women, blacks, and laboring men counting for more than 85 percent of members in 1801. Methodism in Philadelphia also enjoyed strong financial support and civic influence; Philadelphia was home to Methodist printing operations, pension managers, and a powerful cadre of activist women whose family wealth derived from iron foundries and fine textiles, all of which contributed to the Methodists' remarkable influence in the city, especially among laboring people. Methodist preachers and song leaders drew big crowds to the public grounds in front of the state capital. Lay leaders convened intimate class meetings, usually segregated by sex and race, which engaged individuals in small communities of self-disclosure, religious discipline, prayer, and singing. Although all licensed preachers of the Methodist Church were men working under the hierarchical management of Bishop Francis Asbury, the large majority of participants in the Methodist system were women; women exhorted and performed religious exercises, opened their homes to preachers and prayer meetings, and supervised other women and children. In Philadelphia, the percentage of women among Methodists increased from 59 percent to 64 percent between 1796 and 1800, and the relative weight of women's commitment was even greater than these figures indicate; many women joined Methodist societies unaccompanied by men, whereas most Methodist men were married to Methodist women, at least some of whom pressured their husbands to join.[68]

Methodist societies provided religious homes for poor women like the old washerwoman fictionalized by Charles Brocken Brown in *Jane Talbot* and for women like Jane Talbot herself, a single woman unhinged with confusion about whom to trust and what to believe. Brown's Jane was deeply affected, as many single women in Philadelphia probably were, by the revolutionary rhetoric of freedom and self-determination, but too aware of her vulnerability and too fearful of future consequences not to back into the arms of Religion away from the independent-minded skepticism Henry Colden represented. "What a wretch I am!" Jane wrote to Henry at the moment Mrs. Fielding was imploring her to abandon Henry and his irreligious ways. "Never was a creature so bereft of all dignity, all steadfastness," she moaned. "The slave of every impulse; blown about by the predominant gale; a scene of eternal fluctuation."[69] Such feelings of tumult and inadequacy were precisely those that a Methodist class would take as evidence of conviction and repentance to be encouraged and directed toward heartfelt, even ecstatic conversion. Had Jane slipped further down the social ladder to be rescued by Methodist sisters, she might have had a night like Betsy Crooks of Dover, Delaware, who "fell down at prayer Meet*g* last Week" and "was carried at Midnight, from McNatts to her Mothers in an Arm'd Chair, follow'd by all the Class, shout*g* most vehemently all the way."[70]

Henry's calculated move toward religion was a fictional example of the kind of male acquiescence to female pressure suggested by statistics of Methodist membership. "A total change of my opinions on moral subjects might perhaps, in time, subdue the mother's aversion to me," Henry reasoned hopefully. Henry's skepticism had once been a sign of American independence; now it had become a barrier to marriage. Considering removal of that barrier, he concluded that "religion" was the "basis whereon to build the hope of future amendment. No present merit could be founded on my doubts."[71] If Henry's privileged education fit a Presbyterian profile more than a Methodist one, his journey from skepticism to religion was similar to that of many American men at the turn of the nineteenth century who were under pressure from women and their demands for social propriety, supernatural assurance, and the resolution of confusion and doubt.

Jane Talbot is a virtual metaphor for the religious submission that drew Americans together in the early republic. In taking a woman's name for the title, Brown explored forces operating within and upon women that led to their embrace of religion, as well as to the pressures they applied to convert men. But *Jane Talbot* is about more than that; beneath the story of progress toward happy conformity is a tale of intellectual resistance and opportunity lost. Henry's character challenged the central argument evangelicals advanced in their crusade against religious skepticism: skepticism bred immorality. Henry the rationalist was not an immoral, selfish man. To the contrary, he wore himself out with constant self-criticism and good deeds. No one was more dedicated to helping others than Henry Colden, or less interested in advertising his efforts or in seeking reward for them. Insofar as honesty, humility, modesty, compassion for others, self-criticism, and desire for self-improvement counted as moral virtues, Henry the beleaguered skeptic is another kind of metaphor, standing for a kind of rational virtue that was stifled in this period, perhaps as Brown had to stifle it in himself.

Other factors contributed to religion's growing popularity in the early republic; white women were not the only ones who sought voice and protection through religion. No group took religion more seriously or exploited religion's opportunities for respectability more brilliantly than the African American Methodists who joined Philadelphia's Bethel Chapel. For pastor Richard Allen and his congregants, Methodist Christianity was a vehicle for showcasing the humanity and inspiring religious faith of Philadelphia's free blacks. The exemplary Christian faith evident at Bethel challenged everyone in the city who viewed religion as essential to social order to see Americans of African descent as components of that vision, deserving of respect. In the context of white concerns about the fast growing number of blacks in the early republic, amplified fears of black insurrection driven by Toussaint Louverture's revolution in St. Domingue in the 1790s and Gabriel Proser's rebellion in Virginia in 1800, the people of Bethel Methodist posed a challenge, a challenge that white evangelicals were forced to negotiate in the religious terms they were laying down as essential for social order. Battling against skepticism and against the moral corruption and social degeneracy which they presumed to be caused by skepticism, white evangelicals had reason to appreciate black Methodists as allies, despite the challenge to white authority they posed.

Richard Allen's quest for respect through hard work and Christian devotion had not been easy. Born a slave in 1760, probably in Philadelphia, Allen was sold to Stokely Sturgis, a farmer in Delaware, where Allen was converted during a revival and joined the Methodist church in 1777. Convincing Sturgis that religion contributed to his capacity for hard work, Allen reached an agreement with his financially strapped owner to free him once Allen paid him two thousand dollars over five years while continuing to provide unpaid labor on Sturgis's farm. By hauling bricks and cutting wood overtime, Allen bought his freedom in 1785 and became a Methodist exhorter assigned to circuits in Pennsylvania, Maryland, and Delaware. In 1787, he attained recognition in a British abolitionist pamphlet as an example of black virtue, started a chimney-sweeping business in Philadelphia, and helped found the Free African Society, an organization dedicated to mutual aid and public relations. Having suffered numerous insults at St. George's Methodist church, Allen and his followers walked out of a church service in a carefully planned act of separation that led to the establishment of an all-black congregation in 1792 or 1793. Faced with strong criticism for stepping outside the reach of religious government at St. George, Allen asserted his claim to equality as a Christian by appeal to a transcendent realm of authority: "[Y]ou cannot seal up the Scriptures from us, and deny us a name in heaven."[72]

Not without difficulty, Bethel became a center of black community organization and the largest black institution in Philadelphia, with a membership of almost four hundred in 1810, ten times the number in 1794, and increasing to more than twelve hundred in 1813. Whites as well as blacks were drawn to Bethel during revivals. In 1798, Allen and fellow Methodist Jupiter Gibson wrote a church official that "[o]ur churches ar[e] crouded, particularly Bethel" and that "Whites & Blacks" both were "Convincd & Converted." Attracting whites in the process, blacks joined the Methodist Society in numbers that far outpaced their population in the city, counting for forty percent of Philadelphia's Methodists in 1801.[73]

Allen's influence extended well beyond Philadelphia not only as a result of his friendship with Francis Asbury and other Methodist leaders but also through the hymnal he published in 1801, which began with a "spiritual song" that perfectly joined Methodist piety to black freedom. The first verse opened,

> The voice of Free Grace, cries escape to the mountain,
> For Adam's lost race, Christ hath open'd a fountain,
> For sin and transgression, and every pollution,
> His blood it flows freely in plenteous redemption.
> > Hallelujah to the Lamb who purchas'd our pardon,
> > We'll praise him again when we pass over Jordan.[74]

In addition to linking salvation to abolition, Allen's opening hymn reflected the free approach to divine reality typical of Methodists. With images derived from biblical narratives and recast through a prism of abolitionist politics, the song was an exercise in black ownership of the language of Christianity, facilitated by the Arminian theology and expansiveness of Methodist worship. In the hands of Richard Allen and his followers, the accessibility of supernatural realities that Methodists promoted, the pliability of these realities with respect to people's demands, and the relief from censorship obtained through religious devotion all worked together to further the cause of black freedom. Given the increase in black population, poverty, and persecution in the early republic, the advantages of anchoring the cause of black dignity in a supernatural authority respected by whites far outweighed the problems.

The crusade against skepticism—while not Allen's primary concern—contributed to Bethel's growth. Growing respect for the supernatural platforms of evangelical Christianity enabled Bethel Methodists to stand on a par with the white Methodists at St. George's and alongside, if not above, other whites as well. In Philadelphia and elsewhere, evangelical religion lifted blacks up in imagination, onto a transcendent plane from which injustice might be denounced, suffering tended, and hope of new life instilled. In addition to such encouraging effects, this evangelical uplift operated against the poisonous atmospheres of mistrust pervading the early republic and swirling with increasing velocity around blacks.

Other black evangelicals addressed skepticism more directly and perceived it as a threat to a Christian social order that seemed to be the only basis upon which black freedom and racial justice could advance. The Calvinist Lemuel Haynes, tutored in languages and theology by New Divinity ministers in Connecticut, ministered to a small Congregational Church in Rutland, Vermont, from 1788 to 1818, in the western region of Vermont where deism and Universalism were strong. Haynes fought hard against these challenges to Calvinist orthodoxy that threatened to minimize the natural sinfulness of humanity, erase distinctions between the saved and the damned, diminish the absolute sovereignty of God, and undermine fear of God's power to punish the wicked and send unconverted people to hell. A follower of Jonathan Edwards, Haynes made disinterested benevolence an essential component of conversion and true Christian virtue, in opposition to liberal thinkers who regarded Christian virtue more as a matter of enlightened self-interest. For Haynes, self-interest was antithetical to Christian virtue; any attempt to bring the two together was essentially skepticism masquerading as Christianity.[75]

A staunch Federalist, as most New Divinity ministers were, Haynes espoused an organic view of Christian society in which people obeyed Christian rulers and rulers respected people's God-given natural right to liberty, interpreted not as liberty to trespass "on the equal rights of our neighbor" but in strongly communitarian terms as a right to contribute to "society at large." Haynes conceptualized the American Revolution in such organic terms and, like most of his New Divinity brethren, expected that slavery would be abolished in a nation guided by Christian leadership. Sin caused slavery, Haynes believed, and slaveholding was incompatible with Christian life and a guarantee of eternal misery in hell. "People will be examined at the bar of Christ," Haynes warned, "they are by nature under the curse of God's law," and "nothing short of repentance" would save them from a "sin revenging God."[76]

Haynes spoke out strongly against the spread of Universalism in New England, a popular form of anti-Calvinist evangelicalism characterized by skepticism with respect to the existence of hell. A committed Calvinist, Haynes was drawn into debate with the affable Universalist preacher Hosea Ballou, who resided in Barnard, Vermont, between 1803 and 1809 and traveled through Vermont and western New York preaching eternal happiness for all. Ballou also wrote Universalist hymns, many of which lacked the dignified solemnity of orthodox hymns, prompting even a fond biographer to characterize them as "jingle[s]."[77] When Ballou came to Haynes's hometown of Rutland to preach in 1805 and invited Haynes to preach after him in the same pulpit, Haynes resisted, then finally agreed. Reprinted more than twenty times, Haynes's sermon traced Universalism to the Garden of Eden, where "a certain preacher" made his way to Eve, deceiving her with the promise that she might sin without fear of death. Satan is "an old preacher," Haynes explained pointedly: "It is now five thousand eight hundred and nine years since he commenced preaching. By this time he must have acquired great skill in the art."[78]

Equating Universalist disbelief in hell with unrestrained behavior, especially sexual permissiveness, Haynes argued that religious skepticism caused the moral disintegration of society. Noting that Eve was more vulnerable than Adam to Satan's wiles—"Doubtless he took a time when she was separated from her husband"—Haynes quoted Paul: "*For of this sort are they that creep into houses and lead captive silly women.*" Satirizing Ballou's fondness for rhymes as well as his theology, Haynes mocked the Universalist vision of redemption: "The tottering drunkards shall to glory reel, / And common strumpets endless pleasure feel."[79]

In a public letter, Ballou chided Haynes for his "most unchristian-like behavior" in suggesting that Universalism derived from Satan. Remarkably, Ballou did not mention that Haynes was part African American, an indication that evangelical religion was one arena, perhaps the only arena, where blacks might have a chance of participating on equal footing with whites.[80] While Ballou and Haynes could not have disagreed more over the correct doctrine of evangelical theology, both apparently took for granted that evangelicalism was a world for both blacks and whites, and one in which blacks could speak authoritatively.

Ironically, Haynes could not see how focusing on skepticism as America's primary problem shifted the onus away from slavery. Believing that commitment to biblical revelation would eradicate slavery and support racial justice, he was surely disappointed by the rapprochement between slavery and evangelicalism in the South and by the firming racial caste system in the North that subverted any hope of racial equality there. Dismissed by his congregation in Rutland in 1818 after thirty years of service, he preached for a few years in Manchester, where he was something of a curiosity. Summing up the general opinion of her town about Haynes, one Manchester resident acknowledged that he furthered "the interests of the Redeemer's kingdom" though burdened by the "stain upon his skin."[81]

If racial inclusion was a hallmark of evangelical religion, equal treatment of blacks was hardly pervasive in evangelical churches, especially south of

Vermont. As the discriminatory treatment Richard Allen and his followers received from white Methodists at St. George's chapel in Philadelphia demonstrated, separation from white congregations was often the only way black evangelicals could celebrate their equality in Christ. Still, however compromised and imperfect, evangelical religion provided alternative worlds of harmonious racial coexistence that many whites as well as blacks had reason to protect from skeptical dismantling. At a time when slavery was expanding, and free blacks were being subjected to increasing suspicion, evangelical religion not only offered a counterculture that appealed to increasing numbers of blacks; it also offered a supernaturally anchored world of peaceful racial coexistence embraced by whites worried about slavery and racial unrest.

Methodists, Baptists, and Presbyterians all experienced internal division over the question of whether slaveholders should be admitted as members and whether churches should take a public stand against slavery. By 1808, when the importation of slaves into the United States became illegal, but the breeding of slaves and the expansion of slavery through the lower South figured importantly in the growth of the US economy, it became clear that backing off from abolition was the price of evangelical growth, especially in the South. As slaveholders opposed the growth of any institution hostile to slavery, evangelicals focused increasingly on the Christian treatment and behavior of slaves, as well as on otherworldly promises of salvation.[82]

Religious skepticism became increasingly unpopular as evangelicalism came to serve a variety of competing interests with respect to slavery, and evangelical churches in the South and West became increasingly implicated in the operation of slavery. Whites uncomfortable with the dehumanization of slavery found some assuagement of their guilt in the element of racial fairness sometimes associated with evangelical visions of heaven and in evangelical injunctions against un-Christian treatment of slaves. At the same time, those who supported and benefited from slavery appreciated evangelical efforts to promote black honesty, hard work, and humility.

Blacks also had obvious reasons to embrace evangelical religion. It provided some of the few opportunities they had to form any kind of organization or gathering for mutual support, remembrance, and resistance to persecution. Evangelical religion provided platforms for performances of social parity, both real and imagined, where blacks asserted equal or superior moral status relative to whites. Not least, evangelical religion provided a medium through which blacks influenced the white societies around them in a variety of ways—through examples of Christian fortitude that demonstrated the dignity of blacks, through expressions of religious piety that countered efforts to dehumanize them, and through religious practices of shouting, singing, and spirit possession that spread to white evangelicals, altering ideas about Christianity and expanding the opportunities for emotional catharsis that evangelical religion offered.[83]

The growth of Baptist and Methodist communities in the South provided an imperfect solution to conflicts over slavery—conflicts that divided blacks and whites, small farmers and artisans from wealthy planters, and evangelicals from one another. Baptists and Methodists created tight communities where people shared images of divine reality embodied in common forms of discipline and fellowship that they swore to uphold, and these communal exercises, as well as the virtual worlds brought to life through them, relieved some of the pressures associated with slavery. Baptist and Methodist communities eased these pressures in a variety of different, even conflicting, ways—enabling dignity for persecuted blacks, fellowship between blacks and whites, and respect for evangelical religion and those who embraced it as essential contributors to social order and compliance.[84] For this complex means of social easement to work, acceptance of the validity of evangelical religion was paramount; religious skepticism had to be suppressed.

Commitment to a supernatural world floating above politics, civil government, and even religion was fundamental to the strength and legitimacy evangelicals built up in the South and West. Tobias Gibson, a native of South Carolina who preached in Methodist circuits in the lower Mississippi Valley until his death in 1804, stood by his conviction that blacks and whites, "both alike, on the same terms, could enter the kingdom of God if they would," while simultaneously maintaining a strong reputation for "never . . . interfering in a single instance with the civil relation of the parties." Not surprisingly, the hymn Gibson loved best began with "Vain, delusive world, adieu."[85] Coinciding with this investment in a supernatural world, evangelical operations in the South became increasingly enmeshed in the slave economy; by 1810, when cotton had become a medium of exchange among Methodists in the lower Mississippi Valley, "[a]ny member or patron of the Church, wishing to pay his preacher so much money, would deposit to his credit with the gin-holder so many pounds of seed cotton, and take the gin-holder's receipt in favor of the preacher." The fact that the wages paid to Methodist preachers barely reached subsistence level only made this tacit support of slavery seem more honorable: "With this receipt the preacher could make his little purchases."[86]

Before the evangelical arrangement with slavery coalesced in the first decade of the nineteenth century, proponents of the growing slave economy opposed the spread of evangelicalism among blacks and persecuted blacks who dared to preach. In Georgia, the most famous early black preacher was Andrew Bryan, ordained by Baptists in 1788. The "nightly devotions" Bryan led in Savannah "alarmed the fears" of whites who had him "publicly whipped until the blood ran to his heels." By 1803, Savannah boasted three black Baptist churches, all with ties to Bryan. Linking the expansion of evangelical religion in the South to the defeat of religious skepticism, Baptist leaders in Georgia ascribed Bryan's persecution not to any fear that evangelicals might oppose slavery, but to the "Dupes of infidelity" that "infest all parts."[87] For Baptist writers in Georgia as for many white Americans, infidelity—not slavery—had become the primary cause of immorality and social disorder.

Shifting the onus of immorality from slavery to infidelity was not easy. Charles William Janson, an Englishman traveling in the South in the late 1790s, observed that in the Carolinas "[r]eligion is at a very low ebb" and that "Paine's writings were widely read, and the French Revolution influenced the people to a considerable degree." Evangelicals competed with Painites for the hearts of the poor and came in for ridicule because of their loud vulgarity. "In Virginia," Janson observed, "the Methodists bawl out their tenets with the greatest success amongst the lower orders of people." More dangerous from the perspective of slaveholders was the racial inclusiveness of Methodist Christianity and its insinuations of revolutionary equality. Thus Janson reported that Methodists "are said to do great mischief among the slaves, whom they receive into their congregation, and place among the most select part of their white brethren." Janson also believed that Methodist visions of Satan and hell frightened slaves and thus made their misery worse, reporting that Methodists "certainly terrify the uninformed negroes; and, in many instances, serve to aggravate the hardships of their situations, by disordering their minds."[88]

Janson was shocked by the treatment of slaves in the American South, although he strove for an objective tone: "The masters here," he said of South Carolina, "as in the other southern states, regard their slaves, as English farmers do their live stock." Noting the arrival of three shiploads of "prime Congo slaves," he observed, "[a] horse for a man, or a man for a horse, is a common exchange." Aware of the climate of mistrust endemic to this business—"lurking assassins . . . swarm wherever the planter turns his eyes"—Janson also noticed that slavery created opportunities for barbarity that would not otherwise be tolerated; owners could unleash violence upon slaves with impunity, for whatever reason they liked. "Often I have witnessed negroes dragged, without regard to age or sex, to the public whipping-post, or tied up to the limb of a tree, at the will of the owner, and flogged with a cow-skin," the appalled Englishman wrote, "without pity or remorse, till the ground beneath is dyed with the blood of the miserable sufferer. These punishments are often inflicted for an unguarded expression of the slave," Janson explained disapprovingly, "and too often to indulge private resentment or caprice. Sometimes they are fastened on a barrel, the hands and feet nearly meeting round it, are tied together."[89]

Baptists, Methodists, and Presbyterians worked to eradicate this sort of behavior and to maintain some degree of harmony and mutual respect between blacks and whites. In North Carolina, preachers encouraged members to experience their churches as families and to imagine that "Christ's church is a body," whose "beauty and strength ... depend[ed] on its not being maimed." Like other evangelicals, North Carolina Baptists demanded strict discipline and maintained virtuous behavior within their communities by expelling or demanding repentance from miscreants and also by encouraging members to see themselves as agents of that "happy day ... when the kingdoms of this world shall become the kingdoms of our Lord and his Christ." With that virtual world as a model, it was "the duty of every master of a family to give his slaves liberty to attend the worship of God." In a nation where laws and justices of the peace were relatively few and far between, church elders passed judgment on matters that state and local governments were indifferent toward, such as the right to expel members for "break[ing] the marriage of servants."[90]

According to North Carolina Baptist Elder Jesse Burkitt, who brought news of the 1801 revivals in Kentucky and Tennessee back to his state, the accounts of extraordinary manifestations of supernatural power in the Cumberland region generated considerable excitement "among all ranks and societies of people" in North Carolina. As the enthusiasm for heaven in the Great Revival washed south, the notion caught hold that biblical prophecies about the end of time were becoming real, making "ministers all ... ready to cry, *Thy kingdom come.*" This infusion of millennial expectation into slave economies clouded judgments about the growing power of slavery even as it lifted participants into imaginary worlds where that power seemed to be overcome.

As an aid in this process, Burkitt published pamphlets containing some of the "spiritual songs" he had heard in Kentucky and Tennessee together with other songs he knew, distributing six thousand of these pamphlets over the course of two years. "Nothing seemed to engage ... people more," Burkitt testified, "children and servants at every house were singing these ... songs." The songs also became a prominent feature in communal worship, with ministers in some cases walking around shaking hands as everyone sang. With images of the coming Kingdom in the lyrics, and powerful feelings of communal solidarity brought on through this exercise, some reported that singing was the "means of their conviction." Amidst the visible presence of human suffering, which was increasing as the slave industry internal to the United States mushroomed, the demand for self-conviction may have expedited the submission demanded by the slave system. At the same time, the fellowship inspired through singing worship and the promise of a better future must have been a welcome respite. One hymn invited members to "Take your companion by the hand; / And all your children in the band," as the church sang together about "the happy time, / When sinners all come flocking home; / To taste the riches of his love, / And to enjoy the realms above."[91]

In addition to the feelings of happiness, relief, and hope they facilitated, Baptists argued that their worship and discipline transformed "persons of the most dissolute lives" into "sober, punctual, honest, virtuous persons" and that evangelical religion was far more effective than "deism" in creating "better husbands, better wives, better children, more obedient servants, better masters, better neighbours and better citizens." Part of the social work of evangelicalism, Baptist appeals to the "blood of Christ" could soften class distinctions, causing affluent persons to realize their fellowship with others. "Many ladies of quality," according to Baptist Elders in North Carolina, "at times were so powerfully wrought on, as to come and kneel down in the dust in their silks to be prayed for."[92]

CHAPTER FOUR

Church Citizenship

As mistrust abounded and idealism about the new American government became more difficult to sustain, Americans became increasingly devoted to church governments planted alongside local, state, and federal governments and protected, through a variety of arrangements, by their civic authority. Based on allegiance to a heavenly kingdom suspended above the imperfections of American life, religious communities had governments of their own that supplemented—and in important respects superseded—local, state, and federal authority.

In cultivating these religious governments, Americans reworked the social implications of their Revolution. By capturing elements of republicanism within monarchical systems of church governance, religious communities worked out solutions to nagging problems of representation, exclusion, and mistrust that developed in the early republic after overthrowing the British monarchy and creating a new form of civil authority. Operating between fears of moral anarchy unleashed by democracy on one hand and dashed expectations of egalitarian fellow feeling that independence from Britain supposedly should have liberated on the other,[1] devotion to divine governance was a means of sustaining the paternalism previously associated with British authority within the new context of an independent, liberated citizenry.

Sensitive to their exclusion from full participation as citizens of the new political republic, women and blacks sought citizenship in church governments. Church membership provided opportunities for leadership, social influence, and dignity along with the possibility of exalted citizenship in heaven. But such benefits entailed demands for humble conformity, chastened pride, and restrained ambition. The behavior and self-conceptions associated with female piety made it difficult for women in the early republic who sought citizenship in heaven to even dream of political rights on earth. Black aspirations to political equality might be expressed through images of heaven and release from the bondage of sin, but Christian idealization of servitude, coupled with Christian acceptance of slavery, fears of black insurrection, and belief in black inferiority, kept those aspirations bottled up.

Church governments mandated belief in Christ as a requirement for members and disciplined or expelled those who violated it. While differing in many finer points of theology and religious practice as well as in the demographics of church membership, most religious communities at the turn of the nineteenth century were remarkably similar in their understanding of the fundamental relationship between heaven and earth, as well as in their anticipation of a divine kingdom, now held in abeyance in heaven, that sooner or later would govern the earth. The vast majority of religious Americans would have agreed with New York Presbyterian Alexander McLeod, whose 1803 sermon, *Messiah, Governor of the Nations of the Earth*, expressed the relationship between church and state in the simplest and clearest terms: "The Church of Christ is a kingdom not of this world, but the kingdoms of the world are bound to recognise its existence."[2]

In an era when political arguments against monarchy were commonplace, and monarchy routinely equated with tyranny, oppression, and the usurpation of natural rights and liberties, worship of a divine king not only persisted but also enjoyed strong devotion and, in some quarters, wild popularity. Only deists pictured God as a Creator shorn of royalty, and deists were fast disappearing after 1800 through lack of organization and accusations of immorality and atheism. If the popularity of Painite deism in the 1790s revealed a disenchantment with monarchy so thoroughgoing that it could jettison traditional images of God, the upsurge of evangelicalism at the turn of the century revealed a nostalgia for monarchy so powerful that it cast the sanity of deists into question. By 1807, many Americans touched by the upsurge of evangelicalism shared the hope expressed by Boston minister Elijah Parish that the day might finally have arrived when "Ambassadors of Christ will *command* all men to repent." Confident that "God appoints particular times in which he more visibly established his kingdom," Parish perceived the defeat of religious skepticism in his own day as a sign of world transformation and the dawning light of God's kingdom. "The objections of Deists have produced luminous answers from Christian writers," Parish observed, and these manifestations of religious light were part of God's plan for world renewal: "The waters of salvation must be purified from every dangerous defilement, before they are conducted over the fields of the world, before the whole earth becomes the garden of the Lord."[3]

With allegiance to a divine monarchy a means of managing mixed feelings about political independence, religious activists rose up to extinguish the blaze of critical thinking about religion that Paine's *Age of Reason* had popularized. Resisting Paine's political analysis of religion, defenders of religion strengthened their institutions as government agencies superior to, and protected by, state and federal governments. With more aggressive organization than before, religious institutions kept pace with population growth in cities, towns, and throughout the West, filling voids of moral authority, easing fears of social ruin, and working to discredit any intellectual inquiry or political philosophy that did not begin and end with biblical revelation.[4]

The language of divine monarchy was rooted in scripture and tradition, and anyone who turned to the Bible for guidance would encounter it. As deistical attempts to divest God of royalist authority failed, and growing numbers of people turned to the language of divine kingship for solace and courage, ministers exploited nostalgia for monarchy with as much zeal as they responded to popular demands for political representation. Religious Americans desired monarchy as much as they were proud to have overthrown it, and church governments that integrated monarchy with republicanism embraced that cultural ambivalence. Further signaling the complexity of their evolving culture, many Americans accepted the existence of parallel forms of government—civil and religious—while disagreeing with each other about the procedures of decision making and scope of authority proper to each.

The doctrine of two kingdoms—one civil and one religious, "mingled together from the beginning to the end of their history"—had been part of western Christian thought since Augustine's *City of God* in the early fifth century. Bishop of Hippo in North Africa, Augustine prescribed obedience to both earthly kings and the Church headquartered in Rome; God had assigned governance in civil matters to one and given the keys to the kingdom of heaven to the other. Earthly rulers were obliged to protect the Church established by Christ, God's son who died to save mankind and would return to rule the world, sharing his father's dominion as king of heaven and earth. Later, church reformers in the sixteenth century challenged the authority of the Roman Church to control the means of salvation in favor of more direct relations between the individual and God and looked forward to the arrival of Christ's kingdom with renewed anticipation as a result of their religious zeal. During the American Revolution two centuries afterward, numerous writers appealed to those reformation arguments against Roman Catholic authority to justify the overthrow of British monarchy. Thomas Paine thought the Protestant Reformation had helped prepare the way for the liberation of natural reason from all political and religious tyranny; evangelicals hoped that the overthrow of British monarchy would clear the way for Christ's reign and the beginning of the millennial day when Christ's kingdom would dawn on earth.[5]

As evangelical churches grew in size and prestige, along with the evangelical wings of more strait-laced churches, Congregationalists, Presbyterians, Methodists, and Baptists had the largest and most dynamic church governments in the early American republic. All four played major roles in the evangelical upsurge, with Congregationalists and Presbyterians banding together in new efforts to keep up with Methodists and Baptists. In 1776, there were 668 Congregational churches, the vast majority located in New England, 588 Presbyterian churches, mostly in the middle Atlantic and upper South, 497 Baptist churches in the South and in New England, and 65 Methodist societies mostly in the mid-Atlantic region. All four groups expanded during the revivals at the turn of the nineteenth century, with Methodists and Baptists growing the fastest, counting most of their new supporters among women, blacks, and white farmers and laborers. Methodist and Baptist membership accelerated so rapidly that, by 1850, more than 34 percent of all Americans affiliated with a religious institution were Methodists and more than 20 percent were Baptists. Congregationalists and Presbyterians together counted for less than 16 percent of religious adherents by 1850, but they continued to wield a degree of cultural influence disproportionate to the size of their membership. To compete with Methodists and Baptists for members and to extend their own evangelical operations, Congregationalists and Presbyterians exchanged ministers and minimized competition between their churches through a Plan of Union enacted in 1801.[6]

Americans had other religious options, too, including the Catholic Church, whose adherents in Baltimore swelled to 12 percent of that city's population at the turn of the century when the revolution in St. Domingue drove French refugees to a city in the United States where Catholics had maintained a small but devoted presence since founding the colony of Maryland in 1634.[7] The Episcopal Church had begun to recover some of the losses incurred during the revolutionary period, when it was still the Church of England, and vestiges of the parish system built in colonial days offered continuity with the past and contributed significantly to social life in the Atlantic states, especially Virginia. The Society of Friends maintained strong communities in Pennsylvania and New York, though pacifism had kept Quakers out of power since the mid-eighteenth century, and loyalty to Britain during the Revolution and opposition to the growth of American slavery made them objects of suspicion. Lutheran and Reformed churches catered to German populations, and some Dutch Reformed churches participated in the 1801 Plan of Union with Presbyterians and Congregationalists. Universalists, Shakers, Sandemanians, members of the Christian Connection and other radical spin-offs from larger groups also operated in the early republic, as did small congregations of Jews in Charleston, Savannah, New York, and Rhode Island, and adherents of Islam scattered among black populations. Between 1798 and 1812, none of these groups commanded the attention that either Methodists or Baptists did or wielded the conjoined influence of Congregationalists and Presbyterians.

Those four prominent religious groups developed institutional strength in a social environment dominated by partisan politics and, despite efforts by some preachers to keep politics at bay, partisan conflict stimulated the growth of all four religious governments. Highly sensitive to democratizing trends in American politics, Methodists and Baptists drew many of their members from regions and population groups that favored Jeffersonian democracy. Both groups thrived after 1800 as a result of their ability to exploit conflicted feelings about authority and independence among laboring people and also as a result of Jefferson's strong support for separation of church and state; that support helped level the playing field among churches and remove barriers to aggressive recruitment by Methodists and Baptists. But the religious governments that Methodists and Baptists maintained were not democratic. Their church governments revolved around deference to a divine monarch as much as the religious governments favored by Federalist clergy, whom Baptist preachers commonly derided as Tories.

Congregationalists and Presbyterians tended to oppose Jeffersonian democracy, although there were major exceptions among Presbyterians. New Light Presbyterians in Virginia, Kentucky, Tennessee, and North Carolina led the way in spreading enthusiasm for religious revivals in the midst of enthusiasm for Jeffersonian democracy and mistrust of Federalist authority in those states. In the mid-Atlantic states, however, Presbyterians cautioned against religious enthusiasm and radical politics. Thanks to the influence of New Jersey's John Witherspoon, the Presbyterian educator, pastor, and ratifier of the US Constitution who schooled future political leaders on both sides of the partisan divide that developed after his death in 1794, leading men across the spectrum of political opinion were acquainted with Presbyterian ideology. Though Witherspoon's most famous students, James Madison and Aaron Burr, went on to play major roles in the development of Republican partisanship, Witherspoon's commitment to religious influence in civil government contributed even more to Federalist ideology. As if anticipating political division, Witherspoon suspected Thomas Paine as early as 1777 of possessing the "bad character" of a religious skeptic and warned John Adams against him.[8]

Congregationalists were more universally anti-Jefferson than Presbyterians, but even in New England where established Congregational clergy routinely preached Federalist doctrine, there were Republican exceptions. Reverend William Bentley of Salem, Massachusetts, was an ardent Jeffersonian, but Bentley's church was the only church in Salem whose membership declined between 1800 and 1810, and on a few occasions, Bentley's small congregation watched their minister administer communion to himself alone. Like other towns in Massachusetts, Salem had a growing Republican minority during these years, but its members were far more likely to attend Methodist or Baptist meetings than they were to attend the Congregational churches frequented by Federalists.[9]

Congregationalists and Presbyterians believed that their own religious governments supported republican virtue in citizens and that their conceptions of the right relationship between civil and ecclesiastical government had exerted a formative influence on American institutions. Congregationalists and Presbyterians were highly conscious of the synchronicity they thought should exist between their church governments and the American republic. Increasingly on the defensive as the tide of partisan politics turned toward Jefferson, members of these churches resented the laissez-faire approach to religion encouraged by Jeffersonian democracy and worked to bring the nation back to what they considered its original religiopolitical path.

For Congregationalists, this path had been laid out by adherents of "federal theology" in seventeenth-century New England and by the Puritan writers in England who inspired them. According to federal theology, individuals committed to the covenant of grace with Christ were obligated to form church covenants with each other for worship, fellowship, and religious instruction. As the name indicated, Congregational church government operated primarily at the congregational level, though synods of Congregation ministers exercised "federal" oversight over churches for purposes of guidance and peace. Congregational church government was instructional and far-reaching; churches were training schools that required individuals to prepare for citizenship in the kingdom of heaven through all aspects of their earthly lives. The contractual obligations of church citizenship were drawn from the Bible: "The partes of Church-Government are all of them exactly described in the Word of God" and should "continue one & the same, unto the appearing of our Lord Jesus Christ as a kingdom that cannot be shaken."[10]

Congregationalists traced their system of church government to the Westminster Confession written by English puritans in 1646. Amended to emphasize congregational government, the "Platform" of Congregational church governance agreed upon by New England clergy at a synod in Cambridge, Massachusetts, in 1648 stipulated that churches should elect their own ministers and vote on the acceptance of new members. Church members entered into a covenant relationship with one another, agreeing to uphold the ordinances of baptism and communion and to maintain fellowship and affection within their congregation. They also agreed to fellowship and behavioral discipline within marriage and family life, and as participants in local communities and government.

Churches not only performed an important educational function as training schools for civic leadership but also contributed, through the dutiful lives of their individual members, to the governance of society as a whole. It was assumed that some church members would take responsibility for political governance and that all members would be alert to divine oversight and judgment of their nation, local communities, and homes. Christian rulers, citizens, and servants acted as God wanted them to act; otherwise, they were rebels and traitors to his majesty. Civic rulers had special responsibilities toward churches because of the essential contributions churches made to civil life and their own individual obligation to the king of heaven: "The power and authority of Magistrates is not for the restraining of churches, or any other good workes," according to the Cambridge Platform, "but for helping in and furthering thereof." Although church and state each had particular responsibilities, they should "both stand together & flourish, the one being helpful unto the other, in their distinct & due administrations."[11]

The ordinance of baptism evolved in New England as the principal means by which Congregational churches extended their citizenry and maintained religious governance over society. While Baptists abhorred infant baptism as an affront to their insistence on clear biblical precedent and violation of the principle that only believers could be church citizens, Congregationalists practiced that rite as a provisional extension of covenant privilege and obligation to children. Infant baptism bound children to the church and provided a means of watching over families and maintaining their religious order. Reliance on baptism as a means of religious control over New England families led Congregational churches to the Half-Way Covenant of 1662, which extended the rite to children whose parents had not presented themselves as adult candidates for full church privileges, despite being baptized when they were children. Though not without controversy, many congregations in New England opened their doors even wider over the course of time, encouraging parents outside the church to present their children for baptism and thereby accept church oversight of their families.[12]

Except in Rhode Island, New England towns levied assessments on property owners to support local churches conforming to the Cambridge Platform, and the funds collected through assessments provided salaries for duly elected ministers. This arrangement operated under the remote aegis of the King of England, who was also the head of the Church of England, in relation to whom religious heresy amounted to political treason. Though Congregational churches of New England proclaimed allegiance to the British monarch and thus to the Church of England, many church leaders in New England had ambitious plans, not endorsed by the Church or King of England, to create a Christian society in the New World in which the churches, supported by the state, led the way in remodeling society along the lines of the kingdom of God. Numerous problems arose in the attempts to bring this vision to reality, including indifference and outright hostility within an increasingly diverse population, complaints by Baptists and other religious dissenters who resented being marginalized, and British efforts to impose greater religious tolerance in New England.[13]

In the 1770s, the established clergy of New England seized upon the patriotism unleashed in the American Revolution as an opportunity to broaden and reassert their authority as spiritual leaders of God's people. Reviving earlier dreams of a genuinely Christian society, Congregational ministers saw God's plan for the world unfolding through American independence from the King of England—and renewed commitment to the King of Heaven. When the popularity of Thomas Paine's *Common Sense* broke through collective reluctance to separate from Britain, Congregational ministers interpreted enthusiasm for American independence in biblical terms. In Connecticut in 1776, for example, Samuel Sherwood preached that "[t]he time is coming and hastening on, when Babylon the great shall rise to fall no more." Perhaps having in mind Paine's stirring claim, "We have it in our power to begin the world over again," Sylvanus Conant told his Plymouth congregation that "the literal fulfillment" of the prophecy from Isaiah 66:8—"*shall a nation be born at once?*"—had occurred when "thirteen united States . . . were led to declare themselves free and independent of the jurisdiction of Great-Britain, and of all other powers on earth."[14] For Congregationalists as for other religious citizens, America's freedom from all the powers on earth, meant freedom to obey the king of heaven.

Congregationalists agreed that future citizens of heaven worked out their salvation as good citizens on earth and that good citizens built good civil governments according to God's plan. They disagreed with each other, however, about the degree of supernatural transformation required for this process. An elite contingent of Congregationalists centered in eastern Massachusetts tempered their acknowledgment of the pervasiveness of human sin with respect for human reason and leaned toward Unitarian opinions about nature and God that downplayed miracles and emphasized the humanity of Jesus and the potential goodness of humanity. Opposed to these liberal tendencies, Congregationalists in Connecticut and western Massachusetts tended toward extreme or, as they preferred to say, "Consistent" Calvinism, insisting on the thoroughgoing devastation caused by sin and the need for miraculous intervention to effect the total transformation in human nature required for virtuous behavior. A third contingent of moderates honored the orthodoxy of their New England puritan fathers by steering a middle course between the brutal judgments against humanity typical of Consistent Calvinists on one hand and liberal efforts to overhaul the system of Calvinist theology on the other.[15]

Despite these differences, Congregationalists expected civic responsibility and religious life to go hand in hand, and they considered civic virtue to be an outstanding effect of their church polity. They thought virtuous public leadership in a Christian state resulted from the training in self-government and communal government that church membership provided. As Reverend Joseph Lyman explained in a sermon delivered the day before voters chose the electors from Massachusetts who would deny or help Jefferson to a second term, "Rulers, by precept and example, should inculcate the fear of God and the practice of righteousness as the only way civil society can be prosperous or secure." In response to those who would exempt civil magistrates from religious responsibility and "destroy" ministers' "influence in society" through "the fallacious pretext of preventing ministers from preaching politics," Lyman predicted that efforts to remove religion from politics would send the American republic into ruin. Viewing civil government as a means chosen by God to bring his kingdom to earth, Lyman accused magistrates and ministers who advocated separation of trying to "pull down the kingdom they are appointed to uphold—they mar the best privileges and ruin the happiness of their illfated people."[16]

With an underlying sense of civic responsibility more fundamental than their theological differences, Congregational ministers worked in concert with one another and with their Presbyterian brethren who shared similar views about the moral obligations of the state and its citizenry to God. These highly educated men, familiar with ancient languages, the writings of church fathers and the history of protestant reformations in Europe, shared common ideas about America's place in the history of the world and the important role of American civil government in bringing the world closer to Christ. They developed strong ties with one another in colleges and divinity schools and close mentoring relationships that brought younger men into the homes of established clergy for months at a time. Although disputes of various kinds could turn Congregational ministers against one another and theological differences between orthodox and liberal interpretations of scripture were significant, ministers operated as an elite brotherhood occupying a special tier of society with a sense of responsibility to the whole of society. Befitting this shared sense of purpose as the watchmen of society, ministers often exchanged pulpits and presided together during public services on election days and other public events.

A traveler visiting Hartford on election day in 1807 noted a phalanx of two hundred clergy, and was impressed by the spectacle of enormous dignity they presented. The hymn sung at the end of the public religious service that day reflected Congregational ideas about the close relationship between church and state, the privileges of liberty under a watchful ministry, and the divine monarch to whom everyone should submit: "Hail happy land! hail happy state! / Whose freeborn sons in safety meet," the song proclaimed, wedding liberty to thralldom in a way that made perfect sense to many, "Come let us kneel before his face / Devoutly supplicate his grace."[17]

Plagued by doubt in many forms, many Americans in the first decade of the nineteenth century were looking for more order and not less. With politicized mistrust driving public life and dividing the country, a certain element of buyer's remorse had deflated exuberance about American independence. Congregational and Presbyterian clergy offered a solution to these problems of religious and political doubt—the restoration of reason within the framework of biblical revelation and renewed commitment to churches as schools of governance and civic responsibility. Though Paine was discredited, some of his faith in reason could be recovered under the aegis of church government.

The Plan of Union enacted in Philadelphia in 1801 by Congregationalists and Presbyterians strengthened an already existing system of church government and network of religious intellectuals that exerted influence through colleges, Sunday schools, missionary activity, and numerous publishing ventures. Learned clergy were ambassadors of Christ with divine portfolios—ministers of the king with the wisdom and skill to understand the signs of the times, to warn people of dangers facing their society, and to remind them of their civic responsibilities. Fearful of religious skepticism and of the proliferation of preachers poorly informed about church history and government, president of Yale College Timothy Dwight warned that "an ignorant teacher is necessarily a mere Empiric, professing to communicate what he does not possess." While educated ministers studied ancient languages, logic, natural philosophy, rhetoric, and reformed church doctrine, America was full of disseminators of religious "quackery" who "become ministers in a moment; and put on the qualifications for the Ministry as they put on a coat." Education was not all that was required, as Dwight would have been the first to admit, but it was necessary preparation for anyone who aspired to "ascend the sacred desk" and lead "the call of mercy." A learned minister represented Christ's kingdom properly, as it should be represented, so the "Sabbath may dawn with the light of heaven" and the "Sanctuary open the gates of immortality."[18]

When Dwight delivered the inaugural sermon at Andover Seminary, the new postgraduate institution for training ministers and missionaries that opened in 1807, he was not shy about saying where he thought these learned evangelicals would eventually rule. Today is "the birth day of an Institution," he proclaimed with a gesture to Augustine, "destined to furnish a succession of able and faithful ministers for the *City of our GOD.*" Andover men would be "instruments in the hands of the Spirit of God" and literal embodiments of the teachings and institutions connecting earth and heaven: "These are the pillars, on which, in this world, stands that glorious building, the Church of God."[19]

Seeking to forge ahead of Methodists and Baptists in defining the prerequisites for an "Evangelical Ministry," Dwight condemned the "miserable shifts, and impious pretensions" of uneducated preachers, asserting that "men of this character are incapable of the decorum, and dignity, which are indispensable in the desk." He also asserted New England's right to a preeminent role in the religious history of the American nation: "[T]hose eminently good men, who converted New England from a desert into a garden" carried the "*doctrines of the REFORMATION* from Europe," where religious corruption and political tyranny had stymied their growth. The gardens of Christian virtue tended by New England divines had grown precious fruit for many seasons, even feeding Christians in other parts of the world. With their thorough knowledge of reformation doctrines, New England divines created the proper conditions "under which almost all Revivals of Religion have existed."[20]

With ministers trained at Andover Seminary at the head of a new army of righteousness, greater revivals of religion were still to come. "[T]he morning star will soon rise," Dwight predicted, "which will usher in that illustrious day, which is destined to scatter the darkness of this melancholy world, and cover the earth with light and glory." On that wonderful day, Christ would reign unopposed and "[t]he earth shall become one vast temple of JEHOVAH." To play their role in building the kingdom, Andover men must do more than put upstart Methodists in their place; they must "[p]ut on the whole armour of GOD" to vanquish with "boldness and resolution" the common enemy shared by all evangelicals—namely, those "hosts of infidelity" that still plagued the nation.[21]

The victory over religious skepticism would require finesse as well as resolution. Dwight's plan, shared in its broad strokes with that of other Congregationalist and Presbyterian leaders, involved seizing reason from critics of religion and reinforcing its position within the framework of biblical revelation. Thomas Paine's *Age of Reason* had challenged biblical revelation as preposterous on rational grounds and as a form of terrorism that supported political tyranny. Eager to defend the connection between the moral purposes of civic government and biblical revelation, Dwight positioned the rationality of biblical revelation against religious doubt and skepticism. Championing the rationality of biblical revelation and its contributions to civic life, Dwight joined forces with the Scottish school of common sense realism taught from 1768 to 1794 at Princeton by John Witherspoon.[22] Like the Scots-born Presbyterian Witherspoon, Dwight believed that religious doubt had to be quarantined in order for the American republic to work and that the education of ministers was essential in this process.

Others in the Plan of Union were equally vigorous in building strong defenses to support the rationality of the Bible. In his 1803 sermon, *Messiah, governor of all the nations of the earth*, Scots-born Presbyterian Alexander McLeod argued that reason could only be celebrated within boundaries established by religious belief because "[t]he efforts of unassisted reason would never have discovered the great mystery of godliness." Thus McLeod made the Bible the arbiter of reason because of its divine origin. "Having submitted to its authority," he explained, "we must embrace all the doctrines explicitly taught in it, and employ our powers of reasoning in deducing inferences from its established axioms; for when such deductions are legitimate, they are of divine authority."[23]

Religious attempts to capture the power of rational analysis and the cachet of enlightenment respect for reason were hardly new; the enormous theological effort of Timothy Dwight's grandfather Jonathan Edwards could be described exactly that way. But the way that Dwight and McLeod laid claim to reason reflected their immersion in the circular thought of common sense realism. In the 1740s, Edwards had advanced the radically idealist claim that supernatural grace completely transformed the will, enabling the Christian to reason at a higher and more general level than natural men, whose self-love drove every one of their pretentious attempts at objective thought.[24] Sixty years later, in his effort to defend Federalist religion, Dwight jettisoned his grandfather's idealism for an equation between reason and conventional wisdom, thereby ignoring the problem of unexamined assumptions that Edwards had faced, and tried to resolve. Edwards argued that natural reason was perverted by sin, and that only the grace of Christ enabled men to think clearly and truly appreciate biblical revelation. Dwight, like Witherspoon and McLeod, flattened the Calvinist defense of biblical revelation making the authority of the Bible apparent to common sense evidence of the factual truth of its contents.

Edwards advanced his heroic claims about human depravity and the absolute power of God in a political context in which resentment of his ministerial authority was a harbinger of resentment against monarchy and of the groundswell of enthusiasm for the rights of "the people" that would continue to build over the next decades; his parishioners in Northampton fired him for his authoritarian efforts to control their behavior and pass judgment on their souls.[25] Edwards's belief in his God-given authority over others met with a small-scale version of the growing resentment of claims to God-given authority that George III would later face in his effort to wield the power of monarchy over Britain's American colonies.

Dwight and MacLeod, by contrast, incorporated important aspects of republican liberty within their theologies and visions of church government, and their fusion of republicanism and Calvinism met with considerable success. Although Methodists and Baptists were even more popular, Congregationalists and Presbyterians espousing common sense realism made important gains in Jeffersonian America, even as the Federalist candidates they tended to favor for public office were defeated. Expanding their control over American intellectual life, Congregationalists and Presbyterians poured resources into educational institutions erected to promote the connection between religious and civic virtue and to keep religious doubt and skepticism at bay.

Presbyterians had particular reason to be confident about the harmonic relation between the government of their church and that of the United States. In 1787, as delegates to the Constitutional Convention were finalizing the US Constitution in Philadelphia, Presbyterian leaders met in the same city to draft a constitution of their own, which was ratified the following year. Both new governments became effective in 1789, each establishing a representative form of government with a national legislature and chief executive elected by delegates; nothing illustrates the fresh attention to the politics of religious governance stimulated by the American Revolution more clearly than the parallel construction of these two governments. In addition to the parallel elements, there was some overlap in personnel; the first elected moderator of the Presbyterian Assembly was John Witherspoon, who also ratified the US Constitution as a representative from New Jersey.[26]

According to the constitution of the Presbyterian Church in the United States, the state served the church and the king who established it and to whom it was bound and devoted. "*JESUS CHRIST*, who is now exalted, far above all principality and power, hath erected, in this world a kingdom, which is his church," the Presbyterian Constitution declared. As God's kingdom on earth, the church descended from the divine monarchy in heaven and was composed of "all those persons, in every nation, together with their children, who make profession of the holy religion of *Christ*, and submission to his laws." The US government had to observe special rules with respect to this kingdom. As the Presbyterian Constitution claimed, in parallel to what would soon become the First Amendment to the US Constitution, "Civil Magistrates may not . . . in the least, interfere in matters of faith." At the same time, however, the Presbyterian Constitution claimed that officers of the state had a duty to defend the church, and this duty required them to enforce limits on religious expression; officers of the state might not intrude in theological disputes between churches, but they could prevent attacks on the authority of biblical revelation. In strong support of laws against blasphemy, which existed in the colonial era and in some states well into the twentieth century, the Presbyterian Constitution claimed that civil officers were obliged to curtail religiously offensive speech. "It is the duty of civil magistrates to protect the person and good name of all their people," the Presbyterian Constitution declared, such that "pretence of religion or of infidility [sic]" not be allowed "to ever offer any indignity, violence, abuse, or injury to any person whatsoever."[27]

Belief that churches merited honor but not interference from the state was common enough among religious Americans, but Presbyterians stood out from others in having a constitutional government like a nation while also rising above it. With roots in the Kirk of Scotland reformed by John Knox in the seventeenth century, a strong foundation in colonial Virginia, Pennsylvania, New Jersey, and New York, and direct inspiration from the US Constitution, the Presbyterian system of church government in the United States was a three-tiered structure designed for balance and layered government. Congregations governed by ministers and lay elders stood at the base, courts called "Presbyteries" composed of ministers and elders within a geographical district had authority to oversee these congregations, a General Assembly composed of representatives from each Presbytery stood over all as the "highest judiciary" of the Church.[28]

This system of government had a strong republican aspect—congregations chose lay elders to represent them—but like other churches that incorporated lay representation, the declared purpose of the church was worship of the king and preparation for the arrival of his kingdom. In this essential respect, the Presbyterian Church was very different from the US government. Ministers of the church were "ambassadors" of a divine monarch. Though elected by lay people, ministers governed more as representatives of the king than of his people by virtue of being empowered to govern Christ's kingdom on earth. Ministers controlled the keys that opened the door of kingdom to some and shut the door against others. Other ministers and elders could convene to rein in wayward brethren but in the last analysis, ministers represented the exalted prince whose judgments were not to be questioned.[29]

In contrast to Methodist ministers who laid great emphasis on Christ's forgiving side and the suffering he endured for sake of his people, Calvinist-leaning Presbyterians, Congregationalists, and Baptists stressed the judgment of Christ and the fathomless breach separating the saved from the damned. Calvinists celebrated lay representation in church government and criticized Methodists for not having it, but they made up for any departure from royalism in church polity through worship of divine majesty and emphasis on divine judgment. That judgment set the boundaries of "God's pity and compassion," which was reserved for those he made righteous, saving them from "deserved ruin." Happy to say, as Beriah Hotchin explained in a sermon to the presbytery meeting in New Lebanon in 1801, the forgiveness enjoyed by those God elected to forgive "is now displayed in many parts of our land." The absolute power of God to separate the saved from the damned "will appear more fully in the millennial age," Hotchin promised his auditors, and "have a glorious display at the judgment day."[30]

Overlooking any dissonance between the absolute power of God and the representative policies of their church, Presbyterian writers emphasized the essential role that constitutionally appointed ministers played in animating Christ's use of constitutional government to represent his absolute authority. "According to the constitution of the Christian church," Alexander McLeod explained at the ordination of a new minister in New York in 1808, "certain offices are created by the divine Redeemer, and this constitution cannot be put into operation unless persons are appointed to fill these offices." Thus the operation of this constitution depended on lay people to play their part. "There is a striking analogy," McLeod observed, acknowledging lay actors to be the embodiments of religious life that made the whole system come alive, "between a saint and the church."[31]

Like Congregationalists, Presbyterians worried about Methodists who seemed to respect neither learning nor dignity in their aspirations to sainthood and to rely on bodily sensations of grace rather than a process of self-government grounded in rational analysis and directly linked to civic virtue. All four major churches expected self-discipline from their members, but Presbyterians and Congregationalists laid stress on programs of systematic, rational introspection that complemented their devotion to reading and writing and respect for languages and learning. Making rational introspection an essential practice of religious self-government, Congregationalists and Presbyterians defined religious liberty in terms of its purpose of enabling Christian virtue and freeing Christian activism from political corruption and oppressive constraint. Harnessing rational introspection to the higher authority of biblical revelation, Christians had won the freedom to control themselves.

Young Sarah Newman Connell exemplified the Congregational practice of self-control. As a student at Franklin Academy in Andover in 1807, during which time she celebrated her sixteenth birthday, she pursued religious self-analysis and self-instruction with the help of a diary and guidance from her church. "Went to Church all day," she wrote in her diary one Sunday in February: "Religion, thou true source of happiness! Be thou my guide as I journey through life, & at last usher me to realms above, where sorrow is not known." Returning home to Newburyport, Massachusetts, that fall, she confessed to her diary, "My spirits were much depress'd, but," she added, acknowledging her responsibility for self-government, "I always endeavour to cultivate cheerfulness." Enrolling in a new academy lightened her spirits but not her overall self-assessment. On New Year's Day, she gave a summary of herself that did not mention cheerfulness. "When I take a look of retrospection on the past year, I observe many faults which I have committed, many errors in my conduct, which need to be corrected," she wrote, and "look forward to the future with a determination of emendment."[32]

That determination faltered. "Why do I look forward to the future with such anxious solicitude?" she asked herself on January 12. If she worried about finding a husband or the dangers of childbirth that lay ahead, the emotional responsibility of religious self-government weighed on her more explicitly; the anxiety she confessed was itself a religious infraction. She vowed not to complain: "Mature age, may bring with it an increase of sorrow. I will submit to the divine will." Six weeks later, she enjoyed a happy moment and took care to record its components. "We all sat around the fire, enjoyed the sweets of friendly converse, untinctured with envy, discord, or any boisterous passion of the soul." The following Sunday, her minister reinforced her program of rational analysis with arguments aimed at vanquishing doubt about the validity of religious life: "I went to Church all day. Mr. Morse was proving the existence of the soul in a future state, by the works of creation. I was much pleased with him."[33]

In July, Sarah's Aunt Eustis lay at death's door from consumption. Believing that her aunt "has long been prepared to meet the king of terrors," Sarah was ready to take a lesson. "She begged me to forsake the vanities of life, as no satisfaction would be derived from them," Sarah wrote dutifully. "She said I should meet with many disappointments, but I must look to religion for that consolation which the World denies." Sarah read Revelation 21 to her aunt aloud, as Eustis requested, the chapter describing "the new Jerusalem, coming down out of heaven from God, prepared as a bride adorned for her husband," with great glowing walls made of precious jewels. The chosen chapter also described the lake of fire outside the walls of the heavenly city into which "the one who was seated on the throne" sent those who failed to honor him.[34]

Interestingly, Sarah's effort to honor divine will coincided with sympathy for the Republican party. Returning home by stagecoach after a visit to her aunt, Sarah "listened with attention" when her fellow passengers—five gentlemen—began discussing politics. She was particularly impressed with "one Mr. Solmes" who "appeared to be about 60 years old, had an uncommonly pleasant countenance, and appeared to possess as pleasant a disposition." Genial "Mr. S. was a Republican, and spoke with much reason and mildness," Sarah wrote approvingly; by contrast, "[o]n the federal side passion seemed to predominate over reason."[35]

In light of Sarah's commitment to rational self-control, her encounters with Federalist passion show that not everyone with the sensibility of a New England Congregationalist was a Federalist and not all New England Federalists adhered to Congregationalist self-restraint. With Republican majorities in both houses of the US Congress and James Madison's election as president following Jefferson in 1808, more than a few Federalists were bitter. In Newburyport, where Federalist-leaning churches still outnumbered Republican ones, Sarah noted on March 4, 1809, that "Mr. Giles' and Mr. Milton's bell has *rang*, and the rest *tolled* all day, in consequence of Maddison's inauguration."[36]

When the death of the moderate Republican Governor James Sullivan in December 1808 coincided with the anniversary of Jefferson's embargo on foreign trade, Federalists in Newburyport expressed their displeasure in a way that Sarah found offensive. "A long procession has passed through the town," she wrote, and "an Oration was delivered in the public square by an English sailor. All this was done," she explained, "to ridicule the government of the United States. Can it be the steady people of Newbury Port, formerly so remarkable for their *correct habits*, who thus rise up in base sedition against their Country?" Attending a memorial service for Governor Sullivan, Sarah's Republican family became extremely uncomfortable: "We left Church, owing to repeated insults." Fifteen months later on March 13, 1810, Sarah's father was beaten "for daring to support his principles." Following an argument in the courthouse, "he was assaulted by a party of Federalists, from the other side of the river, and abused in a shameful manner. He was brought home by Capt. Ayer, considerably injured." Sarah maintained her commitment to religious self-government, but not without a struggle: "It was with difficulty that I could suppress the resentment I felt at the base treatment my Father had received."[37]

Religious sensibilities did not always fall neatly into political camps, as the Connell family's experience in Newburyport shows. Just as deism attracted people with conflicting opinions about politics in the 1790s, evangelical piety attracted people across the political spectrum in the first decade of the new century. Yet different forms of church government offered different means of managing mistrust and different means of establishing authority, and these differences interacted with the ideological, regional, and demographic divisions of partisan politics.

In certain respects, the Methodist system of church government was the least republican and most like the political monarchy that Americans had overthrown. In its internal governance, the Methodist Episcopal Church of the United States at the turn of the century rejected the republican principle of people's representation; Bishop Francis Asbury controlled ministerial appointments in the United States, and ministers controlled membership and discipline in Methodist societies. Because of this absence of lay representation, Congregationalists, Presbyterian, and Baptists often suspected Methodists of un-American, Roman Catholic tendencies. But if Methodist polity was antirepublican, it attracted more Americans than it repelled—one indication of the nostalgia for monarchical order in the early republic.

The Methodists' extraordinary growth derived from an extremely effective blend of inclusive outreach and hierarchical authority. Methodists brought more people into their societies than any other religious group in the first decade of the nineteenth century, expanding membership from 63,958 in 1800 to almost 175,000 in 1810. No group was more active in recruiting poor people, blacks, and women or more willing to include people that other religious societies belittled. As the liberal Congregational minister William Bentley archly observed about the Methodist invasion in Salem, Massachusetts, in 1798: "The [Methodist] Tabernacle is upon the plan of converting negroes to the faith. And they who can neither read nor write are not left in the Cant of Gentiles but conducted in by a full confession into the Holy of Holies." In managing their rapidly expanding membership, Methodists relied on top-down order and supervision. Thus while Bentley perceived the Methodists as inclusive to the point of ridicule, he did not perceive their organization as democratic. As he observed in his diary in 1802, "Monarchy is the soul of John Wesley's Scheme."[38]

Some insiders agreed. In 1798, the former Methodist Episcopal Church minister James O'Kelly published his notes from the Church's First General Conference held in Baltimore six years before, where his efforts to establish a more democratic form of church government met defeat. He quoted the Conference President Thomas Coke, emphasizing the authority of ministers selected by the Bishop: "[W]e are to all *intents* the *legislature* of the Methodist Episcopal Church: and the government is *Aristocratical.*" O'Kelly and his allies questioned the "absolute power" accorded to Bishop Francis Asbury in appointing ministers and the lack of any provision ministers had to appeal Episcopal decisions. Summarizing arguments against his plea for the rights of ministers to challenge Episcopal authority, O'Kelly wrote, "Others saw, or thought they saw, that such liberty would be injurious to the church, because preachers would ever be appealing." Denying ministers the opportunity to challenge Episcopal authority not only streamlined church governance but also encouraged faith in the bishop's ability to make good decisions and a kind of passive receptivity with respect to his decisions: "It was urged by several, that the bishop always appointed well, as far as they know." O'Kelly was unpersuaded. His ally Richard Ivey "spake with tears . . . crying popery," and O'Kelly was no less critical: "I prayed them not to arrogate infallibility to the bishop."[39]

In their compendium, *The Doctrines and Disciplines of the Methodist Episcopal Church*, Coke and Asbury defended hierarchical authority as the only practicable means of realizing the "grand plan" of extending the Methodist Episcopal Church "to the western states and territories, in proportion to their rapid population." Through a well-organized system of elders and deacons appointed as ministers with responsibility for preachers, exhorters, stewards, and class leaders, Asbury commanded itinerant preachers who rotated monthly around circuits a hundred miles or more in diameter. Asbury also had charge of settled ministers who pastored larger, well-established Methodist societies. With district societies meeting monthly, regional conferences meeting annually, and a General Conference meeting every four years, Methodist advocates extolled their system of church government as a wonderful mechanism: "Everything is kept moving as far as possible; and we will be bold to say, that, next to the grace of God, there is nothing *like this* for keeping the whole body alive from the centre to the circumference, and for the continual extension of that circumference on every hand."[40]

Against complaints that the Methodist episcopacy had too much power and answered to no one, Coke and Asbury maintained that bishops would be burdened with many hardships and that, unlike John Wesley, "the venerable founder (under God) of the whole Methodist society" who "governed without any responsibility whatever," American bishops would be answerable to the General Conference. In the almost unimaginable event that a bishop should exercise "a spirit of tyranny or partiality, and *this* can be proved before the general conference, the whole [authority] will be taken from [him]: and we pray God, that in such case the power may be invested in other hands!"[41]

Members of other religious groups did not hesitate to speak out against the Methodist system of government. At a time when "the rights of man, has attained a zenith unparalleled in the annals of time," Congregationalist James Wilson declared in 1798, "Are not civil and religious rights nearly allied? [M]ust they not in some considerable degree stand or fall together?" The Methodist system of governance was a clear threat to this alliance, in Wilson's view, because it worked to "accelerate and sustain the usurpations and oppressions of tyranny."[42]

Asbury and Coke staunchly defended their governance against such charges. Appealing to reason and scripture (Matthew xviii:15–17), they drew a firm distinction between a minister and "the church" to be governed, declaring that "our Lord invests the minister," not the church, "with the whole authority of judgment and censure." Lay leaders might watch over others under the supervision of ministers, but Asbury and Coke wanted to avoid the dissension and disorder they were sure would arise if lay people acquired governing power. One of the most crucial elements of ministerial authority was the power of excommunication, and only the "minister or preacher in charge of the circuit," Asbury and Coke insisted, had the authority "to exclude a person from the kingdom of grace and glory."[43]

The tight discipline of Methodist polity depended on everyone's willingness to lie in humility before God's throne; loving humility was the lubricant that made the wheels of Methodist organization turn smoothly. To the end of promoting this essential emotion, the handbook *Doctrines and Disciplines*, small enough in size for circuit riders to tuck easily into their saddlebags, instructed preachers to reveal the Son of God as a real presence standing before people and to plead with people to grieve for their insufficient adoration, opening their hearts to receive the Son's atoning grace. The preacher "must bring the mourner to a *present* Savior," the handbook of governance instructed, "he must shew the willingness of Christ *this moment* to bless him." The first question the bishop asked when "trying" ministerial candidates was, "Do they know God as a pardoning God?" This primary emphasis on forgiveness and the all-powerful mercy of God was every preacher's duty to communicate. The need for experiential knowledge of divine forgiveness came with the demand for obeisance. Preachers "must hold forth our adorable Redeemer as . . . a king to reign in us and over us."[44]

Painting images of Christ's anguished suffering on earth and triumphant majesty in heaven, Methodist preachers urged repentance for the sins that made Christ suffer and modeled Christ's transformation into glory with the help of dramatic gestures, singing, and weeping. Accounts of Methodist preaching in the first years after the Cane Ridge revival of 1801, when Methodist growth in the West accelerated, describe how the preachers "spoke loudly and with their whole body; their feet and hands were put in requisition as well as their tongues and eyes," and how they invested images of heaven with emotion: "before their inward eye was ever clearly pictured their expected final haven of repose and joy, the antithesis to this their present painful life of weariness and labor." At the same time, Methodist preachers did not fail to warn listeners of "the dark and unfathomable abyss of perdition . . . open to them" if they failed to accept Christ. "Miltonic descriptions of perdition abounded in their preaching," one early historian recalled. Methodist preachers gave the virtual worlds of heaven and hell "topographical character—as if they had been traveling through certain countries, and were now giving a vivid detail of all they had experienced."[45]

Methodist ministers made entrance into the kingdom a privilege, and one that required interrogation of each prospective member of a Methodist society by a minister acting as a trial judge in one of the lower courts of Christ's kingdom. The western itinerant William Winans left an account of how this process worked in Fayette County, Pennsylvania, during the Christmas season of 1806, when he was eighteen and not yet fully consecrated to Christ. Winans's mother was an active lay leader who hosted itinerant preachers and prayer meetings in her home, and, as a child, Winans had accompanied her to love feasts where he had felt the presence of Christ. But as a young man expected to undergo his own trial of faith, Winans was denied the privilege of participating in any more love feasts. Not expecting to be turned away, he attempted to enter the building where a love feast was about to begin, "when John Collins arrested me on the threshold, referring me to the rule, in obedience to which he barred my entrance." At this rebuff, Winans "felt . . . the anguish which a condemned spirit will feel when it shall see 'Abraham, and Isaac and Jacob, and all the Prophets received into the Kingdom of God, and itself shut out.'" Winans understood that his "exclusion" was the result of his own failure to commit himself fully to Christ, a failure that "might be terminated at my own option." The procedure for entry was clearly visible: "When the Lovefest closed, the door of the house was opened," and he saw the Reverend Collins "in the act of receiving members on trial."[46]

Such emphasis on each believer's ability to exercise the "option" of religious commitment compensated for the absence of lay representation in Methodist discipline. Unlike most Congregationalists, Presbyterians, and Baptists, Methodists stressed the free agency of each individual, and his or her ability to enter Christ's kingdom as a citizen of heaven on equal footing with others. Methodist success in emphasizing individual agency, and in using emotion to create a sense of that agency, put pressure on other churches to relax their attitudes toward predestination. Thus James McGready, the New Light Presbyterian credited for igniting the Great Revival in Kentucky, came close to suggesting that the emotional intensity of the believer's plea opened the door to Christ's kingdom. Those "fainting and almost dying for his presence," McGready wrote, "those who come in this way to the wells of salvation with empty pitchers, crying, give me Christ or I die, . . . these will be feasted at Christ's table on the hidden manna." Under pressure from the Presbyterian Church to reaffirm his commitment to Calvinist doctrine, McGready took care to stress God's control over election when he wrote his sermons for publication, diligently reminding readers of the inadequacy of emotion and other forms of human sensation as agents of conversion. But even then, in urging people to make the effort conversion required, McGready blurred the boundary between Methodism and New Light Presbyterianism. "See him suspended on the cross, pierced with wounds, writhing in the agonies of death," McGready wrote, working hard to stimulate visions and sensations; "Suppose the bleeding, dying Jesus, were exhibited to you upon the cross to-day—all drenched in blood and tears—the blood flowing in scarlet streams from every gaping wound."[47]

Women like William Winans's mother played essential roles in staging Methodist events that demonstrated citizenship in God's kingdom and its ecclesiastical extension on earth. One early historian of Methodism described the Western Conference meeting in Tennessee in 1802, when "[p]opulation was flowing in: the Older settlements were filling up, and new ones being formed," commenting that "[t]he sisterhood, especially at Kingston, were working Methodism on the high-pressure system." Like many preachers at the turn of the century, western itinerant Tobias Griffin counted on women for success: "Among them he formed one of his first, and one of his best, Societies, consisting mostly of the leading ladies of the Swayze, King, Corey, and other families." These women had previously been Congregationalists, and when Griffin demanded more emotional evidence—"He insisted upon a knowledge of personal salvation . . . and to feel the love of God"—they embraced Methodism and "excelled in the eloquence and power of their extemporaneous prayers."[48]

Methodist women in the early republic were never licensed to preach, despite the fact that John Wesley had licensed some women in England, but they often provided the backbone of religious order and membership. Reverend Robert Roberts found that no one would attend his meetings in Harper's Ferry, Virginia, before meeting the approval of one "good lady" whose introduction of him at a quilting bee confirmed his reputation. In Tennessee in 1810, "a woman of great influence" helped Reverend John Brooks restore order in his flock when she rose to call an end to a quarrel dividing the Methodist Society. According to the grateful minister, "The whole assembly, saints and sinners, commenced weeping as she talked," and even "old brethren who had hardly spoke to each other for years, now rose and ran and embraced each other."[49]

Though denied licenses to preach or officiate, women contributed to the government of Methodist societies by exercising considerable influence in the internal politics of these groups, in contrast to their more limited political influence as citizens of the United States. In fealty to Christ, leading women embodied the emotional intensity and single-minded commitment to religious life expected of the citizens of Christ's kingdom. This fealty to Christ operated by analogy to calls for patriotic devotion. As Sarah Jones wrote to her minister, "O, my bro, it is treason, I again say, to the majesty of a Christian, to grow dull." Jones was definitely aware of the need to never allow belief to flag: "O bro, this is the grand secret of Religion, to prove reality by a never-ceasing unweariedness."[50]

Baptists were no less adamant about avoiding treason to Christ and maintaining fealty to his divine kingdom; as a circular letter written in 1802 by Baptist ministers in western Massachusetts proclaimed, "We have solemnly surrendered ourselves up to Christ, taking him to be our prophet, priest, and king, engaging to . . . obey his laws."[51] Baptists operated under a far less centralized governmental system than Methodists, one that emphasized congregational government, the sharp boundary separating them from other people, and strict adherence to the word of God. While a Methodist might say that "[t]he scripture is by no means a sufficient form of government,"[52] Baptists upheld the New Testament as the sole basis of church rule. According to *A summary of church discipline, shewing the qualifications and duties, of the officers and members, of a Gospel-church*, published in 1783 by the Baptist Association in Charleston when the older summary published in Philadelphia went out of print, a church was "a Company of Saints, incorporated by a special Covenant, into one distinct Body, and meeting together in one Place, for the Enjoyment of Fellowship with each other, and with Christ their Head in all his Institutions."[53]

In its purity and separation, each Baptist church was "a garden enclosed" against "the open wilderness" of the profane world.[54] These tightly controlled communal sanctuaries thrived in the South and West, where civil government and other forms of social control were weak. Baptist membership rose from 65,345 in 1790 to 172,192 in 1810, stimulated by western expansion, the laissez-faire policies of Jeffersonian democracy, and growing opposition to Federalist claims to centralized moral authority.

Maintaining a firm boundary between church and profane society, Baptists disciplined members aggressively and excluded nonmembers from participation in rituals. While Baptists generally welcomed revivals as seasons of outpouring grace, they were more leery than Methodists of the visions and physical exercises typical during these seasons. By 1813, concern about the disorder of some revival meetings led Baptist chronicler David Benedict to claim that "Baptists established camp-meetings from motives of convenience and necessity, and relinquished them as soon as they were no longer needful." With emphasis on the church as a well-tended space, he added, "Their meeting-houses are generally small, and surrounded with groves of wood, which they carefully preserved." Eager to distinguish the genuine faith that Baptists painstakingly tended from the artificial religion he perceived Methodists generating, Benedict criticized Methodists for staging camp meetings in an effort to manufacture religious feeling. With insufficient attention to the boundary between church and world, Methodists had stooped to "advertising" camp meetings "in newspapers, &c to collect as large an assemblage of people as possible." Once they drew a big group, the Baptist complained, "then, by preconcerted and artful manoeuvres, and by a mechanical play upon the passions," Methodists went to work "to produce that animation and zeal, which, at (earlier) times . . . were spontaneous and unaffected."[55]

Baptists yearned for revivals of true Christianity when there seemed to be none and then devoted considerable effort to disciplining new members once a revival had passed. In Virginia, Benedict recalled, "many ministers, who laboured earnestly to get Christians into their churches" during the revival of 1785 "were afterwards much perplexed to get hypocrites out." Much the same thing happened in South Carolina after the revivals at the turn of the century, when more than a few men and women ejected from Baptist churches "removed beyond the mountains, to the western States and territories."[56] Rather than impeding overall Baptist growth, excommunicants became candidates for new conversion and fellowship elsewhere. Baptist minister Henry Holcombe testified to the widespread search for forgiveness in the early republic and enormous desire to be made right with Christ: "Men and women are continually confessing their sin and folly, in ever having opposed, or neglected, the interests of his kingdom."[57]

While Congregationalists and Presbyterians promoted self-government through introspection, Baptists maintained tight systems of peer regulation. Attendance at monthly business and disciplinary meetings was required of all members, and behavior during these meetings was closely scripted, with little room for disorder or expressions of disrespect for church procedures or ministerial authority. Members accused of drunkenness, gambling, lying, domestic abuse, swindling, or property destruction heard testimony from their accusers and faced suspension or expulsion if the majority of other members voted against them. West of the Appalachian Mountains where civil courts were few and far between, Baptist churches might be the only source of government in people's lives.[58]

As local government and party politics developed in the West and South, Baptist leaders were prepared for them as a result of the experience they had in church government. Nevertheless, strong Baptist emphasis on the separation between church community and profane society worked against civic engagement outside the church and privileged political activity geared to the protection of Baptist liberty. The common good would best be served by bringing people to the Christian faith and increasing membership in Baptist churches.

Baptist ministers and other elders met in regional associations that assisted in important matters, such as the election of ministers, and intervened in the governance of particular churches when problems arose. The church leaders who gathered in these associations offered guidelines for family discipline and religious instruction of children. They also worked to achieve consensus among churches on important questions—the very essence of party politics— such as whether Presbyterian ordination was valid, whether a woman could be baptized against her husband's will, and numerous matters associated with slavery.[59] In 1789, the General Committee of Virginia Baptists endorsed John Leland's resolution that "slavery is a violent deprivation of the rights of nature, and inconsistent with a Republican government," making it the first religious group in the South to commit to "every legal measure to extirpate this horrid evil from the land."[60] However, by the end of the first decade of the nineteenth century, Baptist associations had backed away from abolition, avoiding internal disagreement as well as external opposition by deciding that the legality of slavery was not a matter about which churches should be concerned. Thus in 1805, the Elkhorn Baptist Association in Kentucky came to the conclusion that it was "improper for ministers Churches or Associations to meddle with emacipation [sic] from Slavery or any other political Subject and as such we advise ministers & Churches to have nothing to do there with in their religious Capcities [sic]."[61]

As Baptist associations grew in size and number, some dissenters balked at participation in the evolving system of American religious organization that divided Christians into competing denominations. Disturbed by the drift of Baptist associations in this direction, as well as by the compromises to pure church government involved, New Hampshire Baptist Elias Smith joined the Christian Connection in 1802, a spin-off movement that eventually merged with western churches led by revivalists Barton Stone and Alexander Campbell. These men wanted to be identified simply as Christians, or Disciples of Christ. For Smith, the markers of Christian life were perfectly clear for those who truly served the *"King of Glory"* and were preparing for "[t]he day of JUDGMENT when a righteous sentence will be passed on all men according to deeds done in the body."[62] Smith called on his fellow Christians to leave churches tainted by association with worldly affairs. Adherence to the rule of Christ's kingdom differentiated Christians so absolutely that distinctions among other people hardly mattered: "I believe, and often tell my hearers," Smith wrote in 1804, "that every natural man is as really an infidel as Mr. Paine."[63]

Baptists agreed that believers were radically different from everyone else and that watered-down versions of faith were not faith at all. Condemning state-supported religion as the usurpation of Christ's authority and a vestige of monarchical control over religion, Baptists supported Thomas Jefferson because his commitment to religious liberty enabled their true Christianity to grow without hindrance from state-supported churches, which Baptists regarded as corrupt, persecutory, and un-Christian. At the same time, Baptists thought Christ's kingdom would come to earth sooner or later and that the government they established within their churches would eventually take over the world. Thus Baptists wanted the nation—and the world—to be governed on their own religious, church-based terms, with as little interference as possible from others and support from civic government.

Baptist ministers embodied the convergence of two aspects of religious citizenship. As elders elected by the voting members of the congregation, and typically already members of that body, ministers were first among equals and responsible to the body that elected them and subject to removal by that body. As ambassadors of Christ, however, they exercised considerable power once elected to office because they represented Christ and his kingdom to his people on earth. As "[m]en fearing God, being born again of the Spirit, sound in the Faith, and of blameless Lives and Conversations," ministers stood for the king in much the same way that the church represented Christ's kingdom. "Churches cannot be too careful in choosing Men to the Ministerial Function," warned *A summary of church discipline*, because they "have the Charge of Souls, and are Leaders in the House of God."[64] Empowered both by God and by their membership, church leaders exercised considerable authority with respect to the order and discipline of members' lives, in contrast to the lack of order and discipline in the moral wilderness around them.

Women held leadership positions in some Baptist churches during the eighteenth century, but lost ground as the Baptists' hypervigilant enforcement of communal order became ever more strongly equated with male headship. Some Baptists in Virginia "held to ruling elders, eldresses, deaconesses, and weekly communion," but when other Baptists in the region spoke out against female leadership, the minority group moved to the Carolinas, where the practice died out. Known for his "strong faith in the immediate teachings of the Spirit," Shubal Stearns and some radical Baptist leaders in Virginia and North Carolina went so far as "suffering women to pray in public," but that practice came to an end around the turn of the century along with the positions of Baptist eldress and deaconness.[65] In 1804, a "quoroum" of men representing the Baptist Church in Mechanicsville, South Carolina, settled all questions about women's official authority by deciding that only "male members should have the privaledge of praying publickly" and participating in church governance. In a church where two-thirds of both black and white members were women, Baptist men made men's government over women a defining characteristic of Christian life. Reflecting the emphatic assertion of male dominance typical in Baptist churches in the South around the turn of the century, the Mechanicsville Baptist Church excluded women from disciplining others, from voting on new members and new ministers, and even from handling money as treasurers of women's donations.[66]

Baptist women in the North were better organized, better able to exert influence in church government, and more fully citizens of the kingdom of God on earth that Baptist churches represented. In Cortland County in upstate New York, settled mainly by immigrants from New England, Baptist records in 1810 show that a few women participated in disciplining others and that women registered opinions about preachers and new members even though they could not vote.[67] But even in New England, where intergenerational networks of religious women were well established, the structures of Baptist church governance strongly enforced men's authority over female citizens of the church.

For women, exclusion from church governance may have been a fair price to pay for the domestic order Baptists insisted upon as a principle manifestation of Christian life. This domestic order could be described very simply: Baptists taught a "Husband and Father how to command and cherish, a Wife or Child how to love, honour and obey." Since Baptists disciplined men who beat their wives and punished drunkenness, adultery, and other forms of disorderly behavior, church membership offered women safety and an element of respect some might not otherwise have enjoyed, especially in regions where officers of law were few, legal redress practically nonexistent, and beatings were not an uncommon way of settling quarrels and expressing pique. In turn, Baptist men benefitted from the loving obedience that church discipline required women to express; men may not have minded stifling doubts about the validity of revealed religion to obtain it.[68]

Baptist churches attracted as many if not more African Americans than Methodist societies did—an indication of the role that church government played in providing some degree of justice and protection for blacks and of the appeal that citizenship in the kingdom of God had for people denied civic respect. Numerous black Baptist churches thrived, as did racially mixed churches, and in some integrated churches blacks and whites sat together. In the upper South, free blacks held offices that entitled them to some authority with respect to whites; in 1797, 1798, and 1801, the African American William Lem served a delegate to the Baptist Association in Glouster County, and in 1806, the Mill Hill Baptist Church in Tennessee decided that the "Black Brethren" should "enjoy the same liberty of Exercise in public gifts as white members."[69] If these signs of respect on the part of whites reflected Baptist visions of racial harmony in Christ's kingdom, they were muted, and white Baptists shied away from involvement in abolition, leaving questions about the legality of slavery to civil government, and after 1800, white supervision of black preachers increased.[70]

To maintain the stark boundary between their churches and civic government, and between their churches and others, Baptists celebrated the baptism of believers by immersion, which New Englander Elias Smith likened to "a *uniform* for all Christ's Soldiers to put on, to shew what Commander they are enlisted under." The "design" of baptism was "to represent a burial and resurrection" that manifested "the believer's faith in the death of his body, and the *resurrection* of the same, at the *last day*." Calling believer's baptism "the boundary of visible Christianity . . . to prevent the confounding of the church and the world," Andrew Fuller emphasized the "interesting and impressive spectacle" it presented to outsiders, as well as the transformation celebrated among insiders.[71]

In Beaufort, South Carolina, in 1799, the baptism of "Mrs. Gedier and Mrs. Jones . . . brought almost the whole City together, as spectators," according to one pleased observer. In Georgia in 1802, minister David Lilly described a baptism that made "[s]everal deists . . . cry aloud for mercy." A crowd of two thousand (or so it seemed to Lilly) was reduced to tears as Reverend Slackford led thirty-six new Christians into a river, including two girls and two boys and "several young ladies of nearly the first respectability in the back country, who were not ashamed to follow Christ through the liquid grave."[72] In North Carolina, "[two hundred] to [one thousand] and more would assemble" to see initiates as they "stood in a row" and then went "hand in hand" in a "march down into the water regularly, like *soldiers* of J, singing as they went."[73]

A French tourist witnessed a winter baptism in Rhode Island when the temperature was below zero and the foot-thick ice had to be chopped open every few minutes. "At length the penitents appeared," the Frenchman wrote, describing the arrival of the church as he watched from the riverbank: "They consisted of the members of the meeting, two and two; then followed the devotees, about twelve in number, of both sexes, in long gowns, resembling a *robe de chambre*." The minister led the way, "alternately praying and singing, in honor of Saint John the baptist: and thus without slackening his pace, or altering his dress," the visitor noted with interest, "he plunged into the freezing stream, till he was nearly breast-high in the water." No less amazingly, "[h]is disciples, with wonderful resolution, hand in hand followed while the members who had already been purified by immersion, ranged themselves along the margin of the deep." A fellow observer on the riverbank recounted the story of an elderly relative who had been dismissed from a Baptist church when he asked the minister to postpone his immersion until spring.

A third spectator in conversation with the French visitor recalled a baptism in Connecticut in which "the minister in the act of immersing the first, he accidentally lost his hold of the unfortunate person, who was in an instant carried down the stream, still running under the ice, and irrecoverably lost." As the Frenchman rendered the story, the minister, "finding his subject gone, with a happy serenity of mind exclaimed, 'The Lord hath given, the Lord hath taken away, blessed by the name of the Lord:—come another of you, my children.'" The minister's willingness to give up others to God created the opposite effect; those waiting to be baptized "lost their faith, and fled."[74]

Although Baptists put the command to believe at the forefront of their practice and made baptism an initiation into a world of belief in which doubt was forever excluded, other religious groups approached belief—and handled doubt—more circuitously. Methodists turned people's attention away from intellectual skepticism to focus instead on the doubts people had about their own self-worth, pleading with them to feel the agony of the king who suffered for their sins, listen for stirrings of repentance and gratitude within themselves, and consider those sensations evidence of divine reality. Belief was simply presumed in this process, and doubt about the existence of God's kingdom circumvented.

Presbyterians and Congregationalists incorporated doubt into their introspective rites for maintaining belief, approaching flare-ups of doubt as opportunities for self-conviction and repentance. In Farmington, Connecticut, in 1799, for example, a twenty-year-old son of the church confessed to his pastor Joseph Washburn that "doubts began to rise in my mind, respect the divinity of the Scriptures." After going so far as to question the existence of God, the young man conceptualized his doubts as "evidence" of the enormity of his sinfulness, the confession of which brought him back to God. In his account of the Farmington revival that year, Washburn included the young man's story of mental struggle as a model for others to emulate and as evidence that a religious revival had occurred.[75]

The assault on skepticism in the early republic contributed to increased support for Christ-centered visions of American political history. Responding aggressively to the waves of religious skepticism that had washed through American colleges, armed forces, and print media in the last decades of the eighteenth century, religious leaders brought natural reason under the aegis of biblical revelation. Few continued to press the problems Thomas Paine had begun to explore, such as the disjuncture between religious governments predicated on monarchy and a federal government founded on its overthrow, the emotional dynamics involved in celebrating liberty from one king and submission to another, and the political confusion that resulted from submission to the authority of biblical revelation. At a time when the democratic implications of the new American system of government were hotly debated, when liberty was ruthlessly exploited by some and denied to others, and when many inspired by American independence also feared what it had unleashed, Americans revitalized Christ and his kingdom with a new and peculiarly American zeal. Few, if any, acknowledged that the deflation of political idealism stimulated the growth of evangelical churches.

Solitary exercises that engaged intelligence and disciplined behavior were part of this political retrenchment. Especially for Baptists and Methodists, group activities were even more important. Through group enactments of fellowship in Christ's kingdom, triumphs over the terrors and anticipations of the thrill of admittance to his throne, Christ and his kingdom became shared, intersubjective realities for people drawn to religious communities. As North Carolina revivalist James Hall explained in 1802, a minister's job was "to encourage God's children to be fervent at the throne of grace, not only in secret, but in social prayer."[76]

Preachers warned that Christ would punish those who rebelled or refused to serve him. Outright skepticism might be an invitation to the Devil, and imagination with respect to that possibility could run wild. In one incident ascribed to a tavern in Vermont in 1801, one of the card players—a native Irishman by birth—swore the Bible "was nothing but a d——d lie, forged by some d——d scoundrel, to impose upon the ignorant, and draw money by." As if by invitation, "the prince of Hell presented himself" at the door, filling the exit way with a terrible dark face, "protuberant eyes that flashed a blue fire," a hissing tongue in a smoke spewing mouth, and "a tail like a whaleman's harpoon."[77]

While stifling doubt and encouraging supernatural imaginings, religious communities simultaneously upheld the need for honesty as the basis of all forms of communication. But religious honesty could not be open-ended, however much soul searching it required. Pictured in terms of the individual's inability to hide from God's omniscient oversight, religious love for truth could not question Christ's authority, and if it did, the Bible should be consulted for correction. As one Reverend Woodard assured his readers, "the word of God . . . will effectually remove many doubts and scruples that lie wavering and depending in some unsettled minds."[78]

With rejection of the Bible an invitation to the Devil and skepticism a sign of disreputable character, belief in a divine government overseeing all provided some assurance with respect to the disturbing aspects of American life. Thus in Pittsfield, Massachusetts, in 1806, Congregational minister Thomas Allen emphasized the importance of not succumbing to doubt or despair but believing that God was firmly in control when history seemed to be veering off course and the tragedies of life seemed overwhelming. He called people to listen "to the instructions of divine providence in the government of the world, upholding, overruling, and disposing of all things in the wisest and best manner for general good and the exaltation of the divine glory." Pushed to the core of his religious beliefs by the death of his son, Allen found it necessary to denounce the kind of self-confidence that Paine had called for in *Common Sense* and the belief inspired by the American Revolution that once they were liberated from tyranny, men would draw on reason and fellow feeling to govern themselves. "Would you assume the reins of government," Allen demanded, "usurp the prerogatives of Jehovah, and carve out your lot in life?" Everyone needed to submit to God, Allen insisted—"it becomes all his creatures to cease their opposition to his government." With full trust in God, Allen concluded that "[t]he affairs of this world cannot be in better hands."[79]

Heightened demand for submission to God coincided with the election and two-term presidency of Thomas Jefferson, a man whose religious and political views were similar to those of Thomas Paine's, as Jefferson's enemies in the Federalist camp liked to point out. Ironically, many of Jefferson's supporters were Baptists and Methodists whose beliefs in the authority of biblical revelation were antithetical to Jefferson's, but who supported Jefferson because of his idealization of the common man and his commitment to religious liberty and the separation of church and state. These evangelicals wanted freedom to establish kingdoms of religion with no interference from the state. If the success of their movements led them toward more expansive political aspirations, their interest in political democracy began by centering on freedom for themselves and their own religious kingdoms.

Religious Federalists differed from religious Jeffersonians in their political opinions about democracy and the common man. Federalists opposed Jeffersonian conceptions of liberty as dangerously naive, fearing democracy as an invitation to demagoguery and resenting the social disorder that followers of Jefferson stirred up. But religious people on both sides of the political divide voiced similar beliefs about the authority of Christ and invoked his kingdom as a model of social order under which the unruly forces of democracy could be contained and restrained and where offenders were sent to hell where they belonged. The virtual presence of Christ's kingdom allayed fears that life in the United States had gone terribly wrong and supported tendencies to hold unbelievers—and political opponents—responsible for the greed and deception that appeared to hold sway.

Religious groups disagreed about many things. Congregationalists and Presbyterians relied on intellectual practices that emphasized introspective self-government, while Baptists relied more heavily on congregational discipline and often resented Congregationalists for linking piety to political leadership and treating them as troublemakers and social inferiors. Methodists disagreed with those who made God seem harsh and forbidding, Baptists disagreed with all those who condoned infant baptism, and Presbyterians and Congregationalists resented those who challenged their learning and authority. Generally more affluent as well as better educated than most Methodists and Baptists, and more comfortably enmeshed in stable social structures, Congregationalists and Presbyterians took pride in their contributions to American independence and to the development of existing structures of government in the United States. Presbyterians and Congregationalists adhered to a mixed approach to church government that replicated elements of American political government, such as balance of power and commitment to both federal and state authority. If the elitism of Presbyterians and Congregationalists alienated many of those drawn to Methodists and Baptists, their importance as agents of cultural formation in colonial America and their cultural prestige as stalwart supporters of American independence in the Revolutionary era contributed to their ability to exert public influence. As learned representatives of Christ and his kingdom, Congregational and Presbyterian ministers cultivated a dignified presence, exercised public influence, and expected public respect.

Differences in worship style may have attracted more attention at the turn of the century than underlying commonalities, but even then, signs of consensus and cooperation abounded. As the numerical strength and organizational reach of religious organizations grew and cross-fertilized to increasing effect after 1800, evangelicalism began to take shape as a quasi party of its own, drawing women, men, and children from across—and outside—the political spectrum into its construction. Like the kingdom of God, this quasi party operated above local, state, and federal government in many respects, but also occupied footholds of public life that grew in size and strength. Over time, evangelicals would attempt to define American democracy in terms of political and religious principles derived from their own church governments. Congregationalists and Presbyterians led the way in educational ventures and social reform, whereas Methodists and Baptists exerted pressure on local mores; though Baptists upheld strong commitments to religious separatism that could discourage public activism, Baptists in Virginia and Georgia founded temperance societies aimed at curbing public consumption of alcohol.[80] Taking up the slack in government authority and managing disillusion about American independence, church governments developed alongside local, state, and federal governments, promoting idealism about the kingdom of God and blaming failures of civility in American life on their religious and political opponents.

Methodist, Baptist, Presbyterian, and Congregational systems of church government were all structured to uphold the divine monarchy of Christ and to promote submission to his rule among women and men who exalted the prospect of citizenship in the kingdom of heaven. That all four groups interpreted this submission as a form of freedom only underscores the willingness to tolerate inconsistency and the depth of investment in a monarchical form of religious government whose political corollary had been overthrown in the American Revolution and was still denounced.

CHAPTER FIVE

Religion in the Formation
of Political Parties

Thomas Jefferson came to power as the result of a democratic wedge between religion and Federalist rule driven by a loose coalition of materialist political leaders and evangelical supporters whose mistrust of Federalism muted their differences. Against imbuing government with sacred rites and symbols that sanctioned what they perceived to be excessive use of government power, Thomas Jefferson and his supporters argued that political authority rested with the people, as did decisions regarding religious belief and practice. Along with resentment of Federalist policies regarding taxes, banks, navigation rights, westward expansion, and immigration, political opposition to Federalism drew on hostility to Federalist attitudes toward religion among some evangelicals, especially Baptists, as well as among political activists skeptical of revealed religion.

The presidential election of 1800 was the first time that voters made the choice between two different philosophies of government—and two different approaches to religion's role with respect to government authority. Prior to that contest, and to the state and local elections in 1799 that generated momentum for Jefferson's victory, voting typically meant assent to decisions made by a ruling elite and to candidates chosen from among them. Popular engagement in political debate and decision-making was a new phenomenon for which opponents of Federalism bore primary responsibility. As Jefferson described this political transformation in the glow of memory two decades afterward, skipping over the partisan dissension it institutionalized: the election of 1800 "was as real a revolution in the principles of our government as that of 1776 was in its form; not effected indeed by the sword, as that, but by the rational and peaceable instrument of reform, the suffrage of the people."[1]

Dissension over the nature of religion and its proper place in the American republic played an important role in this politicization of American life. Followers of Jefferson caricatured Federalist religion as a stalking horse for political power, implying that it was not true religion. Angry Federalists, who thought of religion as the backbone of social cooperation, virtuous productivity, and civic responsibility, defended their conception of religion against political attackers, contributing to the partisan development of religion despite their belief in religion as a cohesive moral agent transcending party. Evangelical opponents of Federalist religion also believed that religion transcended party, but their definitions of religion emphasized its supernatural quality and separation from the world. Ironically, the evangelicals most bent on separating religion from politics contributed most significantly to partisan Republican growth and to the stridency of moral debate within politics.

Four specific forces related to religion brought Jeffersonians to power and forced Federalists to redefine their vision of the future. First, Baptists opposed to state interference in religion formed a pillar of religious support for Jefferson, and their arguments for religious liberty brought them into the political mainstream where their religious separatism supported Jefferson's laissez-faire policies of western expansion. Second, Federalists stung by attack became more aggressive in injecting biblical interpretations of American endangerment into public discourse, propping up visions of a national covenant with God even as they lost control of the machinery of government. Third, the religious skepticism typical of Jefferson and his early supporters receded as a result of campaigns against skepticism by religionists on both sides of the political divide. Fourth, the explosive growth of Methodism among laboring people moved the Methodist Church away from its early association with Federalism toward Jeffersonian democracy, with the effect of increasing public respect for supernatural experience and further muting skepticism of biblical revelation among Republicans. Taken together, these four factors characterize religion's upsurge in the first decade of the nineteenth century, its contribution to the organization of early political parties, and its role in undermining nonpartisan political debate.

In his first inaugural address, Jefferson endeavored to soften the partisanship he had done so much to advance, famously proclaiming, "We are all Republicans, we are all Federalists." He also downplayed the dispute over religion's role in the new republic that had contributed so much heat to partisan division. Proclaiming that Americans were "enlightened by a benign religion, professed, indeed, and practiced in various forms," Jefferson appealed to a common religion, presumably Christianity in its most generic form, which underlay many apparent differences. Upon that vaguely defined common ground, Jefferson asserted his intention to protect religious diversity by upholding "the sacred principle" of minority rights. "[T]hough the will of the majority is in all cases to prevail," he averred, "the minority possess their equal rights, which equal law must protect, and to violate would be oppression." Acknowledging the general government to be "the sheet anchor of our peace at home and safety abroad," Jefferson emphasized its function of protecting an array of different interest groups. In a rosy forecast, he anticipated their harmony under the approving watch of "an overruling Providence, which by all its dispensations proves that it delights in the happiness of man here and his greater happiness hereafter." An "adoring Providence" had bestowed many material "blessings" on the people of America, he added appreciatively, and delighted in their enjoyment of individual rights and freedom.[2]

Among Jefferson's supporters, Baptists played a crucial role in galvanizing popular hostility to Federalism. Though not as important in the early growth of democratic politics as Painite democrats, Baptists figured prominently in the assault on skepticism within Republican ranks. Their millennialism also fed into popular rhetoric about America's providential destiny, especially as that destiny incorporated the uninhibited growth of church governments such as their own.

One of the most ardent supporters of Jefferson's passion for religious liberty, the Connecticut-born Baptist Isaac Backus viewed the simultaneity of Jefferson's election and the outbreak of religious revivals at the turn of the century as evidence that a new age of Christian piety was dawning. Convinced that religious liberty cleared the way for people to turn toward God, Backus had spent a lifetime promoting arguments originally put forward by Roger Williams against the New England Puritan establishment in the seventeenth century. With Jefferson's election, Backus thought Williams had finally been vindicated and that state control of religion would never recover. In 1805, near the end of his life, he exulted that "the liberty that he [Roger Williams] was for, civil and religious, is now enjoyed in thirteen of the seventeen of the United States of America. No tax for any religious minister is imposed by authority in any of the said 13 States, and their power is much weakened in the other 4."[3]

Like Backus, Baptist John Leland resisted Federalist ideas about religion— that their religion was true Christianity, that morality derived from respect for it, and that the state should be invested with its authority. Native to Massachusetts, home to the Puritans who evicted Roger Williams, Leland ridiculed the hypocrisy of the Massachusetts State Constitution in providing for a "general assessment" levied on all taxpayers by the dominant church in each town while at the same time proclaiming innocently that "one denomination of Christians shall have no preeminence above another." Snorting at the provision that members of minority churches might obtain "certificates to draw back their money, after they have paid it," he compared the relationship between a dominant and minority church to park lands owned by "Old Mr. Domineer Bigot" and "Mr. Love Freedom," in which Mr. Bigot could claim that "all the deer in my park, and all that are in the woods, have an animal tax upon their heads, which they are obliged to pay to me, unless you catch them in hunting, or they voluntarily jump into your park, and bear your mark."[4]

While Methodists were new to the politics of religious liberty, Baptists were old hands in the game. Baptists were better organized in their grassroots political resistance to religious establishment than any other group, though they often disapproved of extending religious liberty to non-Christians. In Virginia, minority religious groups led by Baptists could outperform better-known deists in organizing popular political support for religious liberty. While James Madison's famous *Memorial and Remonstrance* against a bill supporting religious establishment in Virginia collected 1,552 signatures in 1785, a second petition against the bill supported by Baptists and other pietists from Westmoreland County collected 4,899 signatures, more than three times as many. Both petitions argued that religious liberty was a God-given right and that Christianity was ill served by religious establishment, but Madison's *Memorial and Remonstrance* was loaded with generic terms meant to be inclusive of low-church Anglicanism and mild forms of deism, such as "the Bill is adverse to the diffusion of the light of Christianity." The Westmoreland County petition was less irenic and more pointed, claiming that the bill ran counter to "the Spirit of the Gospel" and would do little to stop "that Deism with its banefull Influence [which] is spreading itself over the state."[5]

Baptists in Massachusetts were also politically active in behalf of religious liberty, circulating as many as one hundred petitions in 1780 against passage of Article III in the Massachusetts Constitution providing for a religious establishment supported by the state. When that effort failed, they organized resistance to religious taxes in order to test Article III in county courts. Supporting these efforts, sermons and published writings by Isaac Backus drew from John Locke's *Essay on Toleration*, as well as from pious Baptist writers like John Bunyan and from Baptist memories of discrimination over the course of more than two centuries. Reflecting this long history of religious and political dissent, Baptists wove natural rights and Christian election together. "As God is the only object of all religious worship, and nothing can be true religion but a voluntary obedience unto his revealed will, of which each rational soul has an equal right to judge for itself," wrote Isaac Backus in 1779, intertwining rational and pietistic language, "every person has an unalienable right to act in all religious affairs according to the full persuasion of his own mind, where others are not injured thereby."[6]

The alliance between liberal rationalists and Baptists in Jeffersonian America was deeply rooted, deriving from similar alliances during the English Civil War and puritan Interregnum more than a century before. Liberal rationalists and Baptists in Jefferson's day both drew from arguments for religious tolerance advanced by the seventeenth-century English political philosopher John Locke and Locke's arguments, in turn, built upon the argument against religious licensing published in the *Areopegetica* of 1649 by the English scholar, statesman, and religious poet John Milton, whose advocacy of religious tolerance epitomized the confluence of godly piety and liberal rationalism prior to the restoration of British monarchy in 1660. Milton was well aware of the stinging pronouncements against religious persecution published in the 1640s by his radical Baptist acquaintance Roger Williams, whose protests against religious establishment led to his expulsion from the Massachusetts Bay Colony in 1636.[7]

In his famous *Essay on Toleration* first printed in 1667, Locke echoed Williams's complaint against government "meddling" in religion, asserting that the sole business of government was the "peace, safety, or security of the people" and that laws with any other purpose constituted "meddling." Defending his reasoning in 1681, Locke argued that a magistrate has "no more certain or more infallible knowledge of the way to attain" a right relationship to God "than I myself." A generation earlier, in 1652, Williams wrote that, a "minister or magistrate goes beyond his commission who intermeddles with that which cannot be given him by the people," and that it was "but flattering . . . to persuade the rulers of the earth that they are kings of the nation of Israel or church of God." State interference in religion worked "against peace" and was "destructive [of] all civility." Even worse, it was a violent sin against "conscience," the only soil, Williams believed, where God's grace could be planted.[8]

Jefferson's arguments for religious liberty drew directly from Locke, as did arguments advanced by Jefferson's Baptist supporters Isaac Backus and John Leland. Asserting that the effects of religious imposition had been disastrous, Jefferson wrote in *Notes on the State of Virginia* that "[m]illions of innocent men, women, and children, since the introduction of Christianity, have been burnt, tortured, fined, imprisoned"—while the dangers of liberty were practically nonexistent—"it does me no injury for my neighbor to say there are twenty gods, or no god. It neither picks my pocket nor breaks my leg."[9] That comment, which Jefferson's detractors interpreted as a tendency to atheism, echoed Locke's comment in the "Essay on Toleration" that "[i]f I observe the Friday with the Mahomedan, or the Saturday with the Jew, or the Sunday with the Christian, [none] of these, if they be done sincerely and out of conscience, [will] of itself make me [a] worse neighbor."[10]

Again channeling Locke, Jefferson maintained that "our rulers can have authority of such natural rights only as we have submitted to them. The rights of conscience we never submitted, we could not submit. We are answerable for them to our God." John Leland made a similar point: "What can appear more arrogant, than for fallible men, to make their own opinions, tests of orthodoxy, and force others to yield implicit obedience thereto"?[11]

Leland's willingness to consider religious belief a matter of opinion exemplifies the rationalism intertwined in his pietism that enabled his alliance with Jeffersonian deists. Though he believed his own religion was true and would eventually be proven so for all to see, Leland owned the modern term "opinion" as much as anyone, joining Lockean and populist parlance in the title of one of his publications, *The rights of conscience inalienable, and therefore religious opinions not cognizable by law: or, The high-flying church-man, stript of his legal robe, appears a Yaho.*[12] As he observed in a later sermon, "Experience teaches us, that men, who are equally wise and good, may differ in political, as well as in theological or mathematical opinions." Considering that men were "rational beings" who learned from others, there was simply no justification for "the man, who, would rather sink a state or distress a nation, than to be crossed in his own view and opinion."[13]

Baptists obviously parted company with deists in their devotion to biblical revelation and in the religious practices that set them apart from the world, including adult baptism and submission to strict communal discipline. Baptists were even more righteously incensed than deists on the subject of state interference in religion: "What can be more ridiculous," John Leland demanded, "than for Towns to levy a ministerial, as they do a highway tax"? Taxing people to support established clergy angered Leland not simply because it violated the rights of minorities to hold their own religious opinions but also and more importantly because "[s]uch proceedings reduce religion to a level with civil things—treat it as an object of government"—and thus falsely "represent Christ's Kingdom to be of this world."[14]

Baptist demands for the right to worship without impediment enabled the success of Jeffersonian politics. In Virginia, harassment of Baptists by the established Anglican Church since colonial days contributed to popular support for the Virginia Statute of Religious Freedom drafted by Jefferson in 1779 and passed into law in 1786. In Massachusetts and the District of Maine, where Baptists had long been subjected to legal discrimination, Republicans drew heaviest support from towns with strong Baptist churches. Republican political activists counted on Baptists as a base of support in New England and Baptists came through; in John Leland's home town of Cheshire, Massachusetts, Federalists never drew more than 7 out of 241 votes in the years between 1800 and 1812.[15]

Although Jefferson distrusted established clergy, he made a habit of befriending Baptist ministers and other religious leaders who had been or continued to be dissenters from state-supported religions. Jefferson drew some of his strongest support from these people, as well as from men who shared his own materialistic philosophy. As he remarked in 1800, "I have long labored to rally the Physicians & Dissenting Clergy who are generally friends of equal liberty."[16]

As popular participation in politics grew, Republican activists called on Baptists for more political engagement. In 1805, with a snipe at Federalist Anglophilia, the Republican *Independent Chronicle* of Massachusetts called on religious dissenters to rally their troops at the polls in order to "cement the basis of civil and religious Liberty, by confounding the artifices of those *Anglo-federalists*, who would establish an hierarchy in Massachusetts, and suppress the freedom of Divine worship."[17] Under this sort of pressure, Baptists had to deal with the question of how far they could go in political activities without jeopardizing their commitment to religious purity. In 1805, the Elkhorn Baptist Association in Kentucky addressed the issue, questioning whether Baptists should participate in Republican-sponsored events celebrating American Independence. Perhaps it was all the alcohol that flowed during those events, or the violent wrestling contests that ensued, rather than the rousing stump speeches by Republican candidates for public office that compelled the decision, but whatever the precise trigger, the minutes of the annual meeting read as follows: "Quere from Glens Creek Is it right for Baptists to join in & assemble at barbacues on the 4th of July? Answered No."[18]

But John Leland had no hesitation about deep political involvement, celebrating Jefferson's fiscal policies as well as Jefferson's role as a protector of religious liberty. In his Fourth of July oration in 1806 during Jefferson's second term, Leland expressed gratitude to the president for lifting tax burdens imposed by the previous Federal administration for repayment of national debt. Like Isaac Backus, who approved of Jefferson's restraint on government expenditures to lower the national debt, Leland resented the government growth policies engineered by Alexander Hamilton that benefited the wealthy. Taking note that none of the Bible burnings or destruction of church buildings predicted by Federalists had come to pass during Jefferson's first administration, Leland thanked Jefferson for his trust in the people and closed his sermon with "ten thousand times ten thousand more" thanks to Christ "for forgiving us all our debts, and opening the gates of heaven for all who love and obey him."[19]

Jefferson had no compunction, either, about using Leland to taunt his Federalist supporters. When Leland delivered the gift of a 1,235-pound cheese from Republican farmers in Cheshire to the White House on New Year's day in 1802, Jefferson invited him to preach the following Sunday in the chamber of the House of Representatives. Jefferson attended, as did Federalist clergy who wanted to uphold the tradition established by Washington and Adams of convening religious rituals in government buildings for a congregation of church and government officials. Leland preached on the text, "And behold, a greater than Solomon is here," which must have set some teeth grinding. Jefferson would have been entertained not only by such lofty praise but also by the spectacle of Leland's preaching and his opponents' fortitude in sitting through it. As one Federalist cleric complained, Leland "bawled" out the sermon in a "horrid tone," with "frightful grimaces, and extravagant gestures."[20]

While happy to cast the union of American interests in a sacred glow, Jefferson vigorously opposed efforts to invest church authority in the state. In addition to violating the "sacred principle" of minority rights, Jefferson thought ties between church and state had a stupefying effect. As he wrote to James Madison in 1798 about the people of Connecticut, who supported an established clergy, "they are so priest-ridden that nothing is to be expected from them but the most bigotted passive obedience." Equally dangerous was the tendency to monarchy that crept into government when worshipful trappings surrounded affairs of state. As he complained about Washington's administration in 1793, they "seemed ready to hang every thing round with the tassils and baubles of monarchy." As far as Jefferson was concerned, the Republican victory seven years later was as much a defeat for Federalist efforts to infuse the state with religious authority as it was a triumph for democracy. "What an effort, my dear Sir, of bigotry in politics and religion we have gone through!" he wrote jubilantly to his friend Joseph Priestley after the election. "The barbarians really flattered themselves," he gloated, that "they should be able to bring back the times of Vandalism, when ignorance put everything into the hands of power and priestcraft."[21]

Although Baptists hostile to established religion were an essential part of Jefferson's constituency, his political base derived mainly from the Democratic-Republican societies that had sprung up around the country in the 1790s in support of international revolution and democracy. Skeptical of state-supported religious authority in France, Ireland, and the United States, these societies included many sympathetic to Thomas Paine's argument that assent to revealed religion coincided with submission to political tyranny. Reacting against repressive monetary, trade, and anti–free speech policies enacted by Washington and Adams, and with much assistance from newspapers, Democratic-Republican societies laid the groundwork for a popular opposition movement with new strategies for grassroots political organization that engaged new participants and brought new voters to the polls.[22]

For the political activists at the base of this movement, long-standing hostility to the Catholic Church, freshly stimulated by the Church's support of monarchy and opposition to democracy in France, became a handy template for caricaturing the aura of reactionary religion enveloping American Federalism. Thus in 1799, the democratic *Aurora* inveighed against the "despotism" and "tyranny" emanating from the bastions of Federalism in New England, linking religious authority in that region to medieval times. For centuries, "arrogant elites had long demanded that common people "submit quietly" to "*learning*." The *Aurora* reminded readers "how seriously this doctrine has been maintained in the christian church" and how consistently churchmen supported intellectual oppression; "from the mitred bishop to the tonsured priest they were all lords of the conscience."[23]

Jefferson, of course, was passionate about religious liberty as a natural right; he drafted the Virginia Statute for Religious Freedom in 1779, passed by the General Assembly in 1786, which effectively disestablished the Church of England. In the context of the growing national opposition to Federalism at the end of the century, Jefferson and his supporters deployed the rhetoric of religious liberty against his political opponents. Appropriating complaints by Baptists who had been arguing against religious establishment in New England since the seventeenth century, democratic newspapers around the country represented the Standing Orders in Massachusetts and Connecticut mandating taxation to support state-established clergy as evidence of Federalist tyranny.

Defenders of the Standing Orders were outraged; they perceived themselves as champions of individual conscience supporting laws that permitted religious dissenters to give their taxes to a minority church. They also resented the enlarged framework of political interpretation that cast them in the same pool as the supporters of religious establishment in Virginia who sided with Britain in the American Revolution. The black-gowned "regiment" of New England clergy had delivered a stream of arguments for American independence in the 1770s and 1780s, and many had used their pulpits to denounce British tyranny. When the presidential election of 1800 created a national stage for Baptist complaints that New England clergy were illegitimate agents of a repressive political state, Jeffersonians provoked those clergy and their supporters into becoming more partisan, and often bitterly so, thereby undermining the reputation for sober virtue and civic mindedness they labored to uphold. Consequently, Federalists who decried the emergence of "parties" acquired increasing responsibility for politicizing religion and establishing its importance as a driving force in partisan organization.

The democratic critique of Federalist religion coalesced during the election of 1800. Typical of anti-Federalist invective that year, the *Virginia Argus* passed on a report from a Virginia doctor returned from a visit to New England where he attended a commencement in New Haven that involved a large number of clergy. The doctor "could plainly perceive, that the interests of John Adams, & Co, lay nearer their hearts than that of the advancement of the Kingdom of our blessed Redeemer." The doctor also attended the voting for presidential electors and other candidates in Hartford, "which to his surprise was held in a Presbyterian meeting, and the house profit used to political intrigue, artifice cunning, and party."[24]

Seizing the legacy of the American Revolution for use against the Federalist administration, which had assumed that legacy for itself, Jeffersonians likened the Adams administration and its commitment to civic religion to the British monarchy. Thus in November 1800, a Pennsylvania paper reprinted an opinion piece attributed to Charleston Republican Charles Pinckney describing the "opposite political sentiments" of Federalists and Republicans: "The man who is fond of royalty, and considers the British or any other monarchy, as the greatest effort of the human mind, will naturally view standing armies, great power in the judges, even as in England, frequently without the intervention of a jury, high taxes, a well paid and influential clergy" as all entirely good and fitting. By contrast, "a plain republican citizen will shudder at the names of royalty or standing armies, judges without juries, high taxes, or a domineering clergy and an established religion."[25]

In January 1801, a writer for Boston's *Independent Chronicle* attacked the geographer, encyclopedist, and Congregational minister Jedidiah Morse for celebrating the *"Aristocratical balance"* provided by the clergy of Connecticut "as a check to the *overbearing spirit of Republicanism*." Addressing the "Citizens of Connecticut," the critic asked if it were true that "your clergy is an ARISTOCRATICAL BODY" intent on "checking the spirit of Republicanism"? If so, "we cannot but pity your situation." If not, "we expect some severe censures to be passed on the man whose arrogance has led him to give such a statement of your political vassalage." The writer certain that "[t]he YEOMANRY of Connecticut are too enlightened to be priest-ridden."[26] At least one peeved reader complained about such an unfair political attack on the ministers of New England: "When will some writers in the Chronicle . . . cease calling some of our first revolutionary characters, among which are the clergy (as worthy a set of men as live) by the hacknied term of *"Old Tories"*?[27]

Federalist newspapers tried to refute the charge of intolerance. In reaction to Jefferson's inaugural address, an angry Federalist took great exception to the "censure on the former administration . . . implied" by the address and especially the congratulation offered by the new president to his country for "having *banished* from our land, that religious intolerance, under which mankind so long bled and suffered." The writer demanded to know, "What, Sir, is your meaning when you state that we have *banished* from our land religious tolerance?" Aside from "a solitary instance or two of persecution for the sake of religious opinions" back in the seventeenth century, "[w]hen or in what part of our country have men 'bled and suffered' for religious opinions?"[28]

While Jeffersonians felt pressure to proclaim respect for religion and counter their reputation for religious skepticism, John Adams grasped the political advantages of established religious support that he enjoyed. As president, Adams followed George Washington in performances of respect for religion ranging from ostentatious church attendance to calls for days of national prayer and fasting. Even more significant, Adams advanced an essentially political concept of "religion" that served as a useful fiction for obscuring conflict among various sects and implying that some kind of underlying unity existed among them. By insisting on the importance of "religion" for moral order at both state and federal levels, Adams garnered considerable support from New England Calvinists, despite the fact that his own religious opinions verged toward Unitarianism and thus were at odds with those of many of his staunchest religious supporters.[29]

For Adams and his Federalist supporters, religion was the duty to God and community from which political order should derive. While tyranny might also produce political order, it would never be as stable or conducive to morality as that produced by freely offered duty. Considerable latitude existed for individual religious opinion, but political order required that the state be imbued with elements of religious authority embodied, not least of all, in the chief magistrate. As George Washington proclaimed in his farewell address, "Of all the dispositions and habits which lead to political prosperity, Religion and Morality are indispensable supports." Minimizing differences in theology and appealing to common assumption about God's oversight of the nation, Washington explained to his audience that "with slight shades of difference, you have the same religion." Investment in the political aspect of religion and religion's fundamental importance for civil order was essential to the survival of the American republic and its ideals; for example, property ownership would never be secure if judges lost "the sense of religious obligation" in their "oaths" of office. With the implication that religious skeptics were unpatriotic as well as immoral, Washington proclaimed his doubt "that morality can be maintained without religion" or that "national morality can prevail in exclusion of religious principle."[30]

Clergy who provided prayers at state functions and delivered sermons to government officials were among Federalism's most articulate supporters, and the benefits of mutual support cannot have been lost on either side. Opportune moments for cultivating this relationship included days of fasting and thanksgiving proclaimed by the president and solemnized by clergy who created visions of national unity through images of the president's relationship to God. On the occasion of President Washington's proclamation of a day of fasting and thanksgiving in 1795, following the suppression of the "insurrection in the west" known as the Whiskey Rebellion, Jedidiah Morse drew a picture of American Christian unity for his congregants in Charlestown, Massachusetts. "There cannot be a more pleasing sight on earth, than a Christian assembly," he began, "voluntarily convened, as we are today, at the voice of our Chief-Magistrate, to unite with our fellow-citizens, in rendering praise to God." Morse's "delight" in this picture was enhanced by knowledge that "millions" of other Americans were likewise engaged and by the hope that many of them were "true worshippers of God." If such hope might be entertained, with all due humility, "[t]hen our country would this day resemble the heavenly world."[31]

Turning to his biblical text, Morse described the religious faith of Moses and his leadership of the people of Israel "during their memorable forty years journey between Egypt and Canaan." Recalling the sacred laws Moses delivered to his people, Morse invited his people to "contemplate" another "scene," similar but "at least equally calculated to affect, improve and animate our hearts. A nation, far greater than that which Moses addressed," Morse assured his people, "is assembled this day before the Lord, at the recommendation of their venerable political Leader and Father." Eager for his people to reflect on their great blessings, especially in light of the tribulations of other nations, Morse announced, "This incomparable Chief—this Moses of our nation" had called everyone together for a day of prayer and thanksgiving.[32]

Suspicious of Americans with more materialist and secular conceptions of the republic's founding, New England clergymen like Morse led the way in promoting the theory that Democratic societies and Masonic lodges were essentially antireligious organizations conspiring to overthrow the American government. It was certainly true that religious skeptics of various sort found these groups congenial and also that democratic impulses and opposition to religious authority had been intertwined for centuries. But Federalist clergy overstated the degree of organization these groups enjoyed. Inventing connections between various democratic and Republican-leaning organizations and secret societies of Bavarian Illuminati and French Jacobins, Federalist clerics wove conspiracy theories warning that these societies and organizations were developing secret plans to destroy religion and government.[33]

No one pressed the case for organized conspiracy more forcefully than Reverend Morse. As just one example of the "complete and indubitable proof that such societies do exist," Morse asserted in 1799, "I have, my brethren, an official, authenticated list of the names, ages, places of nativity, professions, &c, of the officers and members of a Society of *Illuminati* (or as they are now more generally and properly styled, *Illuminees*)." The particular society to which Morse referred met in Virginia and had a hundred members, including a "deputy" to the "Mother Society in France." This society was part of a broad network of evildoers seeking to undermine the United States's special role in history as a nation in covenant with God. With allusions to Fries's Rebellion in Pennsylvania, Masonic lodges in many towns, and the Tammany Society in New York that Aaron Burr was turning into an effective political organization, Morse warned, "we have in truth secret enemies, not a few, scattered through the country . . . whose professed design is to subvert and destroy our holy religion and our free and excellent government."[34]

Federalist newspapers also carried the message that Jefferson was out to destroy religion. Summarizing the case against him, one opponent contrasted Jefferson with "the great and good Washington" who had passed away the year before Jefferson took power. Washington's "name was, under God, our shield and defense," the writer maintained, because he was a leader who "honoured God, reverenced his Sabbaths, and attended on the institutions of his worship." The contrast with Jefferson was clear. He attended church infrequently according to the writer and, referring to Jefferson's often-cited remark that "it does me no injury for my neighbor to say there are twenty gods, or no god," concluded that Jefferson thought it "a light thing . . . to say there is *no God*." The consequence of electing such a man as chief magistrate would be to signal to foreign nations that Americans were "a weak, a divided, and an irreligious people." At home, Jefferson's election would "destroy religion, introduce immorality, and loosen all the bonds of society."[35]

With conceptions of political government so closely tied to their expectations about how public officials should embody respect for religion, Federalists naturally let their opposition to Jefferson's political philosophy spill into hatred of his character. Arch-Federalist Alexander Hamilton, who equated democracy with mob rule, perceived Jefferson as demagogue who masked his true character as a decadent sensualist beneath a public persona of yeoman simplicity. In a pamphlet published anonymously in 1796, Hamilton called attention to the hypocrisy of Jefferson's professed desire "to emancipate the blacks to vindicate the liberty of the human race," pointing to what he perceived as contradictory assertions about the natural inferiority of blacks in *Notes on the State of Virginia*, the volume Federalists routinely quoted from to demonstrate the inadequacy of Jefferson's religious beliefs. Pointing nastily to deeper motives lurking beneath Jefferson's statement against the enslavement of blacks, Hamilton supposed that "[h]e must have seen all around him sufficient marks of this *staining of blood* to have been convinced that retaining them in slavery would not prevent it."[36]

In the spring of 1800, trying to emulate Aaron Burr's novel strategies for bringing a cross-section of voters to the polls, Hamilton rode horseback from one polling place to another in New York City, almost like a religious itinerant, urging potential voters to send Federalist representatives to the Electoral College and suffering taunts of "villain" and "scoundrel" for his efforts. When city voters overturned precedent to elect a Republican slate, Hamilton feared the worst. As he wrote the Federalist governor of New York John Jay in May, Jefferson's election would mean that men seeking "the overthrow of the government by stripping it of its due energies" would foment "a revolution after the manner of Buonaparte." Leading the country into this ruin, Thomas Jefferson was "an *atheist* in religion and a *fanatic* in politics."[37]

Pressed to defend Jefferson's bona fides as a virtuous man against such attacks, Boston's *Independent Chronicle* asserted that "[t]he attack on his *religious principles* is among the most contemptible arts of his enemies." Sidestepping the matter of Jefferson's personal piety, or lack thereof, the writer thought such attacks ridiculous, given Jefferson's support for religious freedom: "Can any person seriously think, that he would attempt to undermine the cause of religion?"[38] Republican papers circulated news of Jefferson's contributions to a clergyman near Monticello as evidence of his benevolent attitude toward voluntary religion. In an effort to build trust for Jefferson's policies among evangelical groups in Virginia, *The Times* of Alexandria wanted people to know that "Mr. Jefferson constantly supports a very worthy church minister in his neighborhood, when the repeal of certain laws, under the former religious establishment in Virginia, exempts him from the tribute tythes."[39] Others discerned the highest moral virtue in Jefferson's commitment to religious liberty: "Mr. Jefferson stands pre-eminent for his political, social, moral, and religious virtues."[40]

Complaints of hypocrisy flew back and forth, fueling the religious component of partisan mistrust. Defending their man against religious flaws alleged by his opponents to be disqualifications for presidential office, Republicans turned their opponents' political use of religion against them, making Federalists committed to close ties between government and religion seem hypocritical and more interested in religion for self-interested political reasons than for religion itself. Defenders made Jefferson out to be religion's true protector, in contrast to Federalist opponents who imbued their own control over government with religious authority, thereby corrupting and dislodging religion from its proper sphere. "Among the numerous cries set up by the friends of order and regular government, in order to influence the approaching election," wrote a contributor to a paper read in Washington, DC, "are that Mr. Jefferson is an enemy to religion." Pointing out that Jefferson "has been during the course of his life the advocate of universal toleration," the author cast Jefferson's critics beyond the pale of morality, among "those enemies which Virtue always creates, who are in fact the only enemies he has." Turning Federalist hysteria about secret societies around, the writer singled out for particular scorn the clergy centered around New Haven, "those pious Connecticut illuminati men whose piety consists of lust of piety or pelf—whose religion is the things of this world."[41]

Pious Connecticut men and their political allies were beleaguered, but not without resources to fight back, even if they no longer commanded enough votes to keep a Federalist in the White House, or in the governor's office in Massachusetts. The considerable learning of Federalist clergy in New England, their influence over education, and identification with the national covenant struck between God and their puritan forebears inspired them to regroup and set forth new missions for America. Teaming up with Presbyterians active in political affairs and social reform south of New England,

Congregational clergy and their supporters imagined a brighter future ahead as self-appointed bearers of national culture and its outreach to all mankind. Congregational and Presbyterian clergy would take command of American intellectual life and extend freedom in Christ to all the world, while continuing in their efforts to destroy the influence of deistical thinkers and skepticism of revealed religion. As Connecticut-born Reverend Edward D. Griffin told the Presbyterian General Assembly in 1804, "Great events appear to be struggling in their birth. In the eager attitude of hope, many are looking for the dawn of a better day, and even believe that they already see the light purpling the east."[42]

Meanwhile, Baptists and Methodists raced ahead of Congregationalists and Presbyterians in membership, becoming more mainstream and respectable in the process. But while the pillar of Baptist support for Jefferson was deeply rooted in English history, Methodist support for Jefferson was only beginning to develop in 1800. In previous decades, the antidemocratic sympathies of American Methodists were often presumed. During the American Revolution, Methodists were routinely suspected of being Tories and had to curtail their operations, despite efforts to follow the instructions of their English leader, John Wesley, to remain above the fray. When Wesley proclaimed the cause of American independence to be illegitimate, Methodist preachers in America fell under suspicion as British agents. Methodist preacher Thomas Webb spent a year as a prisoner of war in Pennsylvania after escaping execution as British spy. Joseph Hartley and Freeborn Garrison spent time in jail in Maryland, and the travel-obsessed Francis Asbury was forced to confine himself during the war to a neighborhood of loyalist protectors in Delaware.[43]

After Wesley changed his mind in favor of American independence and the Methodist Episcopal Church separated from the Church of England in 1784, Methodist societies in America began to recoup the losses they had suffered during the revolution. But for years afterward, Methodists continued to fall under suspicion as members of a religion whose organizing principles were inimical to American values. Hostile critics viewed the Methodists' hierarchical system of church government as a carryover from Catholicism, which they associated with political tyranny, suppression of individual conscience, and the corruption of authentic Christian faith. As bishop and general superintendent of the Methodist Episcopal Church in America, Asbury still battled against that prejudice in 1803, complaining in his journal about "the ignorance of foolish men," who seemed unable to "distinguish between a pope of Rome," and himself, "an old, worn man of about sixty years," who traveled by horse "five thousand miles a year, at a salary of eight dollars, through summer's heat and winter's cold." The worldly benefits of Asbury's bishopric were few and unpretentious: "[H]is best fare, for six months of the twelve, coarse kindness; and his reward, from too many, suspicion, envy, and murmurings all the year round."[44]

In 1800, many new converts to Methodism drawn from the ranks of laboring people leaned toward the nascent political organization coalescing around Thomas Jefferson. But in the Delmarva Peninsula, where the Methodist Episcopal Church was most firmly rooted, lay leaders tended to be strong allies of the Federalist administration. In Delaware, some of the most powerful Federalists were Methodists, including Governor Richard Bassett. In April 1800, as the presidential contest between Adams and Jefferson moved into full swing, the Republican *Aurora* reported that Governor Bassett had extended a loan of eight hundred pounds to build a meeting house in anticipation of support from Methodist voters for Federalists electors. The *Aurora* also reported that Methodist leaders in Dover threatened to remove supporters of Jefferson from church membership rolls.[45]

Adding to the impression of Methodist hostility to democratic politics, the Methodist Church was still recovering from the sharp decline in membership in Virginia and North Carolina after the departure of James O'Kelly and his supporters, who argued that bishops were not authorized by the New Testament and that installing a more democratic style of governance would bring the Methodist Church more in line with the political principles of the new American republic. When a strong coalition of Episcopal supporters led by Bishop Asbury defeated their efforts in 1792, O'Kelly and thousands of his followers left to form the independent Republican Methodist Church.[46] The O'Kelly schism confirmed the impression that democratic politics and Methodist Episcopal religion were at odds and that Jeffersonians would do better to look elsewhere for political support.

In 1800, as far as Jeffersonian interests were concerned, the political implications of Methodist growth were highly ambiguous. In Kentucky, Methodists were still a tiny minority, and the number of whites belonging to Methodist societies had declined since 1795. In Virginia and North Carolina, where most migrants in Kentucky came from, the best-established Methodists maintained cordial ties with Methodists in Britain, applauded efforts by Washington and Adams to develop commercial and political alliances with Britain, and shared Federalist interest in centralized government, which included deference to ruling elites, as well as investment in a navy and national bank to defend commercial interests. Natural allies of conservative interpreters of the American Revolution, Methodists successful in business and public service had reason to support Federalist policies and to resist the popular opposition to those policies stirred up by Jeffersonians.[47]

But the potential for more cordial alliance between democratic politics and Methodist pietism was soon to be realized. Especially in the West, where Methodist growth was greatest, and where impatience with federal restraints on navigation and occupation of Indian lands was keenest, Methodist societies would become cultures of moral rectitude, florid supernaturalism, and outreach to others in the midst of the speculation, counterfeiting, and the free-for-all rush for land and natural resources permitted by Jeffersonian policy. This symbiotic relationship between libertarian politics and Methodist piety caught on immediately after the Great Revival of 1801. In 1800, only four Methodist circuits served Kentucky, Tennessee, and large parts of Virginia and Ohio, but by 1804, the number of circuits had multiplied almost seven-fold, with twenty-six circuits serving the same area and Methodists leading revivals in all four states.[48]

While the growth of Methodist church government was remarkable in its own right, the impact of Methodist influence in the West was compounded by the alliance that developed between promoters of Methodism and democratic political leaders disinclined toward biblical revelation. In its initial stages, this alliance involved speculation by both parts—political speculation that Methodists might counter Federalist-leaning Presbyterians and religious speculation that skeptical Jeffersonians might be won over to Christ.

Nothing better illustrates the confluence of these speculations than the meeting in Lexington in January 1800 between Kentucky Speaker of the House John Breckinridge and a Methodist preacher seeking funds to build a church in Staunton, Virginia. Breckinridge was a man with considerable wealth, political influence, and skepticism with respect to revealed religion. Since moving from Virginia to Kentucky in 1793, he had built a powerful law practice in Lexington, invested in land, iron foundries and salt works, and established a self-sufficient farm where he bred a variety of animals, including thoroughbred racehorses. With most of his land in the fertile Bluegrass Region, Breckinridge was one of the largest landowners in the new state, owning nearly a quarter million acres at the time of his unexpected death in 1806 at age forty-six. As a political leader, Breckinridge was a founder of Kentucky's first Democratic Society, serving as its first chairman. He also introduced the famous Kentucky Resolutions that challenged the Alien and Seditions Acts of 1798 and brought the term *nullification* into political debate. For his efforts, Breckinridge was elected to the US Senate in 1800, promoted by Kentucky

Republicans as Jefferson's running mate in 1804, and appointed attorney general of the United States by Jefferson in 1805.[49]

Though raised in a family of Scots-Irish Presbyterians, Breckinridge had detached himself from church affiliation as a young man and showed little personal interest in religion afterward. He was not unfamiliar with religious zeal; his ancestors were Scottish Covenanters who fought against Irish Catholics in the seventeenth century and his mother-in-law was adamant about religion. In 1810, his wife Polly received what was probably not the first plea from her mother to convert—"strive to tak the lord & his Christ for without holiness no one shall see the lord & religion is A Blessed & Exemplary practice."[50]

If Breckinridge considered himself enlightened by Christianity, he was not inclined to endorse its prophetic scriptures or participate in any of its denominational forms. As a strong advocate of rationality, education, and freedom of conscience, his correspondence shows no interest in theological discourse or conversion. In family matters, he expressed his feelings in the language of reason. Thus, with regard to the behavior of one of their sons, he wrote Polly, "[W]e have every rational hope from his past & present conduct that he will not disappoint our expectations."[51] Breckinridge paid close attention to the education of his children and extended his intellectual oversight to other family members as well. In a letter to his nephew Joseph, he asked for an account of books the young man had read. Joseph wrote back that he had been studying "History," "Law," and "English Poets," and anticipated forays into "Hume, Robertson, and a few other valuable historians."[52] Possessed of a fine library including books by Gibbon, Hume, Locke, Priestly, Edmund Burke, John Jacques Rousseau, Adam Smith, Jonathan Swift, Shakespeare, and Milton, Breckinridge helped to develop the library at Transylvania University, which served as the leading university in the West into the late-1820s and gave Lexington a reputation as the "Athens of the West."[53]

By way of introduction to this leading citizen, the Methodist preacher presented a letter from Archibald Stuart, an "old affectionate friend" of Breckinridge's since their college days at William and Mary in the 1780s. Stuart wrote Breckinridge that he had warned the preacher that his friend's generosity was much in demand—"I have advised Mr. Monet not to be too sanguine in his expectations from coffers subject to such frequent drafts"—and went on to explain why he thought the man deserved Breckinridge's support. "The society of which Mr. M is a member," Stuart wrote, was not only "becomeing numerous" and "respectable in this quarter" but was also "uniformly republican & aided us much in resisting the influence of the Presbyterians who have been generally hostile to the administration." Stuart's news that the Methodists in the Shenandoah Valley region were uniting behind Jefferson had its effect. On the envelope of Stuart's letter, Breckinridge scrawled: "gave him 5$."[54]

That donation epitomized religion's role in the interplay of local, state, and national interests at a coalescing point in the formative era of American party politics.[55] Political activists like Archibald Stuart maintained ties with activists in other states, like his former schoolmate John Breckinridge, encouraging local opposition to the national policies of John Adams. Feeling their way as their political organizing developed, these party activists became increasingly knowledgeable about different constituencies of potential voters, making friends with individuals and groups representing different class, ethnic, and religious backgrounds. Their expanding efforts reached across the spectrum of grassroots opposition to Federalist policy from Baptists devoted to strict interpretations of biblical revelation to followers of Thomas Paine unmoved by appeals to revealed religion and hostile to what they perceived as its reactionary political influence. Beyond the control of any particular interest group, the coalition supporting Jefferson's bid for the presidency brought rationalists cool about religion and pietists hot for it together in political opposition to Federalist policy. As a result, the Republican party became overwhelmingly popular, and the religious skepticism, which had once been a strong force among Jeffersonians, retreated.

At one level, Reverend Monet's meeting with John Breckinridge replicated the alliance between the Baptist leader John Leland and Thomas Jefferson—a pragmatic friendship between a pious man of the people and a politician passionate for liberty and skeptical of revealed religion. But in contrast to Baptists who had encouraged the development of libertarian politics with respect to religion since the seventeenth century, Monet was charting relatively new territory for a Methodist in reaching out to a religiously indifferent libertarian like Breckinridge for support. Instead of a proud history of religious dissent and reputation for formulating arguments for religious liberty that Baptists enjoyed, American Methodists had only been fully separated from the Church of England since 1784, and that institution had been a target of opposition for Jefferson and his political friends, as well as for Leland and many Baptists in Virginia. Given Jeffersonian opposition to the religious establishment that Methodists had until recently participated in, Breckinridge might have been surprised to see a Methodist preacher come to him with an appeal. If Breckinridge's donation reflected the ad hoc nature of political outreach in 1800, it also suggests the element of political imagination required for Breckinridge and Monet to see each other as potential allies. If Breckinridge anticipated political benefit from the erection of a new Methodist church, his donation was something of a long shot, despite Archibald Stuart's report that Republican Methodists were challenging the influence of Federalist Presbyterians in Virginia.

The meeting between John Breckinridge and Reverend Monet shows how elite Jeffersonians operating outside of religious organizations became allied with networks of religious people who had never actively exercised their political rights before or whose political activity had been stymied by deference to tradition and educated elites. Religious support for political leaders was nothing new; Federalists relied on the support they drew from the most established churches, where preachers lauded the nation's leaders and warned against democracy. But Federalists took their support from religious groups for granted and incorporated elements of religious ceremony derived from colonial linkages of church and state. By contrast, opponents of Federalist policy worked both within and outside church organizations to challenge the lock that elites held on political power. The meeting of Breckinridge and Monet was a sign of the semiorganized, religiously charged political movement that was emerging to challenge and eventually destroy Federalism.

In the form of a neutral currency enabling such transactions from one world to another, Breckinridge's donation of five dollars—the equivalent of seven days paid labor or a cord and a quarter of hard wood[56]—bridged the divide between his rational materialism and Methodism's reputation for unleashed emotion, supernaturalism, and disregard for learning. Breckinridge did share one bit of common ground with Methodist preachers—a knowledge of horses. Methodist itinerants were famous for riding hundreds if not thousands of miles in preaching circuits that encompassed large territories, especially in the West. But while Methodist preachers exhorted against horse racing for sport and often had to cope with any horse they could get, Breckinridge began purchasing brood mares in 1795 and, despite problems with thieves, owned 128 horses in 1806. In 1801, he acquired use of the seven-year-old, sixteen-hand, retired racehorse "Speculator," bred in England by the Duke of Bedford. With an appreciation of fine horseflesh, a growing fortune in business and real estate, and "Speculator" as his stud, Breckinridge launched what eventually became a world-famous breeding operation for thoroughbreds.[57]

Natural reason and the right to liberty were so basic to Breckinridge's understanding of human happiness and the course of history that he treated them more as tenets of natural philosophy than of religion; opponents of natural reason and the right to liberty could only be men who sought to impose tyranny on others. Like his friend Jefferson, Breckinridge believed that the Creator had given men the vast world of nature to develop and that opening the American continent to US expansion followed the general thrust of divine purpose at the time of creation. The American government should expedite this expansion rather than stand in its way. In 1793, in protest of President Washington's closure of American navigation on the Mississippi River to prevent antagonizing Spain, as well as New England legislators who feared geographical expansion would jeopardize government oversight, Breckinridge declared that "the rights of man" justified "the free Navigation of the Mississippi" and that "[i]t cannot be believed that the beneficent God of Nature would have blessed this country with unparalleled fertility, and a number of navigable streams," and not have expected Americans to use the Mississippi. "The God of nature," Breckinridge declared, "has given us both the right and the means of acquiring and enjoying it; and to permit a Sacrifice of it to any earthly consideration, Would be a crime against ourselves and our posterity."[58]

In 1803, when faced with the question of the constitutionality of the Louisiana Purchase as a US senator, Breckinridge appealed to the "Goddess of Liberty" who could not be restrained. Though committed to a narrow interpretation of federal authority that forced him to think twice about Jefferson's bold and probably unconstitutional move in acquiring Louisiana, Breckinridge's investment in the sacred principle of liberty enabled him to rationalize the legality of the Louisiana Purchase as an extension of the federal government's power to make treaties. If his appeal to the Goddess of Liberty suggested that religious assumptions were involved in this line of thinking, he cast them into a metaphor for a principle deeper than any particular religious opinion or affiliation, or lack thereof.[59]

Breckinridge may have seen Reverend Monet as a political ally and fellow admirer of the Goddess of Liberty and her unfolding natural bounty, but not someone with whom he shared more particular opinions. Unlike Methodist preachers whose outspokenness against slavery drew considerable resentment at the turn of the century, Breckinridge made major contributions to the Republican defense of slavery. As part of their property, he and Polly brought twenty-five slaves with them from Virginia to Kentucky in 1793; when John died, Polly inherited fifty-seven slaves, making her one of the largest slave owners in the state.[60] Although he believed that slavery should eventually be abolished, Breckinridge led the way in defeating a bill to institute general emancipation in Kentucky in the 1790s, arguing that if slaves were taken away from owners, all property rights would be jeopardized.

Tall and handsome, Breckinridge exuded worldly success, learning, and self-confidence, while Methodists were perceived even by their most ardent supporters to be lacking in precisely these qualities. Among the few Methodist preachers in Kentucky in 1800, one of the best known was Valentine Cook, the principal of Bethel Bible Academy, beloved for the contrast between his inward beauty and his uncomely exterior: "stoop-shouldered to such a degree, that his long neck projected from between his shoulders almost at a right angle with the perpendicular of his chest," the man's "remarkably low forehead, small, deeply-sunken hazel eyes, a prominent Roman nose, [and] large mouth" contributed to his "eccentric" look, as did his utter lack of self-confidence: "On many occasions his brethren and friends had to hunt him up and bring him from his knees to the sacred desk." According to one admirer, Cook "was so thoroughly convinced that without the agency of the Holy Spirit no merely human preparation could suffice for the successful proclamation of the gospel, that he was never willing to enter the sacred place without a conscious sense of the divine presence." Once entered into that presence, though, Cook became transformed. Like the Jesus he loved, Cook tapped the glory inside his sorry exterior to convey the power of God's love with a fervency that made others weep. One worshipper remembered hearing Cook read a hymn that culminated in a vision of the dying Jesus, suffering for each believer:

> I saw one hanging on a tree
> In agony and blood;
> He fixed his languid eyes on me,
> As near the cross I stood.[61]

John Breckinridge had little use for this sort of piety and may even have been uncomfortable about encouraging political activism in a religious group known for such enthusiasm. Still, he and his friends needed voters. As Methodists joined Jeffersonians in political opposition to Federalist elites fearful of ordinary people gaining political power, their presence not only swelled the Jeffersonian party but also altered its religious face, marginalizing the relative skepticism and religious coolness of deists like Breckinridge.

The general decline of religious skepticism after 1800 became evident in the Breckinridge family as three sons of John Breckinridge abandoned their father's materialistic philosophy and confidence in natural reason to return to the Presbyterian faith of Breckinridge ancestors. After Polly lost John unexpectedly in 1806 and cried so incessantly that some family members believed her blindness in later life stemmed from that grief, she took up religion and encouraged her sons John, William Lewis, and Robert Jefferson Breckinridge in their education and careers as Presbyterian ministers. William, born in 1803 and converted in 1818, became head minister of Louisville's prominent First Presbyterian Church, moderator of the Presbyterian General Assembly, President of Centre College in Kentucky, and President of Oakland College in Mississippi. Son John, who was nine when his father died, became even more religiously conservative. After his graduation from Princeton Theological Seminary in 1822 and service as chaplain of the US House of Representatives, he became a professor at Princeton, general agent of the Presbyterian Board of Foreign Missions, and died as president-elect of Oglethorpe College in Georgia in 1841. In the mid-1820s, this namesake of his father challenged the liberal ethos of Transylvania University, whose fine library his father had helped to create, forcing the resignation of the university's religiously liberal president, Horace Holley, in 1827.[62]

Robert J. Breckinridge, born in 1800 and described by his father as "superior to all the rest," started out in law and politics like his father but turned toward Whig policies of national union and away from his father's emphasis on the right of states to challenge federal laws that they deemed unconstitutional. Robert also reverted to the anti-Catholic fervor that had animated his Scottish Covenanter ancestors. As a Presbyterian minister in Baltimore who married into the hyperorthodox Warfield family, he was accused of fomenting a mob to attack a Catholic convent and then indicted for libel in 1840 for a vicious diatribe against a Catholic who had the temerity to proselytize in an almshouse supported by county funds. As president of Jefferson College in Pennsylvania, head minister of Lexington's First Presbyterian Church, and president of the Danville Theological Seminary in Kentucky, Robert J. Breckinridge pursued a career as a Calvinist writer and journal editor committed to exposing Catholicism as the "most hateful to God, of all apostasies" and promoting the fundamental position that only a predestined few would attain salvation and that orthodox protestant religion was "the only parent of virtue—as God is the only source of all good."[63]

Like others critical of or indifferent toward revealed religion, the John Breckinridge who passed away in 1806 did not leave a legacy of religious skepticism strong enough to withstand the tide of religious fervor that swept over the country in the early decades of the nineteenth century. Through the political alliance that Jeffersonians like him struck with Baptists and Methodists, pietists acquired a popular leverage they had not previously enjoyed, and critics of revealed religion, once popular but never well organized, found themselves out of step or forgotten. Meanwhile, religious commitment to

American political unity continued unabated even as Federalism declined and disappeared after 1812. Congregationalists and Presbyterians would not grow with the blazing speed of Baptists and especially Methodists, but their influence on religious language about American nationalism was on the rise. The skepticism of religious authority that characterized Jefferson's vision of liberty was on the wane.

As this process of national religious and political formation was coalescing around 1800, the Methodist contribution to Jeffersonian politics was not at all clear. Even as Bishop Asbury and the preachers under his supervision succeeded in making inroads against perceptions that Methodists were closet Tories and crypto-Catholics, the Methodist system of top-down Episcopal government continued to generate suspicion. Efforts made by prominent Methodist laymen to support Federalist leaders and policies contributed to the impression that Methodists were authoritarian and opposed to democracy. On the other hand, Methodist commitment to free will, individual conversion, and uninhibited religious expression complemented democratic impulses. Asbury's vigilant efforts to keep his preachers' eyes on heaven and above the political fray drew attention away from the elements of political conflict implicit in Methodist organization. Only an astute political observer—perhaps Archibald Stuart or John Breckinridge—might have seen that the Methodist system was slowly transforming to align with the economic and political liberalism of Republican politics. Correspondingly, as religious preachers like Reverend Monet must have hoped, Republican politics was slowly transforming to accommodate evangelical religion, breaking the powerful connection between democratic politics and skepticism of revealed religion that Breckinridge represented.

Passion for liberty was an important point of convergence between Methodists and Jeffersonians. Both celebrated the will power of ordinary people and argued against restraining it. While Methodists explored supernatural worlds with relatively unrestrained enthusiasm, Jeffersonians claimed liberty over the land and its resources as a natural right. In the developing convergence of these two forms of libertarianism, Methodists enjoyed some advantage over Baptists, whose long-standing commitment to congregational autonomy worked against organized missionary outreach on a national scale. As Asbury poured his considerable energy and brainpower into managing the expansion of a sprawling system of Methodist itinerancy, recruiting an army of fanatically devoted preachers who proclaimed their version of liberty through uninhibited worship, moral discipline, and grassroots community organization, Methodism spread like wildfire, especially in the West, where Republicans were strong. By 1810, Methodists in Kentucky, Tennessee, North and South Carolina, Ohio, and Indiana had emerged as reliable supporters of Republican political policies and resisters of Federalist elitism.[64]

Thus in Ohio, Edward Tiffin, an ordained Methodist deacon who preached around Chillicothe, was elected in 1803 as the new state's first governor. Thomas Scott, secretary of the Ohio Senate until 1809 and chief judge of the Ohio Supreme Court in 1810 was a Methodist, as was Thomas Worthington who had worked with Tiffin, Scott, and other Methodist Republicans to wrest control of political institutions in the Northwest Territory from Federalists and became governor of Ohio in 1816. The editor of the Republican *Scioto Gazette* during Worthington's governorship was also the minister of Chillicothe's Methodist church. From their stronghold in the Scioto Valley, these Methodist politicians sought to balance religious and political concerns to make Ohio a libertarian state where men were free to follow their own economic interests and emotional experiences of God. Unlike Congregationalists and Presbyterians clustered around Marietta, who put more emphasis on doctrinal order, formal worship, and restraint of individual liberty, political leaders in the Scioto Valley preferred a more insistent focus on the individual's relationship to God and a political philosophy that emphasized both individual liberty and resistance to federal intrusion in local affairs.[65]

Through this convergence between Jeffersonian politics and Methodist religion, Jeffersonian resistance to investing moral authority in government would exert liberalizing pressure on Methodist church government, eventually leading to elements of lay representation that moderated the authoritarian system laid out by Asbury and Thomas Coke. Conversely, Methodist religion would mediate and help legitimate the libertarianism of Jeffersonian democracy. While the explosive growth of Methodism overpowered the skepticism of biblical revelation prominent in the early stages of democratic political organization in the United States, Jeffersonian opposition to restraints on individual liberty caused Methodists to back off in their adherence to religious principles that challenged individual property rights. The clearest example of this libertarian political pressure involved slavery.

Initially, Methodist leaders wanted to stand by the arguments John Wesley made in his 1744 treatise, *Thoughts on Slavery*, that slave holding was incompatible with Christian life. At the famous Christmas Conference of 1784, when the Methodist Episcopal Church in the United States emerged as an independent entity, church officials declared slavery to be "contrary to the Golden Law of God on which hang all the Law and the Prophets, and the unalienable Rights of Mankind, as well as every Principle of the Revolution." They also set forth procedures for manumission that Methodist slave holders were required to follow, with deadlines depending on the age of each slave. In the spring of 1785, the Virginia conference of Methodist preachers submitted a petition calling for emancipation to the state legislature, where it failed to gain a single vote and set off a firestorm of opposition. Counterpetitions supported slavery, declaring that the American Revolution had "seald with our Blood, a Title to the full, free, and absolute Enjoyment of every species of our Property" and that Methodist leaders must be "contemptible Emissaries & Hirelings of Britain" bent on driving "their fellow Citizens in Distress & Desparation" and "their Country in inevitable ruin." In the summer of 1785, Asbury and his co-leader Thomas Coke agreed to a suspension of the rules against Methodist slavery instituted six months earlier. While some Methodist ministers continued to preach that slave owners were no better than *"horse thieves & Hogstealers, Knaves, &c,"* calling them "Oppressors, Rogues, & men destitute of even heathen honesty," such arguments fell on a growing number of deaf or hostile ears as slavery expanded along with Methodism in the South.[66]

In response to what some perceived as the alarming spread of slavery, the Methodist General Conference restated the Church's opposition to slavery at its quadrennial meeting in Baltimore in 1796. Struggling to stem the tide of accommodation to slavery among Methodists in Virginia, Asbury worked on an agreement for settled preachers to sign, which made them promise not to own slaves. "It appears to me," Asbury wrote in his journal in 1798, "that we can never fully reform the people, until we reform the preachers." An earlier ban against itinerant preachers owning slaves had not been effective in stopping the problem: "[H]itherto," Asbury admitted, "except purging the traveling connexion we have been working at the wrong end." Prohibiting slavery among settled, as opposed to itinerant, preachers was essential if the Church was going to make any headway in exterminating the practice among lay people. Asbury wrote, "[I]f it be lawful for local preachers to hold slaves, then it is lawful for traveling preachers also; and they may keep plantations and overseers upon their quarters: but this reproach of inconsistency must be rolled away."[67]

When Methodist preachers in the South spoke against slavery, they often met with resistance, both from fellow Methodists who owned slaves and from opponents of the Church who feared the spread of Methodism because of its reputation for abolitionist agitation. In some cases, local authorities prevented Methodists from meeting, interpreting their stand against slavery as an incendiary threat to civil order. In 1800, the General Conference of the Methodist Episcopal Church reiterated its support for the position that slaveholding was incompatible with Christian life; the same year, peace officers in South Carolina carried out state orders to disperse Methodist meetings held behind closed doors. In 1801, a South Carolinian outraged by one of Asbury's statements against slave ownership challenged his interpretation of Christian morality, proclaiming that "there were no arguments to prove that slavery was repugnant to the spirit of the gospel." Asbury strongly disagreed, but would not let his belief that slavery was repugnant to the gospel stand in the way of his primary goal of spreading the gospel. Asbury and other Methodists were still concerned about slavery but shifted their focus to the humane treatment of slaves by Christian masters and to hopes that individual owners might someday free their slaves. A journal entry in 1803 indicates how Asbury's commitment to abolition had softened. After a chapel service at "brother Mark's house" in Georgia, Asbury noted that Mark was planning to build a separate chapel once the house was finished and that "he is a kind master to his slaves, and hints at the probability of his liberating them by will, but he may change his mind before he dies."[68] Whatever Mark put in his will, the Methodist chapel would be built by slaves.

When the General Conference met again in Baltimore in 1804, Asbury had come to accept the fact that some Methodists would continue to own slaves. He also seemed more receptive to arguments that releasing vulnerable people from bondage was a bad idea for slaves, as well as an economic hardship for slave owners. The General Conference tried to slow the increase of slavery among Methodists with rules prohibiting Church members from purchasing new slaves, but its refusal to back down from the principle that slavery was essentially incompatible with Christianity created increasing problems for the Church as Methodist membership more than quadrupled in the West between 1796 and 1804. To mollify proslavery Republicans in the West and South, the General Conference relinquished its principled opposition to slavery in 1808, placing all decisions regarding the ownership, sale, and purchase of slaves in the hands of regional conferences.[69] To expand their operations in the South and many parts of the West, especially Kentucky, Methodists would accommodate Republican slave owners.

Methodist accommodation to slavery coincided with accommodation to a code of white male supremacy that elevated manly honor and positioned free men in relation to the subordination of women and blacks. Working to contain and minimize the egalitarian aspects of Methodist conversion and religious experience, white preachers incorporated aggression, dominance, and pride into their celebrations of Christian life. While restraining aggression in their black brethren, white preachers Methodist preachers gloried in their own "combative powers." Thus John Brooks described how he grabbed a "noted infidel" in Tennessee and "threw him into a large fire and put my right foot on him to hold him there." Similarly, James Finley delighted in the rumor, spread during a camp meeting in 1816, that, "as I was a Kentuckian, I carried a long dirk in my waistcoat, and that I would as soon stab a man as not."[70]

As they adopted Republican views on political liberty, property rights, and manly honor, Methodists backed away from any hope they might have harbored that southern states would adopt a principled religious stand against slavery. They also helped dispel the impression that Jeffersonians were hostile to religion. Support from minority groups famous for intense piety enabled Republicans to present themselves as the true friends of religion and to attack Federalists as priest-ridden hypocrites whose shows of piety boiled down to nothing more than reverence for their own social status and political power. As Jeffersonians stifled charges of irreligion with growing numbers of evangelicals in their ranks, partisan claims about religion became an ingrained feature of American politics, a powerful and volatile ingredient in the formation of political parties.

CHAPTER SIX

Honor into the Breach

Under the Speaker's canopy in the US House of Representatives on the first day of April in 1812, Henry Clay received President James Madison's *"confidential* Message" recommending a law prohibiting ships from leaving American ports for sixty days.[1] Taking the president's request as a final step to war, the thirty-four-year-old leader from Kentucky cleared the chamber of unofficial persons and convened a secret session. Clay and his "War Hawks" had been pressuring the hesitant president for several years, and their support had ensured his second inauguration the previous month. Like Shakespeare's dashing hero to whom he was compared, this "Harry of the West" declared manly honor to be a compelling reason for war.[2]

In an editorial published April 19, Clay summarized his argument for combat, insisting that "it is by open and manly war only that we can get through it [the present crisis] with honor and advantage to our country." If the nation failed to defend its honor by declaring war now, "[f]uture attempts to retaliate the wrongs of foreign powers & to vindicate our most sacred rights, will be in vain."[3] Here and elsewhere, Clay's appeal to manhood resembled that of Shakespeare's Harry, who proclaimed in his famous "band of brothers" speech in *Henry V*, Act IV, Scene III that, "if it be a sin to covet honour, then I am the most offending soul alive."

Honor would unify the nation as religion could not, inspiring passionate feeling as effectively as religion could, especially among young white men. For all its effectiveness in people's lives, religion's role as a unifying cultural force was disrupted by conflicting, partisan notions of its relationship to politics and civic authority; while Federalists thought of religion as the wellspring of government responsibility for the common good, Republicans emphasized its independence, with some relegating religion to the margins of public life while others proclaimed its superior authority. Religion's role in public life was further complicated by its diverse and conflicting truths, ambivalence with respect to ordinary reality, and circuitous and often defensive modes of reason. Religion was increasingly prevalent and influential in politics, but too complex and inconsistent in its effects to operate as a unifying cultural force.

The term *sacred honor* was hardly new to American politics; in the final words of the Declaration of Independence, the signers agreed to pursue independence with everything they had—"our lives, our fortunes, and our sacred honor." But in contrast to the signers' confidence in reason, an ill-reasoned mania to defend honor had come to the fore among Republican politicians led by Henry Clay. The War Hawks' eagerness to plunge the nation into war reflected the toll taken by two decades of partisan mistrust, more than a decade of hyperactive religious emotion, and the failure of critical reason to withstand their onslaught.

Much had changed since the 1790s, when proponents of political equality followed Thomas Paine in challenging submission to biblical revelation as an obstacle to reason. With religious people in Republican as well as Federalist camps having demonized Paine, Henry Clay would not call attention to Paine's role in the development of democratic interpretations of republicanism even though, like Paine, he championed democracy and common sense. More sophist than idealist, Clay parried questions about the moral reasoning behind his clamor for war as if such questions were signs of cowardice. The bravado he and his fellow War Hawks shared derived from a variety of sources, including appeals to nature to justify American expansion and war with Britain, widespread tolerance for blatant forms of circular reasoning, and obsession with perceived slights to manhood.

Among Republicans, appeals to national honor operated as a substitute for religious unity, bridging the gap between materialists like Clay and evangelical Baptists and Methodists upon whom Republicans counted for votes. Especially in the West and South, where men sensitive to insinuations of lying or cheating often defended their honor with pistols, ritualized combat in defense of honor finessed problems associated with skepticism; as long as honor remained unsullied, religious differences, including the extent to which a man believed in religion, might be overlooked. Appeals to honor provided cover for men indifferent to organized religion and offered something to uphold as sacred, without that obligation to the common good so often expressed with annoying condescension by Federalists.

Evangelicals on the Republican side would never elevate manly honor as high as Christian piety, but they did nurture images of God's honor that allowed the two to coexist in a relationship of mutual support. Much as the separation between religion and politics promoted by Baptists facilitated libertarian politics, as well as Baptist church growth, commitment to national honor could grow along with readiness to defend God. Thus even the most extreme pietist had room for "honor" in his lexicon; in his 1807 defense of revivalism, for example, the Shaker leader and former New Light Presbyterian Richard McNemar praised those who lived "not for their own pleasure, and aggrandizement; but for the honor of God." Singling out individuals who continued to experience traumatic episodes of bodily convulsion after the Great Revival of 1801 had subsided, he praised them for wearing religious enthusiasm as a "badge of honor."[4]

The cult of honor held Republicans together, along with devotion to what John Breckinridge had called the Goddess of Liberty. Not surprisingly, Federalists like Timothy Dwight criticized honor as a sorry substitute for biblically derived moral principles aimed at protecting the common good and restraining liberty from evil. With a handful of allies in Congress and considerable support from institutions and print media outside of Congress, Dwight was Clay's most formidable foe. But the Federalist party that Dwight supported was in decline, and efforts to build a third party—dubbed Tertium Quids by their leader, Virginia Republican John Randolph—failed to coalesce, further smoothing the Republican path to war.

In the spring of 1812, with Madison's recommendation of war finally in hand, Clay worked to galvanize Congress. Though Republicans controlled three-quarters of the House and four-fifths of the Senate, as well as the presidency, they were split into contentious factions. Clay's principal antagonist in the House was the Quid leader John Randolph. A sarcastic and conservative adherent of Jeffersonian philosophy who condemned foreign entanglements, centralized government, and military expansion, Randolph was not happy with congressional secrecy, either. When Clay announced that any effort by his fellow congressmen to resist Madison's "war measure" would "cover ourselves with shame and indelible disgrace," Randolph rose to protest.[5]

"Sir," Randolph began, "we are now in conclave. The eyes of the surrounding world are not upon us." Suggesting that the Speaker had convened something like a papal assembly, without the transparency government ought to have, "We are shut up here from the light of heaven; but," he added reprovingly, "the eyes of God are upon us. He knows the spirit of our minds."

Calling for honest self-reflection and an end to the distortions produced by factional posturing, Randolph insisted, "We ought to realize that we are in the presence of that God who knows our thoughts and motives, and to whom we must hereafter render an account for deeds done in the body." With that plea for critical distance, Randolph went on to say that Madison's message was not such a clear call to war as Clay supposed, the country was not equipped for war, and no new causes for war had arisen since the previous Congress. Young men's lust for war was the real stimulus behind the call to arms, he implied, admonishing his colleagues to proceed with caution: "[W]ar is not to be considered as a matter of pleasure." Alluding to the Speaker's immaturity and impetuous nature, Randolph "hoped we would not act as a thoughtless young couple sometimes do, who are in a hurry to marry first, and then look around to get something to make the pot boil."[6]

Taking the floor again, Clay objected in the first place to Randolph's presumptuousness in giving members of the House a religious lesson: "[T]he gentleman from Virginia need not have reminded us, in the manner he has, of that Being who watches and surrounds us." The reasons for war, as everyone knew, included British impressment of American sailors, incitement of Indian attacks against American settlers, and British efforts to promote internal division in the United States. Emotion played a major role in this calculus, too, and the Speaker was not ashamed to say so: "Although he felt warm, he prided himself upon his feelings, and should despise himself if he was destitute of them."[7]

Clay's reprimand to Randolph for religious intrusiveness was more than a show a personal annoyance. Deflecting religious criticism of war by appealing to popular resentment of sanctimonious elites, Clay implied that Randolph's reminder about God was needless and possibly insulting. While Clay's own commitment to biblical revelation was minimal, he drew support from Baptists and Methodists, as well as from aggressive materialists like himself. Surprising in certain respects, the alliance between Republican evangelicals and belligerents like Clay would carry the nation to war, destroy Federalism, and privilege the political interests of the West and South over those of New England and commercial regions along the Atlantic coast. However close in his personal beliefs to what evangelicals would call infidelity, Clay's passionate commitment to honor bridged the difference between evangelical and materialist worldviews, enabling naturalists like himself to hide their indifference to revealed religion under the cover of shared resentment of religious elites. Defense of American honor would consolidate a variety of different perspectives, valorizing grandiose tendencies already present among adherents of God's kingdom while compensating for lack of religious enthusiasm among proponents of national expansion.

In his reprimand to Randolph on the House floor, Clay alluded to the standard Republican argument about the proper relationship between religion and government that had developed over the course of thirty-five years. His comments reflected a transformation in how the American Revolution had come to be understood. They also reflected the profound demographic shift that had taken place among ardent defenders of American liberty.

In the revolutionary era, proponents of American liberty challenged the sanctity enveloping the British monarchy as part of their claim to political independence. Later in the 1790s, as opposition to the authoritarian policies of George Washington and John Adams developed, democratically inclined Republicans scorned clerics who used their religious office to support the authority and presumptive sanctity of federal government in the United States. Growing into a political majority after 1800, democratic-leaning Republicans continued to link the bogus piety they attributed to Federalists to haughty British arrogance. Congregationalists and Presbyterians in the Federalist camp found that deployment of revolutionary rhetoric infuriating; their clergy had used their pulpits and pens to support independence during the revolution, while other religious groups had hesitated about, or opposed, rebellion. Times had changed, and a new generation, familiar with the emotionalism of both revivalism and partisan politics, had sprung up in defense of American liberty against British assault. Claiming the mantle of the American Revolution for themselves, these activists were eager to assert their manhood against British tyranny and to charge Federalists with lack of honor for supporting it.

Republicans who hated Federalist religion and its connection to British interests went so far as to accuse American Congregational and Presbyterian missionaries of collaborating with the British to incite Indian hostility against American settlers in the West. A "Map of the Seat of War," published in Philadelphia in 1812 and promoted in Republican newspapers, used icons of tomahawks to indicate the location of missionary villages. Revealing "the practical correspondence between the *bible* societies and the tomahawk," the map offered "at a glance the points of our country, where the scalps of infants ... were taken in the cause of the friend of the blacks," as well as allies of "*British* religions." With "Mahomedan ferocity and butchery," according to the Republican *Aurora*, Indians served the interests of the British Empire, having been recruited to that cause by religious fanatics from New England. According to the *Aurora*, the "savage of the wilderness was allured from the forests" with "the aid of the Connecticut blue laws, and the history of the witches."[8]

Clay's honor-bound drama worked itself out against a background of chaotic national expansion. The unruliness of American life, especially in the West and South, included confusion and dispute about how men and women should relate to each other, and a wide range of opinion with respect to how freely, as well as how aggressively, girls and women might be expected to behave. The rapid growth of slavery in the lower South and parts of the West fueled a culture of violence in those regions, where owners could treat their property any way they liked and slaves endured vicious beatings without any legal right of redress. Confusion and conflict over Indian treaties, disputes among Indians over assimilation to western culture, and growing Indian resistance to American expansion added to the chaos. A quick survey of the volatility of American life and the limited effect of attempts to control it will highlight the dynamism and complexity of the society Clay and his War Hawks sought to harness.

In the West as elsewhere, Republican-friendly churches intervened sporadically in the process of national expansion, functioning to contain violence, discipline aggression, direct ambition, and channel emotional expression. But while religion figured importantly in the process of national expansion, honor was really the common denominator; even among evangelicals, disagreements about religion were common. Federalists longed for the days when religion and government worked together, and their nostalgia would bear fruit in subsequent decades as state and federal courts enforced evangelical mores and a mythology developed about the puritan roots of American empire.[9] But as the nation headed toward war in 1812, Federalist religion provoked strident resentment, as the Republican newspaper linking Mahomedan ferocity with Connecticut blue laws indicated, while Baptists and Methodists were focused on their own aggressive expansion. A new kind of symbiotic relationship between religion and government had emerged based on commitment to the protection of competing interests. Honor operated in this context as a way of defending competing rights and creating a national outlet for unifying aggression.

War Hawks hailed mainly from the West and South, where personal honor defined morality for many white men, and ritual combat in drinking, wrestling, shooting, horse racing, cock fighting, and politics established bonds of rivalry and friendship.[10] One English visitor clearly disapproved of the sort of behavior he observed in the Carolinas: "The lower class in this gouging, biting, kicking country, are the most abject that, perhaps, ever peopled a Christian land," the Englishman reported, noting that the same individuals "are extremely tenacious of the rights and liberties of republicanism. They consider themselves on an equal footing with the best educated people in the country." Primitive accommodations for traveling and socializing supported the erosion of distinctions. "In the taverns in this part of the US," the visitor explained, "there is generally no other accommodation than a large sitting-room, in common, where the governor of the state, and the judge of the district, in travelling, must associate with their fellow-citizens of every degree."[11]

Some women appeared to thrive in this culture of rights and liberties. Timothy Dwight's orphaned niece Margaret, on her way to Ohio to live with cousins in 1810, stopped at an inn "kept," Margaret reported in her diary, "by 2 young women, whom I thought *amazoons*—for they swore & flew about 'like *witches*' they talk & laugh'd about their sparks &c &c till it made us laught so as almost to affront them." Margaret Dwight could not help but express some admiration for these strong and forthright creatures: "[T]here was a young woman visiting them who reminded me of Lady Di Spanker," she wrote, referring to the forceful horsewoman in Maria Edgeworth's novella, *Mademoiselle Panache*, "for she sprung from the ground to her horse with as much agility as that Lady could have done—They all took their pipes before tea," Margaret added, perhaps a bit envious of their freedom and camaraderie.[12]

If meekness was a Christian virtue among women, Christian women did not always practice it. In the spring of 1812 in Missouri, itinerant preacher William Winans recounted the story of one Methodist "Lady" whose "very cordial invitation to her house" he was happy to accept. Winans's diary is full of romantic mishaps with women, and his judgment of women seems not to have been particularly keen. In any event, Winans quickly discovered the limits of Christianity's effectiveness in suppressing female aggression in this Methodist woman, who turned out to be "an unrivaled scold, termagant, and tyrant." She treated Winans well, "but her husband and her servants were objects of almost unceasing, unreasonable and outrageous abuse and vituperation." The servants were "marked, scarred and spirit-broken" as a result of being "accustomed to receive at her hand the most violent treatment." Winans learned that even, "once in her rage, she plunged a knife into the abdomen of a servant child." Not least on Winans's list of the woman's bad actions was her readiness to challenge her husband for authority: "[S]he and her husband sometimes attempted to determine their rival claims to supremacy, by the law of the strongest bearing rule" and "she did not hesitate to resort to sharp-pointed arguments in the establishment of her claims."[13]

However indicative of domestic violence in the early republic, the termagant from Missouri certainly did not conform to Methodist expectations of domestic harmony or female piety. More typical in that regard was the Methodist family Margaret Dwight met in the Pennsylvania Mountains on her way to Ohio. One Sunday morning in 1810, waiting with her party beside a creek for the water to recede so they could get across, she described her tranquil resting spot. "An old man & his wife live here, & appear to be very kind clever people, & what is more than we have found before, they appear to regard the Sabbath," Dwight added with some relief. "They are Methodists," she added, and "This is a small log hut, but clean & comfortable—There are no waggoners here." The contrast between waggoners and Methodists could not have been sharper; Dwight had just left Phelps's Tavern where she had a brush with a "drunken waggoner, who came up to me as I stood by the door waiting for a candle, he put his arm round my neck, & said something which I was too frighten'd to hear." Hoping to avoid any more run-ins with that lot, "I shall be oblig'd to colour my frock I believe, for it attracts the attention of those creatures so much, that I dare not go in sight of them scarcely." The contrast with Dwight's former home in New England was remarkable. On her way to Ohio, she wrote, "We find no books to read, only at the bakers to day I found part of a bible, a methodist hymn book & a small book containing an account of the progress of M[ethodi]sm throughout the country; in letters from Ministers & others."[14]

Piety helped regulate interactions between men and women, and the link between impiety and access to dishonorable women was often presumed. On his way West in 1804, William Winans generalized about the lives of riverboat men and the temptations that beset them: "The tedious navigation, accumulated in them an immense amount of excitability," he thought, and this excitability combined dangerously with "drinking, gambling, boxing matches" and insufficient acquaintance with "decent Female Society." As far as the young preacher could see, riverboat men enjoyed a good deal of indecent female society: "The females, with whom they did associate" were "effective instruments of their degradation and ruin. At every principal landing-place on the whole route, these obscene Harpies were congregated." When it came to describing the women "at N. Orleans, the principal Depot of Flat-boat transportation," only a biblical term would do—"their number was Legion."[15]

Piety regulated relationships between married people as well, and here the relationship between religion and emotional trust came to the fore. New Light Presbyterian James McGready singled out mistrust between husband and wife as one of Satan's most destructive "devices." Generalizing from his acquaintance with married people in Kentucky, he was sure that once a husband began to question the need for Christian piety, perhaps by hearing some of his friends "satarize religious exercises," Satan often "tempts him to speak harshly to his wife—to whom suspicions of his attachment are suggested." The consequences of such a lapse in trust might come fast and furious: "She retaliates—answers him with tartness and severity. . . . the man becomes enraged, and abuses her, sometimes in the most shocking, barbarous manner."[16]

For McGready, such ruptures between husbands and wives were one awful variant of America's fundamental problem, namely, lack of trust—lack of trust in God, lack of trust in others, and willingness to deceive others for purposes of selfish gain: "Use every effort to acquire riches upon any terms"—that was the road to hell Americans too often travelled. "In horse-swapping, land-jobbing, and all other kinds of trade, take every advantage in your power," McGready explained in his bitter summary of how American society operated in Kentucky: "deviate from the truth; extol any property you may wish to sell to fifty times beyond its value; tell what extravagant prices you have been offered for it." Such vaulting ambition operated by its own rules: "[T]reat all as your inferiors . . . leave religion to the vulgar . . . Cherish all manner of deceit."[17]

The expansion of slavery added significantly to the deceit that appeals to religion—and to honor—aimed to combat. Fueled by the invention of the cotton gin, aggressive speculation in real estate, and systematic exploitation of slave labor and slave breeding, the exportation of cotton from the Deep South more than doubled between 1804 and 1807. The boom in American cotton production made many fortunes and contributed to national wealth and productivity, but also created resentment among British merchants whose West India cotton was being undersold and escalated social tensions throughout the South. "One can see how gnawing is the anxiety," one observer reported from the Deep South after the Louisiana Purchase. Another observer described life there as "Pandemonium."[18]

The onus, brutality, profitability, and religious acceptance of slavery placed defenders of American liberty more on the defensive than in the 1790s, when many people still hoped and believed that slavery in the United States would gradually disappear. The importation of slaves became illegal on January 1, 1808, in accordance with agreements made twenty years before, but the legal status of slaves as property became more firmly entrenched and slavery expanded, operating more systematically and with increasingly efficiency, especially in the lower South. At the same time, the number of Methodist societies and Baptist churches increased dramatically as evangelicals attempted to contain violence and create oases of divine rule in an unruly and deceitful world. Methodists and Baptists backed away from earlier condemnations of slavery in order to expand their religious influence without opposition from slave owners, and their political leaders followed suit. Riding the wave of democratic populism, Henry Clay turned away from the ardent call for emancipation he had voiced in 1799 as other policies he favored—especially westward expansion—entailed alliance with increasingly powerful slaveholding interests.[19]

Social turbulence and mistrust escalated in the borderlands of Indiana and Illinois, Michigan Territory, and Upper Louisiana, where Americans vied with Indians for land. Despite paternalistic efforts by Congregational and Presbyterian missionaries, Native American suffering intensified everywhere Natives remained. Mistrust between Indians and Republican-voting Americans led to efforts on both sides to control volatile situations. These efforts exposed the sheer force of Republicans' devotion to their own liberty, and the limits of Native resourcefulness in confronting it.

Opposition to the United States hardened among Natives as a result of US policies undermining Native autonomy, as well as in response to the constant pressure of Americans impinging on Indian lands. While proclaiming friendship, Jefferson had systematically chipped away at Indian landholdings by negotiating American access to rivers, purchasing land around rivers for the United States, and encouraging Indian indebtedness to the US government as a stimulus to these transactions. Exploiting Indian poverty and playing rival chiefs off against each other, Jefferson's Indian policies pushed the boundaries of American settlement farther west and north, culminating in the 1809 Treaty of Fort Wayne, which consolidated US claims and overrode Indian protests about their validity. Tension between Indians and American settlers in the borderlands often broke into violence, with accounts of Indian savagery appearing regularly in western newspapers.[20]

The political and religious opposition movement led by the Shawnee brothers Tecumseh and Tenskwatawa gained traction once the Treaty of Fort Wayne made it clear that Indian rights were not a US government priority. Confronting the American juggernaut rolling over Indians, the Shawnee brothers appropriated evangelical strategies for creating social order while reviving ancestral traditions about chaos arising in the form of an evil monster from the sea. Indians from different tribal backgrounds gathered at Tenskwatawa's religious community on the Wabash River in Indiana where his apocalyptic visions borrowed from biblical revelation. His emulation of Jesus as "The Open Door" to salvation announced in John 10:9 drew adherents that made Prophetstown similar to the supernaturally driven communities founded by Tenskwatawa's Shaker admirers.[21]

The opposition movement led by the Shawnee brothers reflected the volatile dynamics of life in the West, as well as the brothers' imaginative efforts to control them. A gifted speaker and keen observer of American culture, the Prophet's brother Tecumseh achieved renown among soldiers and missionaries for his ability to translate Native concerns about the morality of American attitudes toward land in metaphorical terms that whites could understand; Tecumseh may have been the first to proclaim that Indians worshipped "Mother Earth," a romantic counterweight to American devotion to the Goddess of Liberty. His buckskin tunic and advocacy for a return to Native dress were obvious signs of commitment to Native independence that resonated, at the same time, with the American idealization of homespun and boycotting of foreign goods. Tecumseh's efforts to build an intertribal, pan-Indian confederacy emulated the United States, while also harking back to resistance movements against English colonists led by Pontiac, Metacom, and earlier Indian leaders. An American observer at a council meeting in Ohio in 1807 sensed the parallels between rival nationalists when he compared Tecumseh to Henry Clay.[22]

As in the West more generally, the relationship between religion and politics at Prophetstown was unstable, with Tecumseh struggling to unify disparate people against external forces while religious enthusiasm in the millennial commune led by his brother grew relatively unhindered. The Prophet's visions of a millennial day when invaders would be expelled and pristine life restored built enthusiasm for Tecumseh's political and military plans, but the supernatural credulity unchecked at Prophetstown also led to political and military disaster. Declaring his followers invulnerable to disease, that bullets would not harm them, and that the Creator had invested them with special powers mediated through the Prophet's rituals of purification, Tenskwatawa came to an impulsive decision, in his brother's absence, to engage General William Harrison's army in battle at Tippecanoe in 1811 with incantations but little ammunition, a foolhardy venture that resulted in the complete destruction of Prophetstown, Tecumseh's base of religious support.[23]

In comparison, the American War Hawks' commitment to war against the British was not a supernaturally driven fiasco, but it did emerge out of a background swirling with violence, deceit, impulsive behavior, sporadic discipline, and weak government. In Britain, Americans faced a superior military opponent whose power over trade highlighted American weakness. Unlike American designs with respect to Indians, however, British imperialism was not a direct or immediate threat to American land or ways of life. As internal stresses on American idealism escalated, feelings of insecurity mounted, and tendencies to blame Britain for American problems intensified until the impulse to replay America's glorious war for independence from Britain became irresistible.

Economic hardship contributed to the escalation of stress and mistrust prior to 1812. The prosperity that many white Americans had enjoyed during Jefferson's first administration declined sharply as a result of the trade embargo Jefferson pushed through Congress in 1807. That rash act of commercial warfare made it illegal for American ships to engage in foreign trade. Aimed principally at Britain, the embargo crippled American commerce, wrecked economic productivity, and left many laborers, artisans, and farmers in dire straits; John Randolph likened it to an effort to "cure corns by cutting off the toes."[24]

Jefferson's embargo intensified regional and partisan conflict, pushing New England Federalists to despair over government regulations that seemed designed to destroy them. When officially recorded profits from American exports crashed from 108 million dollars in 1807 to 22 million dollars in 1808, economic depression hit most regions of the country, increasing the strain on idealism about American freedom already exacted by slavery and partisan conflict. Congress did repeal the embargo, substituting milder nonintercourse laws in 1809, but the economy was still depressed when Madison called for a new embargo in the early spring of 1812. When that embargo took hold, the *Hartford Courant* declared that the "ruinous policy of the national administration, has brought our country to the verge of destruction."[25]

As social turbulence increased, efforts to manage it intensified. Political and religious institutions became better organized and more entrenched, though still weak in comparison to the strength they gained after the War of 1812. Though factionalized by conflicting regional interests and disputes over centralization, Republican organizations dominated politics and government, with Republican rhetoric, patronage, caucuses, newspapers, barbecues, balls, holiday celebrations, and spokesmen commanding influence, shaping opinion, and relegating Federalists to minority status outside their New England base.

The separation between religion and politics championed by Republicans enabled Henry Clay to get on with the business of declaring war with little religious interference. Conversely, free to build religious kingdoms based on biblical revelation and supernatural forms of communication, some evangelicals found Clay's call to defend American honor compelling. In Ohio, where Methodists figured importantly in Republican politics, the General Assembly resolved "[t]hat we will, at the call of our country, rally round the standard of freedom." Religion contributed to this resolve: "Relying, constantly, on the interposing protection of Heaven," the assembly declared, "we will meet, with firmness, every event."[26] With equally firm reliance on "him who rules in Heaven," the *Republican Star* of Maryland called her sons to war in 1812: "Gird on your swords, your musket seize/Be all prepared for battle; / Go forth to conquer or to die, / The cause is good, is glorious, / And sacred Union will ensure / The final end victorious."[27]

The Methodist leader in Ohio, James B. Finley, expressed regret at how the call to war intruded in religious communities: "Many that once walked with us to the house of God and took delight in the services of religion, now marched off in rank and file to become disciplined in the arts of war," he complained. Anticipating the day "when the Prince of peace shall obtain his dominions, 'swords shall be beaten into plowshares and spears into pruning hooks,'" Finley would have liked his converts to focus on tending their gardens of piety. Nevertheless, he was pleased in 1812 when one of his auditors sent him "a very neatly-turned maul with a slip of paper wrapped around the handle" containing a poem that suggested why some Methodists might have considered going to war a complement to the fervor of their religious piety. The culminating stanza read, "Lift up your voice and loudly call / On sinners all around, / And if you can not make them hear, / Take up this maul and pound."[28]

Militant expressions of piety were a commonplace. Such expressions reveal the inroads of manly honor into evangelical rhetoric, as well as the long-standing evangelical defensiveness about gardens of piety separated from the corruption and deceit of the outside world. When one of the most effective itinerant preachers in the West died in 1804, his Methodist brothers called for swords to protect their plowshares. "We cannot afford to withdraw our forces and give up the contest," they asserted: "We dare not abandon the field brought into successful cultivation by the dying labors of the sainted Gibson, and which is now the repository of his mortal remains."[29]

The dearth of printed sermons by Methodists and Baptists who prized extemporary preaching, in contrast to Congregationalists and Presbyterians who wrote out their sermons and prized publication, makes it difficult to gauge the extent to which Baptist and Methodist preachers lent support for war against Britain. But it is evident that some of their most prominent leaders were cautious and intent on maintaining an elevated position above politics and war. In the summer of 1812, Francis Asbury did preach to Pennsylvania volunteers, invoking Republican rhetoric in reference to the war "between our people and the English people" and shaking hands with each man afterward. But he also referred to the war as an "unhappy subject" and the biblical text from Jeremiah 2 that served as the launching point for his homily was no call to arms or boost to morale: "For my people have committed two evils; they have forsaken me the fountain of living waters, and hewd them out cisterns, broken cisterns, that can hold no water." Not surprising, commanding officers did not invite Asbury to preach to soldiers again.[30]

Asbury was not a pacifist; during the Indian wars of the 1790s, he devised a plan in case of Indian attack that involved "mak[ing] a rope long enough to tie to the trees all around the camp when we stopped at night, except a small passage for use to retreat, should the Indians surprise us," and positioning it "to strike the Indians below the knee, in wh[ich] case they would fall forward, and we would retreat into the dark and pour in a fire upon them from our rifles."[31]

Though not entirely averse to combat, Asbury understood the importance of elevating Methodist religion above politics and war. Mindful of the difficulties Methodists faced that were caused by suspicions about their ties to the British in the American Revolution, he must have known that many of his new constituents were Republican and that Republican emphasis on the separation of church and state facilitated Methodist growth.

Baptist minister Thomas Baldwin took advantage of religion's purchase above politics to push an aggressive religious campaign. In a sermon to the interdenominational Massachusetts Bible Society immediately prior to passage of the Congressional war bill, aware that his audience included Federalist opponents of war as well as Baptists like himself, Baldwin focused on the promise of missionary work expanding around the globe, comparing the opportunities of the present day to the spreading the gospel to heathen lands during "the Apostolic Age." To those who cautioned "that there are some things peculiarly unfavourable at the present time; that we daily hear of wars, and rumours of wars," Baldwin reminded his audience that "the walls of Jerusalem were built in troublous times." Looking to that millennial day when "the noise of war may no longer assail the ear, nor the eye be pained by seeing garments rolled in blood," he predicted that religion would solve all of the political problems that currently beset mankind: "the art of war shall become extinct, and ambition and tyranny no longer be suffered to spread desolation and misery over half the world."[32] Baldwin did not chide Americans for fighting tyranny; he focused on the glorious day when that fighting would no longer be necessary and the whole world showered with the blessings of religious freedom, virtue, and truth.

Republican patriots had already begun to appropriate the millennial rhetoric and its intimations of American power in the world. In 1804, after Barbary pirates in Algiers captured the American ship *Philadelphia*, Stephen Decatur and a small crew of American seamen snuck into the harbor at Tripoli and burned the ship. Federalists failed to see this act as a victory, but the Republic press burst with pride at the defense of American honor and at Jefferson's demand that the United States be treated as a sovereign nation by foreign powers. A young lawyer from Maryland, Francis Scott Key, wrote a poem about Decatur's raid the following year, a poem he later rewrote to commemorate the sight of America's flag after the bombardment of Fort McHenry in 1812. In the 1805 poem, Key described how "triumphant they rode" as Decatur and his crew "stain'd the blue waters with infidel blood." By "infidel," Key was not referring to the men Federalists hated—Tom Paine, Jacobin revolutionaries, and Voltaire—but to those who lived under "the Crescent, its splendor obscur'd / By the light of the star-spangled flag of our nation." In this prescient bit of artistry, Key touched on the fusion of patriotic enthusiasm for American freedom and millennial visions of Christian missionary triumph that would come to exert such a powerful force in American identity, as he paid homage to the flag in which "each flaming star gleam'd a meteor of war, / And the turban'd head bowed to the terrible glare."[33]

As the multiple and conflicting elements of this fusion of evangelicalism and patriotism swirled about, religious groups weighed in on both sides of the demand for international respect, heightened by disrespect from Barbary pirates, that prompted trade embargoes and war. In the commercial centers of the United States, most Congregationalists, Presbyterians, Episcopalians, and Quakers considered American belligerence foolhardy. Baptists, on the other hand, tended to stand with other Republicans in their hatred of British tyranny and animosity to Federalists. Several Baptist churches went so far as to censure members who openly questioned Republican embargoes and war against Britain. In April 1809, the Baptist church in Halifax, Vermont, disciplined an elder for saying that "our rulers have brought difficulties on us, and if they do not immediately remove them they will bring down the judgement of God upon us." In 1812, the church excommunicated ten members for joining the Washington Benevolent Society, a Federalist club. Baptist churches in Wallingford, Vermont, and Templeton, Massachusetts, debated whether to exclude from church membership anyone who joined the Federalist Party.[34]

Feeding partisan rancor, Republican resentment of religious elites figured in the background of the riots that broke out in Baltimore immediately after the declaration of war. A town of fifty thousand people with a rough boom-and-bust economy, Baltimore had become heavily Republican, to the displeasure of its Federalist elites. Home to thousands of Irish, German, and French immigrants, it was also the most religiously dynamic and diverse city in the nation by 1808 and one of the most religiously active; the percentage of at least nominal churchgoers approached 50 percent of the city's population between 1810 and 1812, and all the city's churches—Catholic, Methodist, Episcopal, Presbyterian, Lutheran, Baptist, German Reformed, Quaker, United Brethren, and Swedenborgian—enjoyed numerical growth from the early 1800s through 1815. Ecumenical cooperation was also on the upswing, but ethnic and cultural rivalries dominated the politics of religious institutions. Irish and German Catholics suffered condescension from wealthy French Catholics, relationships between affluent Methodists and the poor who flocked to the chapel at Fell's Point were uneasy, and Baptists nursed a long history of animosity to the Church of England and her Episcopalian successors.[35]

Republicans hoped that war would fuel patriotism and bring Americans together. But in Baltimore, the upsurge of patriotism quickly spun out of control, unleashing unmanaged rage. On June 22, four days after Madison signed the bill declaring war on Britain, a crowd of thirty to forty men descended on the *Federalist Republican*—that "temple of Infamy," as opponents described the city's Federalist newspaper—destroying its office and printing press. That patriotic outburst inspired more violence, with little resistance from the city's Republican officials. Mobs roamed the streets night after night, vandalizing property and threatening people. Outraged by the half-hearted and ineffective efforts of city officials to restore law and order and refusing to be intimidated, editor Alexander Hanson and some of his supporters set up a new office and printing press in another house in Baltimore, armed themselves, and prepared to defend their constitutional rights.[36] The next issue of the *Federalist Republican* portrayed the assault of the previous month as "a daring and desperate attempt to intimidate and overawe the minority, to destroy the freedom of speech and of the press." Attributing the assault to "a system of French revolutionary terror," Hanson suggested that it was a deliberate act intended to keep men in political office who would otherwise have been thrown out by the paper's "exposure of their misdeeds, folly, and infatuation."[37]

As news spread that the *Federal Republican* was back in town, hecklers gathered outside the new printing office and boys started throwing stones. Aiming to scare off the crowd, Hanson and his supporters fired their muskets. Some in the crowd fired back and hauled in a cannon directed at the newspaper office. Violence escalated as an estimated 1,500 to 2,000 people—men, women, and children—rushed into the melee. The militia finally arrived and negotiated the Federalists' safe retreat to the city jail. As the editors and their supporters walked the mile to the jail under militia escort, they were pelted with jeers and cobblestones along the way. When the militia disbanded after locking up the men, the crowd seized nine of them from jail, beat and tortured them over the course of several hours, stabbing their faces with knives and pouring hot candle wax into their eyes to test if they still lived. Two old Revolutionary War generals were among the victims—Light Horse Harry Lee and James Maccuban Lingan—left almost naked in a pile in front of the jail.[38]

The *New York Post* called the riots in Baltimore "the worst tyranny that can happen—in all other grievances you have redress against the aggressors, but in a mob it is almost impossible to discover and detect the culprits." Fueled by economic crisis and a declaration of war, Republican hatred of Federalists had erupted in a spasm of mob violence. Religion was also a factor, supplying rhetoric and emotional zeal. Maryland's *Republican Star* blamed the Federalist newspaper in Baltimore for causing the riots: "The consecrated fire on the altar of freedom is not to be quenched," the *Star* proclaimed. "If *Tories* would be tolerated, they must renounce their heresies. The awful vengeance of a people who have appealed to the God of Battles," the paper warned, "is not to be insolently wantonly roused."[39] On the other hand, the Federalist *New York Post* speculated that those who agreed to serve in Madison's war would be among "those who, without repentance, cannot enter into the kingdom of heaven."[40]

Mobs had gathered previously in America to express collective anger against repressive policies or obnoxious elites, and property associated with particular grievances had sometimes been destroyed. In New York City in 1788, rioters destroyed the printing presses used by John Greenleaf to attack the recently ratified US Constitution, and in 1811, Federalist faculty at Columbia College were rudely jostled when they withheld a diploma from an outspoken Republican.[41] Prior to the Baltimore riots, however, mob violence against persons had been minimal. By the summer of 1812, economic crisis, religious rhetoric, and democratic populism weakened traditional constraints against personal violence directed at perceived elites. As news of unrestrained violence in Baltimore spread, Federalists were quick to condemn Republican politicians whose demagoguery, they believed, had set it loose; the *Hartford Courant* blamed "those furious Jacobins who govern the democrats—who cause them to meet and resolve and pledge their *sacred honor* to support the government of the U. States."[42]

While highly partisan on the Federalist side, the *Hartford Courant* correctly identified "sacred honor" as the drumbeat sounded by War Hawk patriots to galvanize patriotic support for war against Britain. Supplementing the rhetoric of liberty—and supplanting the fellow feeling of revolutionary egalitarianism with touchy self-defense—appeals to manly honor figured prominently in Republican attacks against the tyranny of Britain and her Federalist allies. Though hardly a new concept, manly honor had become more democratic and populist, seized by orators like Henry Clay from the culture of gentlemen and offered to the common man as a hallmark of national identity and personal pride.

Newspapers played an important role in explaining to a broad public how ritualized combat in defense of manly honor applied to a second war with Britain. When the story of a free black American who chopped off his own arm after being seized by a British vessel reached Tennessee in 1811, the *Carthage Gazette* wagged its finger at cautious politicians in American government: "What a lesson might a pusillanimous congress draw from this manly act! A nation of six millions souls submits to British impressment! while a 'black seaman' maims himself to break his yoke." When Britain did its best to avoid war by offering to revoke the Orders in Council, which had been used to justify the seizure of nine hundred American ships and was often cited by Americans as their principal grievance against Britain, Charleston's *City Gazette* declared it would never be appeased, citing "the honor of America" and "the dignity of manhood" as principles forbidding rapprochement with Britain. In New Hampshire, the *Democratic Republican* published General William Hull's address to the people of Canada depicting the American invasion of their country as a matter of honor. Inviting Canadians to join the United States and escape British tyranny, Hull explained that Americans had to put pressure on British Canada: "[T]he insults and indignities of Great Britain have once more left them no alternative but manly resistance or unconditional submission."[43]

The image of America as a man eager to defend his honor had antecedents in an earlier, but less reckless image of America as younger man able to stand on his own. In the revolutionary era, proponents of American independence declared that Britain violated her parental responsibility by treating her colonies as children after they had reached maturity. In 1775, Philadelphia minister Jacob Duché declared, "We venerate the parent land from whence our progenitors come," but had to draw the line at Britain's effort to prevent American maturity; we "cannot but think that they began to be jealous of our rising glory, and from an ill-grounded apprehension of our aiming at independency, were desirous of checking our growth."[44] Thirty-five years later, a new generation, used to independence and buoyed up by the millennial rhetoric cascading out of the Great Revival and by the vast increase in territory acquired by the United States during Jefferson's presidency, thirsted for glory. Simultaneously on the defensive as a result of insecurity about being able to fill the shoes of revolutionary heroes, an insecurity amplified by mistrust, fear of skepticism, and impatience with critical thought, the War Hawks in the Twelfth Congress jumped up belligerently to defend the manhood it insisted that Britain had insulted. While in 1775 Duché had prayed for the recovery of "that delightful union and intercourse which hath heretofore subsisted betwixt us and our Parent-land," the War Hawks regarded Britain as an offensive rival and demanded a duel.

The same code of honor that led Henry Clay to demand a duel with the Kentucky Federalist Humphrey Marshall for calling him a liar in 1809, an encounter from which Clay was lucky to have escaped with a flesh wound in his thigh, applied to America.[45] Speaking against an amendment watering down a bill for nonintercourse with Britain and France, Clay equated British trade sanctions and impressment of sailors with insults to American honor that threatened the rights of all free American men. "Britain stands pre-eminent in her outrage on us," Clay exclaimed on the Senate floor, "by her violation of the sacred personal rights of American freemen." Failure to retaliate would further sap the strength of a nation that had already withstood humiliation. After "years contending against the tyranny of the ocean," he warned, the vigor of America had lessened—"the sensibility of the nation is benumbed by the dishonorable detail" of British insult.[46]

Expanding upon his theme, Clay observed that the memory of revolutionary heroism was fading along with old heroes themselves. "The withered arm and wrinkled brow of the illustrious founders of our freedom are melancholy indications that they will shortly be removed from us," Clay opined nostalgically; "Their deeds of glory and renown will then be felt only through the cold medium of the historic page." To restore American glory, Clay declared, "We shall want the presence and living example of a new race of heroes to supply their places." Clay had no patience for the view that America was less than the equal of Britain or France: "When resistance to Britain is submission to France, I protest," Clay insisted, "against the castigation of our colonial infancy being applied in the independent manhood of America."[47]

A hotspur like Shakespeare's Harry, with a penchant for gambling, horse races, and snuff, the "Cock of Kentucky," as Randolph called him, Clay embodied the passion and aggressiveness of many of his Kentucky constituents, along with an appealing leaven of sentimentality. Credited with coining the term "self-made man," Clay defended himself against better-educated men by claiming he had risen on his own "genius," having received from his father only "infancy, ignorance, and indigence." (Randolph added "insolence" to the list.[48]) The leading Federalist in the House of Representatives, Josiah

Quincy of Massachusetts, who thought Clay was more responsible that anyone for taking the nation to war, described him as "[b]old, aspiring, presump-
tuous, with a rough, overbearing eloquence" shaped by "contests with the
half-civilized wranglers in the country courts of Kentucky, and quickened
into confidence and readiness by successful declamations at barbecues and
electioneering struggles."[49] The story of Clay jumping on a sixty-foot tavern
table causing one hundred twenty dollars damage to perform his version of
a *pas seul* derived from French dance lessons,[50] epitomized his readiness to
seize elements of the culture of gentlemen and rework them in the idiom of
the common man.

If Quincy viewed Clay and his fellow War Hawks with New England condescension, he also seized upon their devotion to the Moloch of honor. In a
speech against Jefferson's embargo in April 1808, while Clay was still in Kentucky as a leader in the state legislature, Quincy thought that if America was
going to be anthropomorphized, it should be described as a self-aggrandizing
adolescent "giddy with good fortune,—attributing the greatness of our prosperity to our own wisdom," rather "than to a course of events and a guidance over which we had no influence." Acknowledging that rhetoric calling
for defense of American honor reflected the spirit of the times, Quincy feared
the "vanities" and "inflated fantasies" of a young nation that would rush to
"vengeance . . . for some real or imaginary wrong." If maturation was to be the
metaphor, "we are now entering that school of adversity the first blessing of
which is to chastise an overweening conceit of ourselves."[51]

Quincy's critique of the belligerent rhetoric of Republicans leading up to
the War of 1812 reflected his familiarity with New England arguments discred-
iting the rationale of manly honor that had emerged in the context of efforts
to rid the nation of dueling. Leading the way in these efforts, Quincy's older
friend Timothy Dwight, a leader in Federalist circles as president of Yale College, parsed the logic of dueling, finding two arguments that he endeavored
to expose as petty, mean-spirited, and un-Christian. The "chief argument, on
which duelling rests," Dwight claimed in a sermon prompted by the demise
of Alexander Hamilton in 1804, was "the shame of neglecting to give, or refusing to accept a challenge." Essentially, duelists believed that if a man "does
not fight, he shall be disgraced; and that this disgrace is attended with such
misery, as to necessitate, and to justify, his fighting." Avoidance of disgrace
combined with the second reason for dueling, namely, revenge. Beneath the
pretty "varnish" of language about manly honor, "[r]evenge for a supposed
affront, revenge for wounded pride, for disappointed ambition, for frustrated
schemes of power, dictates the challenge." Dwight had much to say about the

un-Christian nature of revenge and fear of disgrace, but more pointedly, he condemned them both as childish. There was no real honor "in giving, or taking, affronts easily, or suddenly; nor in justifying them on the one hand, or in revenging them on the other," Dwight asserted. "Very little children do all these things daily," and "[t]hose who imitate them in this conduct," he concluded, "are only bigger children."[52]

Federalists did not reject manhood rhetoric, but their versions centered more on duty and self-command. From the Calvinist-tinged perspective of many Federalists, the demand for personal recognition so prominent in War Hawk rhetoric seemed dangerously impetuous and essentially sinful. The *Hartford Courant* praised Connecticut's refusal to call up a militia as "manly resistance" to the "[f]olly, rashness, blind obstinancy, and a total disregard to the public interests" that "mark the present war."[53] Genuine "honor," Josiah Quincy asserted, involved duty, self-restraint, and careful consideration of the common good. Along with true "freedom" and "independence," Quincy told his fellow congressmen in his first speech on foreign relations in 1808, honor "consists in taking the nature of things, and not the will of another, as the measure of our rights. What God and Nature offer us we will enjoy in despite of the commands, regardless of the menaces, of iniquitous power." Jefferson's embargo, which Congress was preparing to extend in 1808, represented none of that self-command and no real menace of iniquitous power. Instead, obeying British demands to stop trade with France, and French demands to stop trade with Britain, "in direct subserviency to the edicts of each, we prohibit our citizens from trading with either." That was not all. "As if unqualified submission was not humiliating enough, we descend to an act of supererogation in servility; we abandon trade altogether." Such irresponsible behavior crippled American commerce and wrecked the US economy. And, "what has become of our American rights to navigate the ocean? They are abandoned in strict conformity to the decrees of both belligerents."[54]

Proudly adhering to an ethic of self-restraint and obligation to public good inculcated by the religious culture of New England, as he freely acknowledged, Quincy viewed the clamor for war from the West and South as essentially immoral, much as he and other Federalists regarded dueling as a form of barbarity. As one of the few congressmen willing to confront Republican rhetoric head on, Quincy withstood considerable abuse, including efforts to force him to defend himself in a duel. Writing to his wife that he had "been handled a little roughly," Quincy described how "provoked" he became when the Republican editor of the *National Intelligencer* altered his speech against the extension of Jefferson's embargo to make it read like gibberish while giving the author of a rebuttal the chance to polish his speech before it went to press. "Really, Mr. Speaker," Quincy had protested in December, 1808, in response to disparaging remarks about the people of New England made by Congressman Troup of Georgia, "I know not how to express the shame and disgust with which I am filled when I hear language of this kind cast out upon this floor." Quincy was aware that "such vile substances were ever tempering between the paws of some printer's devil" and might be "played off from the top of a stump or the top of a hogshead, while the gin circulated, while the barbecue was roasting" on election day when, in certain regions "those who speak utter without responsibility, and those who listen hear without scrutiny." But he never anticipated "that such odious shapes would dare to obtrude themselves on this national floor among honorable men." Proclaiming inability to express the depth of his feeling on this point, "I want language to express my contempt and indignation."[55]

In 1808, when Quincy attracted national attention by criticizing the Republican ideology of manly honor, Henry Clay was honing that rhetoric as Speaker in the lower house of the Kentucky State Congress. Clay's popularity in his home state took him to the US Senate, where he called for more federal aid for internal improvements like roads and canals, moving beyond other Republicans in his willingness to expand the power of federal government for both economic and military purposes. Frustrated by the hesitancy of fellow senators to respond to British activity harmful to US interests, and out of his league with respect to age and education, Clay ran for election to the US House of Representatives in 1810. With his reputation for hotheaded leadership preceding him, the War Hawks in the House elected him Speaker of the House in November 1811, immediately upon completion of his Senate term. Observing the haste of that appointment, John Randolph perceived Clay to "stride from the door of the Hall as soon as he entered it to the Speaker's Chair." During his tenure as Speaker, Clay transformed the office into the second most powerful position in the US government, departing from the custom of previous Speakers in exercising his right as a member of the House to participate in debate. He managed votes through persuasion and compromise and controlled committee appointments to award positions of influence to fellow War Hawks including Langdon Cheves and John C. Calhoun of South Carolina, Richard M. Johnson from Kentucky, Felix Grundy from Tennessee, George M. Troup from Georgia, Peter B. Porter from New York, and John A. Harper from New Hampshire.[56]

The immediate challenge Clay faced in the House was John Randolph, the representative from Roanoke whose biting intelligence intimidated others as much as his high voice—apparently an effect of a childhood fever that stunted his growth—irritated them. A slight, swarthy descendant of Pochahontas and John Rolfe, Randolph behaved cavalierly, dominating debate for extended periods, bringing dogs and sometimes a slave attendant with him into the House, resting his spindly legs on his desk while others were speaking, flamboyant in a hunting jacket or blue great coat and silk cravat, his long dark hair gathered carelessly in a ribbon. Intent on bringing Randolph under control, one of Clay's first acts as Speaker was to order Randolph's large dog removed from the House.[57] The Virginian embodied the strain under which Jeffersonian philosophy labored as the nation moved toward war, as well as the eccentricity that philosophy of small government in its pure form had acquired.

Randolph was more Jeffersonian than Jefferson, whom he recoiled against in December, 1805 when, as president, Jefferson attempted to buy West Florida from Spain through Napoleon with funds secretly procured from Congress. The Quid party led by Randolph objected to Jefferson's willingness to build up the powers of federal government, thereby violating the commitment to local control and state's rights central to Jeffersonian philosophy. Quids also objected to Jefferson's deceitfulness and willingness to betray the vision of America under which he operated; alluding to the Grand Academy satirized in Jonathan Swift's *Gulliver's Travels*, Randolph dubbed his former hero "that Prince of Projectors, St. Thomas of *Canting*bury." Randolph's religious attachment to Jeffersonian ideals meant that any political compromise amounted to betrayal. "The *Old* Republican party is already ruined past redemption," he moaned in 1806, "New men & new Maxims are the order of the day." Temporarily turned out of office in 1813 for his opposition to war, he stuck to his guns: "No man can reproach me," he wrote Francis Scott Key, with "the abandonment of my post in a time of danger and trial. 'I have fought the good fight, I have kept the faith.'"[58]

In addition to sharing in opposition to war with Britain, Quids and Federalists criticized the harsh treatment of Indians on the frontier and deplored the excessive force used in battling Indians at Tippecanoe in 1811.[59] Quid resistance to the War Hawk's aggressive nationalism might have split Republicans more decisively than it did. It also might have led to bipartisan alliance between Quid Republicans and Federalists. No bipartisan, interregional resistance to war developed, however, partly because of Randolph's failure of leadership, overweening devotion to the State of Virginia, and investment in an idealism about decentralized government that had lost much of its charm. Quincy maintained cordial relations with Randolph; the two shared a strict ethic of honesty and belief in an overseeing God who discerned deceit. But

Quincy criticized Randolph for caring only about Virginia and lacking commitment to national interests. More than a decade of hyperbolic animosity between Federalists and Republicans made any political alliance between them unlikely, as did the underlying conflict between Federalist respect for government, commitment to commercial development, and desire for military preparedness on one hand and Quid suspicion of government and idealism about pastoral life on the other.[60]

With opponents of the war too divided to mount an effective countercampaign, Clay delivered his appeal to defend American honor with an approach to oratory that many Republicans found compelling. In an era when government leaders could still be shy and inept in public speaking, and the most charismatic, emotional, and histrionic speakers around were Methodist and Baptist preachers, Clay was among the first to bring an evangelical style of self-expression to political oratory. Like his mentor George Wythe and his senior law associate John Breckinridge, whose mantle of Kentucky leadership Clay inherited when Breckinridge died in 1806, Clay had little interest in organized religion or supernatural claims to revelation. But unlike these older and more formally educated deists, Clay absorbed certain aspects of evangelical culture even as he remained immune to evangelical conversion. He was not a trained orator, schooled in rhetoric and declamation, but like his hero Patrick Henry who was famous for fiery rhetoric and for defending Baptist preachers, Clay was an extraordinary public speaker, one of the most famous of his day. Impassioned, personal, sensitive, and flamboyant, he knew how to engage an audience and to rouse people to stand up, clap, and shout.[61] His oratorical skill fortified his bridge to evangelicals, making him similar to them in style, despite underlying differences in religious belief.

When Clay rose to speak against Josiah Quincy's plea for moderation with respect to Britain, the rhetorical structure as well as the emotional energy of his oration carried similarities to evangelical preaching. Extolling personal liberty as the mark of honor separating virtuous men from others, he could have been contrasting Christian saints from ignorant sinners. "[T]here is a remarkable difference between the Administration and the Opposition," Clay proclaimed; "it is in a sacred regard for personal liberty," which the Federalist opposition clearly lacked. With the common ground of liberty bridging the gap between evangelicals and materialists like himself, Clay pointed to the difference between true believers and hypocrites: willingness to defend liberty set men who truly loved her apart from others. "True to our principles," he asserted, "we are struggling for the liberty of our seamen against foreign oppression. True to theirs, they oppose the war for this object." Drawing a further distinction similar to that drawn by evangelicals between true Christians and hypocritical pretenders, Clay warned against those who only made an outward show of respect for the sacred principle: "They have lately affected a tender solicitude for the liberties of the people," he cautioned, but true Americans should not be confused by their pretense: "it is evident. . . . that they speak in a foreign idiom."[62]

In Clay's skillful hands, the appeal to national honor operated as a means of political organization. Already known for his commitment to internal improvements in roads, banking, and military affairs, Clay applied his organizational genius to emotional dominance over the US House of Representatives. As Pennsylvania Republican Jonathan Roberts described Clay's sway over that chamber, the Speaker from Kentucky "reduc'd the chaos to order." But the order Clay created in Congress involved a belligerent demand for unity that created more problems than it resolved, pushing the United States into a war that escalated social distress, leaving the nation's capital city in flames, the president in danger of enemy seizure, and exposing the ineptitude of the War Department and the inferiority of American forces in battle with a few notable exceptions, especially Andrew Jackson's astonishing defeat of the British in the Battle of New Orleans. The order Clay created out of congressional chaos involved misrepresenting the war as a victory for the United States when, in fact, the Treaty of Ghent that ended the war in 1815 simply restored peace between the United States and Britain without addressing the causes that led the United States to declare war.[63] For all Clay's effectiveness in organizing legislative process, his success in reducing chaos was more akin to the ritual order of revenge than to an open and searching process of legislative decision making.

Although Clay resisted realistic assessments of American military preparedness and the disadvantages of plunging the nation into war, he appealed to "reason" as if he possessed what his opponents lacked of that virtue. When opponents of military power cited instances from history—Carthage, Genoa, and Venice—in which possession of a navy led to military downfall, Clay questioned their rationality: "Have they attempted even to show that there exists in the nature of this power a necessary tendency to destroy the nation using it?" Certainly not. "Assertion is substituted for argument; inferences not authorized by historical facts are arbitrarily drawn; things wholly unconnected with each other are associated together—a very logical mode of reasoning!" he exclaimed in ridicule. He insisted it would be just as specious to argue that because Greece and Rome no longer existed, their investment in freedom must have been the cause. Outdoing his opponents in sophistry,

Clay compared their argument against the establishment of a better navy to an attempt to make American liberty seem ludicrous: "In the same way he could demonstrate how idle and absurd our attachments are to freedom itself."[64]

Clay's opponents may have fumed at his distortions, but the pretense of engaging in fair-minded debate was common enough, as was the presumption that people with whom one disagreed must be irrational. Such appeals to reason were hallmarks of religious discourse at the turn of the nineteenth century, especially in religious appeals to reason to refute skepticism. As the Kentucky revivalist James McGready asserted in one of his sermons, "There is no subject, which the human mind has investigated, that is supported by more clear, convincing, and undeniable evidence, than the divine authority of the Bible, the certainty of divine revelation, and the blessed reality of the religion of Jesus Christ." McGready proclaimed great respect for reason and insisted that claims to evidence not based on faith in the divine authority of Bible were irrational: "[D]eists and infidels of the present day," he asserted, argued "in opposition to the noonday splendor of the light of evidence."[65]

McGready's approach to evidence and his attack on the illogic of his opponents' arguments provided a model for Clay to follow, as well as a sterling example of the influence of religion on politics. McGready upheld biblical revelation as the beginning and end of sound reasoning and proper consideration of evidence; Clay upheld defense of liberty's honor in much the same way. With liberty a sacred cause to be asserted and reasoned from, but never questioned or systematically examined, appeals to sentiment in support of liberty were perfectly appropriate, much as emotional appeals to religious faith were expected.

As defense of liberty and American honor commanded popular sentiment, supported by a powerful if tenuous alliance between War Hawks and Republican evangelicals, opponents of the war resorted to bitter religious condemnation. When President Madison recommended that governors call for a day of prayer and fasting shortly after the declaration of war, Federalist Governor Caleb Strong declared a day of fasting in Massachusetts on July 23, during which he took the opportunity to deliver a public address enumerating a few of the terrible consequences of the war of which he heartily disapproved, including unjust treatment of Indians and an open invitation to French infidelity. Reverend Jedidiah Morse leapt to the governor's call for prayer and fasting with morning and afternoon sermons that portrayed the war as a terrible disaster, beginning with the assertion that "[o]ur Country, in the providence of God, and as a just punishment for our national sins, is now involved in a state of calamity and danger." Stopping just short of condemning Madison for taking the nation to war, Morse emphasized the horror into which America had descended: "A darker day for our country, I believe, was never witnessed by the oldest of the present generation, and probably by none of our ancestors."[66] The ancestors to whom Morse referred were, of course, the New England puritans whose biblical framework of self-understanding Morse applied to the whole American nation. Those ancestors had survived many dark days, instructed by ministers who explained disasters and disappointments as punishments for immorality and rebellion against God.[67]

Morse's bitter outrage about the Republican takeover of the country pushed his rendering of American iniquity to the brink of no return. America had descended so far into evil and corruption that she had actually become the enemy of God's people, who were reduced to the status of refugees in an unholy land. Not only was it "unnatural" to engage in war "against the nation from whom we are descended," he claimed, but Britain was "still the bulwark" of Christianity and doing more than any other nation to spread the gospel around the world. Britain "embosoms a great many devout men and women," Morse warned, "whose prayers, like a cloud of incense, daily ascend up before the throne of God for protection." With the good British nation "sheltered behind a shield of omnipotence, our rulers have been permitted, in the righteous providence and displeasure of God, to engage our country, not in a *defensive*, but in an *offensive* war."[68]

Timothy Dwight, president of Yale College, joined in the enthusiasm for biblical commentary with several fast-day sermons that summer. In two sermons prepared for the July 23 fast, he fed the thirst for apocalyptic interpretations of current events that he and Morse had been stimulating for twenty years, focusing on the pouring out of the sixth and seventh vials of destruction preceding Christ's millennial reign prophesied in the book of Revelation. This outpouring of divine wrath was triggered by French infidelity, beginning with Voltaire, who "formed a set design to destroy Christianity," and was now culminating in America's descent into war with Britain, a war that would lead America to closer alliance with unholy France. Between these two events, "[b]ooks were written, and published, in innumerable multitudes, in which infidelity was brought down to the level of the peasant, and even of children," Dwight lamented, and "poured with immense assiduity into the cottage, and the school" and "into the shop, and the farmhouse," and to "the university." Dwight warned against French contagion—"To ally *America* to *France* is to chain living health and beauty, to a corpse dissolving with the plague." In this *"day of the Lord's vengeance,"* when God's *"indignation is upon all nations, and his fury upon all their armies,"* Christians in America should isolate themselves from France and all the corrupt nations of Europe to repent, reform, and *make the eternal GOD our refuge.*"[69]

The following month, Dwight preached another pair of sermons in which he announced a more triumphal path, an alternative to simply protecting Christians from a violent and corrupt maelstrom. Rather than centering on the infection of French infidelity, his second version of Christian history took the destruction of the Church of Rome that began in the sixteenth century as a springboard for the argument that Satan's reign was now entering its final throes. Rather than feeding the sense of catastrophe that would lead to the final judgment and the end of the world, as he did in the earlier pair of sermons, Dwight looked to higher ground through the prospect of Christian missionaries spreading the gospel throughout the world in anticipation of the brightening light of millennial day. "The angel, Religion, is now descending from heaven *over the region and shadow of death*," Dwight proclaimed. With a nod to the numerical predominance of women as church members, he predicted that millions of heathen people would soon turn to God with the help of religion's womanly touch: "With a voice sweeter than the harps of cherubim, she proclaims to the wondering millions beneath, *Behold, I bring you glad tidings of great joy*." Recasting Thomas Paine's famous declaration of 1776 that "we have it in our power to begin the world over again," within a millenarian framework that would resurface much later in the political rhetoric of Ronald Reagan, Dwight announced, "It is the springtime of the world" and "the morning of the great Sabbath of mankind."[70]

In making the transition from the apocalyptic doom of dying Federalists to the millennial optimism of nineteenth-century evangelicals, Dwight had to perform some deft biblical exegesis. To convince his audience that the day of judgment was not upon them and that they should not turn away from the world but commit to its redemption, Dwight cited biblical texts from Daniel and Revelation as evidence that Christ would return to earth only at the end of a long, full, and glorious millennial day. The darkness of the present hour was not the sign of Christ's imminent return, as his earlier sermons that summer might have led auditors to believe, but the end of night, the time in which millennial dawn was gradually but inevitably breaking. Savvy enough to see that Federalist culture in its current defensive and embittered form was doomed, he constructed a millennialist narrative about America's role in world history in which the essence of Federalist commitment to the engagement of religion in politics would be reborn to vanquish chaos and doubt. Thus Dwight entered the War of 1812 at the level of biblical interpretation, with a strategy for waging a cultural war that showed every promise of success. If the War of 1812 was the darkest day America had ever seen, it was also a golden opportunity for ministers to reassert America's providential role in history, and call for national repentance and conformity to God's will.

Dwight's vision of America's providential role in history was an answer to Clay's call for defense of America's manly honor. While Clay directed his call to white men and to their sense of beleaguered manhood, Dwight made sure to include women in his call for cultural awakening and missionary outreach. While Clay's rhetoric of manly honor appealed to slaveholders and Indian fighters, Dwight's rhetoric of millennial dawn cast the sordid world of politics, slavery, and war as a transient world that would fade, like night into day, as religion gained ground.

Building on his grandfather Jonathan Edwards's *History of the Work of Redemption*, which was reissued in 1808, Dwight envisioned Christ's reappearance as the capstone of a Christian world constructed over time. Reworking Edwards' *History*, Dwight outlined a postwar vision of America in which the close relationship between religion and politics associated with New England Federalism would reemerge from the chaos of war, economic crisis, and partisan political conflict to shape national memory and identity. He emphasized the gradual nature of religious recovery, opining that "the Millennium may be justly expected to begin, long before the times, to which its commencement has been postponed by many commentators." Dwight acknowledged that darkness still held sway, particularly with respect to the idolatrous rage for politics among many American men. "They worship; What?" he demanded, "not GOD, but the leader of a party." How foolhardy: "will party politics carry you to heaven?" Certainly not. "Believe me," Dwight warned, "this preference of politics to Religion [will] soon *pass away*." The prospect of millions of souls in many dark corners of the world turning to Christ, inspired by the missionary zeal of Christians in America, heralded "the dawn of immortal day."[71]

In a sermon in 1813 to the young American Board of Commissioners of Foreign Missions (ABCFM), Dwight spelled out his expectations for the interdenominational missionary agency that would grow into the nation's largest and most far-reaching exporter of American culture in the nineteenth century. Galvanizing supporters, Dwight signaled that female citizens of heaven and saints of all colors would achieve recognition before God. Their piety would help transform the very "[d]isposition of man," expunging that "self-gratifying consciousness of superiority, and that ambition, which is the desire of it" that Christians like Dwight found so distressful. As part of this revolution in men's character, their "[*p*]*ublic conduct*" will be "extensively inverted," he predicted, "there will not be an electioneering trick, a cabal, or a demagogue. No candidate for office will proclaim his merits to the public; slander a rival, or solicit a suffrage." This wonderful transformation would occur as people looked to Jesus as their shepherd, "the beautiful figurative language," Dwight explained, that called to mind "the affectionate mother, smiling over her beloved infant." With self-gratifying ambition thus reduced, people of different races and classes would cooperate to close the gap between heaven and earth: "[M]en will be willing to walk to heaven together, although the color, or fashion, of their clothes shall differ."[72]

If religion never achieved the ascendance over politics that Dwight anticipated, it did persist as a companion and contributor, and his conception of the dawning millennium contributed to the salience of religion as a solution to America's political problems. Over the next several decades, American millennialists led numerous efforts, from temperance to the abolition of slavery, to change US law. Representatives of the ABCFM formed friendly relations with foreign leaders hospitable to protestant Christianity in the Near and Far East, with lasting effects on American foreign policy. Most important, millennialists contributed to a sense of national destiny grounded in divine providence, in which America was a beacon of hope and freedom for the whole world.[73]

What champions of this exceptionalism often overlooked, however, was its entanglement in the partisan conflict and general ethos of mistrust it sought to overcome. A profound element of denial figured in Dwight's biblically derived vision of America, denial with respect to the ambition to control the levers of power—recalling Thomas Paine's characterization of Federalist religion as a stalking horse for politics—and denial with respect to the fabulous nature of the assumptions on which it depended. With skeptical reasoning equated with immorality, these millennialist assumptions were protected from critical scrutiny. Still, the underlying fictive aspect of American exceptionalism could be sensed, maintaining what had become a habitual, culturally instinctive effort to hold skepticism at bay.

With a millennialist message about America, and America's role in the world, Dwight and his successors Lyman Beecher and Charles Grandison Finney hitched the wagon of New England's covenant theology to the freedom-loving horses of Methodist and Baptist supernaturalism. Without relinquishing the religious investment in politics and public welfare they derived from puritan tradition, these influential Americans let out the reins of optimistic millennialism that Calvinist preoccupation with original sin had held close. While the Federalist political party Dwight identified with would die out, the religious vision of American destiny he helped engineer brought biblical destiny right to the center of American politics, where New England's virtuous founders knew it should be. Congregationalists like Dwight and their Presbyterian allies would not let Baptist and Methodist liberty run off without them but would reassert their commitment to public order and common good through broader interdenominational cooperation.

Baptists and Methodists enjoyed even greater success, benefiting from increasing public status and popularity, and from their ability to accommodate the cult of manly honor, much as they accommodated slavery. Baptists' belief in their replication of Biblical rule and Methodists' belief in their access to supernatural reality contributed to a more general belief, however unsubstantiated in reality, that religion operated above politics. The pervasive respectability these beliefs came to enjoy made open expressions of religious doubt a lonely and politically perilous endeavor. Opponents of doubt appealed to deeply rooted memories of British tyranny and Federalist arrogance to make failure to adhere to some form of popular belief appear elitist and un-American.

In increasingly well-organized efforts to galvanize sentiment, both religious and political leaders created strong organizations while avoiding the underlying problems of social conflict and mistrust their idealism was supposed to resolve. As religious institutions grew, feeding popular piety through increasingly effective means of communication, new forms of political organization fed partisan conceptions of patriotism. Wedding desire for the resolution of doubt to idealism about the kingdom of God, the American Revolution, and American manhood, emotion could be stirred and even manufactured. A response to the mistrust and suspicion that escalated during economic crises, as well as a means of repressing skeptical criticism in both religion and politics, the jerry-built fusion of organizational efficiency, sentimentality, and hostility to open-ended inquiry became an American way of life.

Doubt about God and country could be guarded against and even denied, but not extinguished; efforts expended against doubt reflected its feared strength. In the context of partisan mistrust and evangelical growth, efforts to resolve doubt became national practice and a hallmark of American identity. The War of 1812 crystallized this process; a heedless near disaster that the United States was fortunate to survive without forced payment of reparations to Britain, it was celebrated as a victory for freedom.

Francis Scott Key, the son of a Revolutionary War officer, captured the national habit of doubt, as well as the means of resolving it, in the poem he wrote watching the fighting at Fort McHenry during the battle of Baltimore. In what later became the national anthem, the poem's first stanza is really couched as an expression of doubt, starting with a question about the flag being still there: "O say, can you see" it? Although "[t]he rockets' red glare ... gave *proof* through the night," the stanza ends with a reiteration of doubt: "O say, does that star-spangled banner still wave / O'er the land of the free, and the home of the brave?" The poem's later stanzas, now largely forgotten, are more positive, broadcasting certainty against the doubt-filled mood that Key captured almost inadvertently in his famous first stanza.[74]

The poem resolves the question it asks about the continued existence of the flag—the symbol of American integrity and idealism—with an implied "yes," drawing the reader into participation in the poem's narrative as the one who knows the outcome and supplies the "yes." Every time the national anthem is sung, participants go through the same process, raising the doubt again and resolving it by implication before the uncertainty in the question can sink in. In much the same way, the highly effective presidential campaign slogan, "Yes we can," begged the question of confidence and trust in America by answering it. This national practice of defending against doubt, even before its existence can be acknowledged, memorializes an approach to religion and politics established in the early republic.

NOTES

INTRODUCTION

1. Rufus Hawley, "An Account of a Revival of Religion in Avon, Conn., in the Year 1799," in *New England Revivals, As They Existed at the Close of the Eighteenth, and the Beginning of the Nineteenth Centuries*, ed. Bennet Tyler (Boston: Massachusetts Sabbath School Society, 1846), 220–26, quotations from 221–22.

2. Hawley, "An Account of a Revival," quotation from 222.

3. Josiah B. Andrews, "An Account of a Religious Revival in Killingworth, Conn., in the years 1801, 1802, and 1803," in Tyler, ed., *New England Revivals*, 282–300, quotations from 288–89. For background, see Jeffrey L. Pasley, *The Tyranny of Printers: Newspaper Politics in the Early American Republic* (Charlottesville: University Press of Virginia, 2001); David Waldstreicher, *In the Midst of Perpetual Fetes: The Making of American Nationalism, 1776–1820* (Chapel Hill: University of North Carolina Press, 1997); Simon P. Newman, *Parades and the Politics of the Street: Festive Culture in the Early American Republic* (Philadelphia: University of Pennsylvania Press, 1997); and Len Travers, *Celebrating the Fourth: Independence Day and the Rites of Nationalism in the Early Republic* (Amherst: University of Massachusetts Press, 1997).

4. Ronald P. Formisano, "Deferential-Participant Politics: The Early Republic's Political Culture, 1789–1840," *The Journal of American Political Science* 68, no. 2 (June 1974): 473–87; Ronald P. Formisano, *The Transformation of Political Culture: Massachusetts Parties, 1790s–1840s* (New York: Oxford University Press, 1983); and Ronald P. Formisano, "The Concept of Political Culture," *The Journal of Interdisciplinary History* 3, no. 3 (Winter 2001): 393–426.

5. Formisano, *Transformation of Political Culture*, 13–15, 30–33; see also David Waldstreicher, *In the Midst of Perpetual Fetes*; and Matthew Q. Dawson, *Partisanship and the Birth of America's Second Party, 1796–1800* (Westport: Greenwood Press, 2000).

6. David McCullough, *John Adams* (New York: Simon and Schuster, 2001), 493–507, quotations from 501 and 505.

7. *A Dictionary of Americanisms on Historical Principles*, ed. Mitford M. Mathews (Chicago: University of Chicago Press, 1951), 954.

8. *Connecticut Courant* (Hartford), September 29, 1800, 1.

9. Jon Butler, *Awash in a Sea of Faith: Christianizing the American People* (Cambridge, MA: Harvard University Press, 1990), 194–224; and David L. Holmes, *The Faiths of the Founding Fathers* (New York: Oxford University Press, 2006).

10. Kerry S. Walters, *The American Deists: Voices of Reason & Dissent in the Early Republic* (Lawrence: University of Kansas Press, 1992), quotations from 1–2; Kenneth Silverman, *Timothy Dwight* (New York: Twayne Publishers, 1969), 97; and Lyman Beecher, *The Autobiography of Lyman Beecher*, ed. Barbara M. Cross, 2 vols. (New Haven: Yale University Press, 1961), quotation from 1:27.

11. Charles William Janson, *A Stranger in America* (New York: The Press of the Pioneers, 1935; orig. 1807), 101, 8–9, quotations from 101; John B. Boles, *The Great Revival: Beginnings of the Bible Belt* (Lexington: University Press of Kentucky, 1996; orig. 1972), 12–24, quotations from 13 and 14; and William Warren Sweet, "The Churches as Moral Courts of the Frontier," *Church History* 2, no. 1 (March 1933): 5–8, quotation from 5.

12. James McGready, *The Posthumous Works of the Reverend and Pious James M'Gready, Late Minister of the Gospel, in Henderson, Kentucky*, ed. James Smith, 2 vols. (Nashville: Lowry and Smith, 1833), quotations from 2:167.

13. "Preface," in *Memoirs of Mary Wollstonecraft Godwin, author of a vindication of the rights of women* (Philadelphia 1802), quotation from 1.

14. Patricia U. Bonomi, *Under the Cope of Heaven: Religion, Society, and Politics in Colonial America*, rev. ed. (New York: Oxford University Press, 2003; orig. 1986).

15. Charles H. Lippy, *Being Religious American Style: a History of Popular Religiosity in the United States* (Santa Barbara: Praeger, 1994); and David D. Hall, ed., *Lived Religion: Toward a History of Practice* (Princeton: Princeton University Press, 1997).

16. *By the House of Delegates, January 8, 1785. Resolved, that it is the opinion of this House, that the happiness of the people, and the good order and preservation of civil government, depend on morality, religion, and piety* (Annapolis: Frederick Green, 1785). For initial laws regarding religion in other states, see Edwin S. Gaustad, *Faith of Our Fathers: Religion and the New Nation* (San Francisco: Harper & Row, 1987), 141–74; and John F. Wilson and Donald L. Drakeman, eds., *Church and State in American History: Key Documents, Decisions, and Commentary from the Past Three Centuries*, 3d. ed (Cambridge: Westview Press, 2003; orig. 1965), 1–82.

17. David W. Kling, *A Field of Divine Wonders: The New Divinity and Village Revivals in Northwestern Connecticut, 1792–1822* (University Park: Pennsylvania State University Press, 1993), 54–62.

18. Andrew Fuller, *The practical uses of Christian baptism a circular letter from the ministers and messengers of the several Baptist churches of the Northamptonshire Association, assembled at Northampton, June 15, 16, 1802, to the churches in their connexion composed by Andrew Fuller* (Burlington, NJ, and Philadelphia: Stephen C. Ustnick and Thomas Ustnick, 1802), quotation from 11.

19. William Warren Sweet, "Churches as Moral Courts," 3–21, esp. 11–12; see also William Warren Sweet, ed., *Religion on the American Frontier*, vol. 1, *The Baptists 1783–1830, A Collec-*

tion of Source Material (New York: Cooper Square Publishers, 1964; orig. 1931); Monica Najar, *Evangelizing the South: A Social History of Church and State in Early America* (New York: Oxford University Press, 2008); and Mark Dementi Kaplanoff, "Evangelizing the South: A Social History of Church and State in Early America" (PhD dissertation, University of Cambridge, 1979), 76–80.

20. Thomas Jefferson to Gideon Granger, October 18, 1800, *The Papers of Thomas Jefferson Digital Edition*, ed. Barbara B. Oberg and J. Jefferson Looney, main series, vol. 32 (Charlottesville: University of Virginia Press, Rotunda, 2008).

21. John Leland, *Politics sermonized exhibited in Ashfield on July 4th, 1806* (Springfield: Andrew Wright, 1806), quotations from 22; and William G. McLoughlin, *Isaac Backus on Church, State, and Calvinism; pamphlets 1754–1789* (Cambridge, MA: Harvard University Press, 1968), 229.

22. *American State Papers Bearing On Sunday Legislation, Revised and Enlarged Edition*, compiled and annotated by William Addison Blakely, ed. Willard Allen Colcord, rev. ed. (Washington DC: Religious Liberty Association, 1911).

23. For the shift toward libertarian politics, see Joyce Oldham Appleby, *Capitalism and a New Social Order: The Republican Vision of the 1790s* (New York: New York University Press, 1984); Douglas R. Egerton, "The Empire of Liberty Reconsidered," in James Horn, Jan Ellen Lewis, and Peter S. Onuf, eds., *The Revolution of 1800: Democracy, Race, and the New Republic* (Charlottesville: University of Virginia Press, 2002); Rachel N. Klein, *Unification of a Slave State: The Rise of the Planter Class in the South Carolina Backcountry, 1760–1808* (Chapel Hill: University of North Carolina Press, 1990); and Adam Rothman, *Slave Country: American Expansion and the Origins of the Deep South* (Cambridge, MA: Harvard University Press, 2005). For the shift toward evangelicalism, see Butler, *Awash in a Sea of Faith*, 225–56; John B. Boles, *The Great Revival: Beginnings of the Bible Belt* (Lexington: University Press of Kentucky, 1996; orig. 1972); Roger Finke and Rodney Stark, "How the Upstart Sects Won America: 1776–1850," *Journal for the Scientific Study of Religion* 28, no. 1 (March 1989): 27–44; and Nathan O. Hatch and John H. Wigger, "Introduction," in *Methodism and the Shaping of American Culture* (Nashville: Abingdon Press, 2001), 11–22.

24. Nathan O. Hatch, *The Democratization of American Christianity* (New Haven: Yale University Press, 1989).

25. Notably, Christine Leigh Heyrman, *Southern Cross: The Beginnings of the Bible Belt* (Chapel Hill: University of North Carolina Press, 1997); Cynthia Lynn Lyerly, *Methodism and the Southern Mind, 1770–1810* (New York: Oxford University Press, 1998); and Monica Najar, *Evangelizing the South*.

26. For example, Myra C. Glenn, "Troubled Manhood in the Early Republic: The Life and Autobiography of Sailor Horace Lane," *Journal of the Early Republic* 26, no. 1 (Spring 2006): 90; and Robert Wuthnow, "Democratic Renewal and Cultural Inertia: Why Our Best Efforts Fall Short," *Sociological Forum* 20, no. 3 (September 2005): 365.

CHAPTER 1

1. Thomas Paine, *The Age of Reason* (Secaucus: Citadel Press, 1974; orig. 1794 and 1795), quotations from 60, 68, and 54–55.

2. Ibid., quotations from 60, 68, and 72; Eric Foner, *Tom Paine and Revolutionary America*, 2d ed. (New York: Oxford University Press, 2005; orig. 1976), 211–47.

3. Sophia Rosenfeld makes a similar argument about Paine's use of the term "common sense" in "Tom Paine's Common Sense and Ours," *The William and Mary Quarterly* no. 4 (2008): 56 pars, http://www.historycooperative.org/journals/wm/65.4/rosenfeld.html, last accessed August 13, 2010.

4. Paine, *Age of Reason*, quotation from 54.

5. Edward Gray, "The Architect and the State: Political Economy in Tom Paine's Iron Bridge," Florida State University working paper cited with the author's permission.

6. Letter from John Adams to Abigail Adams, March 19, 1776, in *Adams Family Papers: An Electronic Archive* (Boston: Massachusetts Historical Society), http://www.masshist.org/digitaladams/, last accessed June 17, 2011. See also David McCullough, *John Adams* (New York: Simon and Schuster, 2001), 97, 101, and 373.

7. Paine, *Age of Reason*, quotations from 49–51.

8. Carroll D. Wright, *History of Wages and Prices in Massachusetts: 1752–1883* (Boston: Wright and Potter, 1885), 58 and 43–44 for conversion from pounds to dollars.

9. Lyman Beecher, *The Autobiography of Lyman Beecher*, ed. Barbara M. Cross, 2 vols. (New Haven: Yale University Press, 1961), quotations from 1:27.

10. Robert Stuart, "Reminiscences, Respecting the Establishment and Progress of the Presbyterian Church in Kentucky," in Robert Stuart Sanders, *The Reverend Robert Stuart, D.D. 1772–1856: A Pioneer in Kentucky Presbyterianism and His Descendants* (Louisville: Dunne Press, 1962), quotation from 68.

11. For Paine's popularity in the 1790s, see Alfred F. Young, "The Celebration and Damnation of Thomas Paine," in *Liberty Tree: Ordinary People and the American Revolution* (New York: New York University Press, 2006), 265–95; and Simon P. Newman, "Paine, Jefferson, and the Strange Career of Revolutionary Radicalism in Early National America," University of Glasgow working paper cited with the author's permission.

12. George W. Ranck, *History of Lexington Kentucky, Its Early Annals and Recent Progress* (Cincinnati: Robert Clarke and Co., 1872), 188, 193; and J. H. Spencer, *A History of Kentucky Baptists from 1769 to 1885* (Lafayette: Church History Research and Archives, 1976; orig. 1886), 500–501, 481, 195, quotations from 500.

13. Spencer, *History of Kentucky Baptists*, 481, 195; Elkhorn Association of Baptists, *Minutes of the Elkhorn Association of Baptists. Held at Cooper's Run, August 8, 1795, and continued by adjournment until the 10th* (Lexington: Elkhorn Association, 1795), quotations from 4; and *Stewart's Kentucky Herald* (Lexington), October 30, 1798, 3.

14. "IMPORTANT," *Stewart's Kentucky Herald* (Lexington), November 11, 1796, quotations from 2.

15. Newman, "Paine, Jefferson," quotation from 18.

16. Paine, *Age of Reason*, quotations from 50.

17. Foner, *Tom Paine*, 1–6.

18. Rosenfeld, "Tom Paine's Common Sense"; and Thomas Paine, *Common Sense*, ed. Isaac Kramnick (New York: Penguin Books, 1986), quotations from 63 and 82.

19. John Adams to Abigail Adams, March 19, 1776, *Adams Family Papers*.

20. Gary B. Nash, *The Unknown American Revolution: The Unruly Birth of Democracy and the Struggle to Create America* (New York: Penguin, 2005), 189; and Rosenfeld, "Tom Paine's Common Sense," quotation from par. 44.

21. Foner, *Tom Paine*, quotation from 86.

22. Vikki J. Vickers, *"My Pen and My Soul Have Ever Gone Together": Thomas Paine and the American Revolution* (New York: Routledge, 2006), 51–52; see also Eric Slauter, *The State as a Work of Art: The Cultural Origins of the Constitution* (Chicago: University of Chicago Press, 2009); and Olivia Smith, *The Politics of Language, 1791–1819* (Oxford: Clarendon Press, 1984), 42–57.

23. Paine, *Common Sense*, quotations from 76–77.

24. Ibid., quotations from 76 and 87.

25. Rosenfeld, "Tom Paine's Common Sense"; Sophia Rosenfeld, "Before Democracy: The Production and Uses of Common Sense, *The Journal of Modern History* 80, no. 1 (March 2008): 1–54, http://www.journals.uchicago.edu/doi/full/10.1086/529076, last accessed June 18, 2011.

26. Young, "Celebration and Damnation," 278–81.

27. Newman, "Paine, Jefferson," 5–7.

28. Thomas Paine to Samuel Adams, January 22, 1803, in *Paine versus religion, or, Christianity triumphant containing the interesting letters of Sam. Adams, Tho. Paine, and John Gemmil to which is added, Mr. Erskine's celebrated speech at the trial of the age of reason* (Baltimore: G. Douglas, 1803), quotation from 6.

29. Rosemarie Zagarri, *Revolutionary Backlash: Women and Politics in the Early American Republic* (Philadelphia: University of Pennsylvania Press, 2007); James Horn, Jan Ellen Lewis, and Peter S. Onuf, eds., *The Revolution of 1800: Democracy, Race, and the New Republic* (Charlottesville: University of Virginia Press, 2002); and Adam Rothman, *Slave Country: American Expansion and the Origins of the Deep South* (Cambridge, MA: Harvard University Press, 2005).

30. Benjamin Trumbull, *Twelve discourses, comprising a systematical demonstration of the divine origin of the Holy Scriptures of the Old and New Testaments; designed for the benefit of Christians of all denominations: and especially for the instruction and edification of young people; to establish them in a rational and full persuasion of the truth and importance of the Scriptures; to excite their early and earnest pursuit of divine knowledge, and awaken their highest solicitude to walk with the wise, and fly the way of evil men* (Hartford: Hudson and Goodwin, 1799), iii–v, quotations from iii and v.

31. Thomas Paine to Samuel Adams, January 22, 1803, in *Paine versus religion*, quotations from 7.

32. Samuel Adams to Thomas Paine, Boston, November 30, 1802, in *Paine versus religion*, quotations from 4.

33. Ibid.

34. A True Baptist [John Leland], *The age of inquiry; or, Reason and revelation, in harmony with each Other; operating against all tyranny and infidelity: intended as a clue to the present political controversy in the United States. To which is added, some remarks upon the report of the committee of the legislature of Connecticut, upon the Baptist petition, presented at*

their session of May, 1802 (Hartford: for the author, 1804), 7–9, quotations from 9; see also John Leland, *A Storke* [stroke] *at the Branch* (Hartford: Elisha Babcock, 1801), 7.

35. [Leland], *Age of Inquiry*, quotation from 7.

36. Foner, *Thomas Paine*, 252–53.

37. Peter Gay, *Deism: An Anthology* (Princeton: D. Van Nostrand, 1968).

38. Carol Smith-Rosenberg, *This Violent Empire: The Birth of an American National Identity* (Chapel Hill: University of North Carolina Press, 2010), 191–95.

39. G. Adolf Koch, *Republican Religion: The American Revolution and the Cult of Reason* (New York: Henry Holt and Co., 1933), 51–79; Elihu Palmer, "Principles of the Deistical Society in the State of New York," reprinted in Koch, *Republican Religion*, quotations from 78–79; and Philip S. Foner, ed., *The Democratic-Republican Societies, 1790–1800: A Documentary Sourcebook of Constitutions, Declarations, Addresses, Resolutions, and Toasts* (Westport: Greenwood Press, 1976), quotation from 31.

40. "Discourse of Thomas Paine, at the Society of the Theophilanthropists, at Paris," *Temple of Reason* (New York), January 3, 1801, quotation from 68.

41. "From the New-York Gazette," *Trenton Federalist*, November 8, 1802, quotations from 1.

42. "Wood's Exposition of the Clintonian Faction," *Temple of Reason* (Philadelphia), September 25, 1802, quotation from 246; John Wood, *A Full Exposition of the Clintonian Faction, and the Society of the Columbian Illuminati* (Newark: printed for the author, 1802); and Koch, *Republican Religion*, 98–106.

43. Koch, *Republican Religion*, 103–13, quotation from 112.

44. Dewitt Clinton, *An address delivered by the most worshipful, the Hon. Dewitt Clinton, Esq. to the Grand Lodge of the State of New-York at his installation into the office of grand master, on the 19th of June, 1806* (New York: Brothers Southwick and Hardcastle, 1806), quotation from 11; see also Stephen C. Bullock, *Freemasonry and the Transformation of the American Social Order, 1730–1840* (Chapel Hill: University of North Carolina Press, 1996); and Catherine L. Albanese, *Sons of the Fathers: The Civil Religion of the American Revolution* (Philadelphia: Temple University Press, 1976), 129–42.

45. "The Mason's Prayer," *Odes and Hymns; Festival of St. John—June 24, 5801* (Portsmouth: n.p., 1801).

46. William Bentley, December 2, 1800, and July 11, 1801, *The Diary of William Bentley, D.D., Pastor the East Church, Salem, Massachusetts*, 4 vols. (Salem: Essex Institute, 1905–14), quotations from 1:357 and 1:379.

47. Bentley, August 21, 1798, *Diary of William Bentley*, quotation from 1:278.

48. David L. Holmes, *The Faiths of the Founding Fathers* (New York: Oxford University Press, 2006), 59–71.

49. Jeremy Belknap, *Dissertations on the Character, Death & Resurrection of Jesus Christ* (1795), in Conrad Wright, *The Beginnings of Unitarianism in America* (Boston: Starr King Press, 1955), quotation from 243.

50. Bentley, June 18, 1809, and September 25, 1805, *Diary of William Bentley*, quotations from 3:441–442 and 2:107; and Koch, *Republican Religion*, 208–20.

51. Richard Watson, *An apology for the Bible, in a series of letters, addressed to Thomas Paine, author of a book entitled, The age of reason, part the second, being an investigation of*

true and of fabulous theology (New York: John Bull, 1796), quotations from 19 and 240–41; and Kerry S. Walters, *The American Deists: Voices of Reason and Dissent in the Early Republic* (Lawrence: University Press of Kansas, 1992), 2.

52. Gideon Yaffe and Ryan Nichols, "Thomas Reid," in *The Stanford Encyclopedia of Philosophy* (Winter 2009 edition), ed. Edward N. Zalta, http://plato.stanford.edu/archives/win2009/entries/reid/; and E. Brooks Holifield, *Theology in America: Christian Thought from the Age of the Puritans to the Civil War* (New Haven: Yale University Press, 2003).

53. Mark A. Noll, *America's God: From Jonathan Edwards to Abraham Lincoln* (New York: Oxford University Press, 2002), 93–113.

54. Holifield, *Theology in America*, 353; Jeffry H. Morrison, *John Witherspoon and the Founding of the American Republic* (Notre Dame: University of Notre Dame Press, 2005), 45–69; Daniel Day Williams, *The Andover Liberals: A Study in American Theology* (New York: Octagon Books, 1970), 5–16; and Joseph Haroutunian, *Piety versus Moralism: The Passing of the New England Theology* (New York: Harper and Row, 1970; orig. 1938), 249–55.

55. "Communication," *Daily Advertiser* (New York), August 19, 1800, 16:4841, quotations from 2.

56. "Ancient Chronicles, Chapter XX," *Connecticut Courant* (Hartford), September 29, 1800, 35:1862, quotations from 2.

57. Daniel Boorstin, *The Lost World of Thomas Jefferson* (Boston: Beacon Press, 1960; orig. 1948), 21–24; on the iron bridge, see Thomas Jefferson to Dr. Joseph Willard, March 24, 1789, *The Life and Selected Writings of Thomas Jefferson*, ed. Adrienne Koch and William Peden (New York: Modern Library, 2004; orig. 1944), 430–31; and Edward Gray, "The Architect and the State: Political Economy in Tom Paine's Iron Bridge, Florida State University working paper cited with the author's permission; for the White House meeting, see Kim Tousley Phillips, in *William Duane, Radical Journalist in the Age of Jefferson* (New York: Garland Press, 1989), 117.

58. Quotation from Foner, *Tom Paine*, 264.

59. Foner, *Tom Paine*, 103–5; Leo Marx, *The Machine in the Garden: Technology and the Pastoral Ideal* (New York: Oxford University Press, 2000; orig. 1965).

60. Thomas Jefferson, *Notes on the State of Virginia*, ed. William Peden (Chapel Hill: University of North Carolina Press, 1954; first English edition published in London, 1787), quotations from 47 and 53–4.

61. Jefferson, *Notes*, 43–47.

62. Boorstin, *Lost World*, 89–93.

63. Quotations from Boorstin, *Lost World*, 91 and 157.

64. Jefferson, *Notes*, quotations from 138 and 143.

65. Ibid., quotations from 138 and 230.

66. Wallace, *Jefferson and the Indians*, 208–9, 221.

67. *American State Papers, Indian Affairs*, vol. 1 (Washington: Gales and Seaton, 1832), quotations from 650; and Anthony F. C. Wallace, *Jefferson and the Indians: The Tragic Fate of the First Americans* (Cambridge, MA: Harvard University Press, 1999), 218–22.

68. Wallace, *Jefferson and the Indians*, 214; and Gregory Evans Dowd, *A Spirited Resistance: The North American Indian Struggle for Unity, 1745–1815* (Baltimore: Johns Hopkins University Press, 1992), 161–65.

69. Jefferson quotation in Wallace, *Jefferson and the Indians*, quotations from 317.

70. For the argument that Jefferson compartmentalized different aspects of his life and thought, see Joseph J. Ellis, *American Sphinx: The Character of Thomas Jefferson* (New York: Alfred A. Knopf, 1996).

71. Nancy Isenberg, *Fallen Founder: The Life of Aaron Burr* (London: Penguin Books, 2007), 263 and see also 119–21, 212–13, 405–14.

72. Matthew L. Davis, ed., *Memoirs of Aaron Burr, With Selections From His Correspondence*, 2 vols. (New York: Harper and Bros., 1837 and 1838), quotation from 1:45; see also Mary-Jo Kline, "Historical Introduction," in *Political Correspondence and Public Papers of Aaron Burr*, 2 vols. (Princeton: Princeton University Press, 1983), 1:liii–lxx. In regards to Bellamy's library, see Arthur Goodenough, *The Clergy of Litchfield County* (Litchfield: University Club, 1909), 26;

73. Samuel Hopkins, "Honoured Sir, Newport 1802," in Kline, *Political Correspondence and Public Papers of Aaron Burr*, quotations from 2:747–49.

74. Joseph Bellamy, *True religion delineated; or, Experimental religion, as distinguished from formality on the one hand, and enthusiasm on the other, set in a scriptural and rational light. In two discourses. In which some of the principal errors both of the Arminians and Antinomians are confuted, the foundation and superstructure of their different schemes demolished, and the truth as it is in Jesus, explained and proved. The whole adapted to the weakest capacities, and designed for the establishment, comfort and quickening of the people of God, in these evil times* (Boston: S. Kneeland, 1750), quotations from 188–90; see also Jonathan Edwards, *A careful and strict enquiry into the modern prevailing notions of that freedom of will, which is supposed to be essential to moral agency, vertue and vice, reward and punishment, praise and blame* (Boston: S. Kneeland, 1754).

75. Bellamy, *True religion delineated*, quotation from 40.

76. Richard Douglas Shiels, "The Connecticut Clergy in the Second Great Awakening" (PhD dissertation, University of Massachusetts, 1976), 304 and 311.

77. Joanne B. Freeman, *Affairs of Honor: National Politics in the New Republic* (New Haven: Yale University Press, 2001), 209 and 231, quotation from 231; and Nancy Isenberg, "The 'Little Emperor': Aaron Burr, Dandyism, and the Sexual Politics of Treason," in Beyond the Founders: New Approaches to the Political History of the Early American Republic, ed. Jeffrey L. Pasley, Andrew W. Robertson, and David Waldstreicher (Chapel Hill: University of North Carolina Press, 2004), 134–35.

78. Isenberg, *Fallen Founder*, quotation from 119; and Isenberg, "Little Emperor," quotations from 136.

79. "Friday, August 3," *New-York Evening Post*, August 3, 1804, quotations from 2; see also Isenberg, "Little Emperor," 136.

80. David Hume, *A Treatise of Human Nature*, book I, parts IV and VII (London, 1739).

81. "Timothy Dwight to Aaron Burr," New-Haven, March 1772, reprinted in Davis, *Memoirs of Aaron Burr*, quotation from 41.

82. Richard N. Côté, *Theodosia: Theodosia Burr Alston: Portrait of a Prodigy* (Mount Pleasant: Corinthian Books, 2005; orig. 2002), 236–40.

83. Ibid., 64–75; and Isenberg, *Fallen Founder*, 80–83.

84. Aaron Burr, "To Mrs. Burr," February 8, 1793, and Aaron Burr, "To Mrs. Burr," February 16, 1793, both reprinted in Davis, *Memoirs of Aaron Burr*, quotations from 1:363 and 1:363.

85. Mary Wollstonecraft, *A vindication of the rights of woman: with strictures on political and moral subjects* (Boston: Peter Edes, 1792) quotation from 247.

86. Aaron Burr to Theodosia Burr, January 4, 1799, in *Correspondence of Aaron Burr and His Daughter Theodosia*, ed. Mark Van Doren (New York: Stratford Press, 1929), quotation from 46–47.

87. Ibid., quotations from 66 and 76.

88. Côté, *Theodosia*, 259–69.

89. Bernard Mayo, *Henry Clay: Spokesman of the New West* (Boston: Houghton Mifflin, 1937); 261–66; and Isenberg, *Fallen Founder*, 271–316.

90. "A parallel, drawn from Antiquity," *Enquirer* (Richmond), January 3, 1807, quotations from 3.

91. Henry F. May, *The Enlightenment in America* (New York: Oxford University Press, 1976).

92. "New-York, Oct. 25," *Albany Centinel* (November 2, 1802), 2.

93. "Baltimore, November 1," *Philadelphia Gazette & Daily Advertiser*, November 2, 1802, quotation from 3.

94. "From the Gazette of the United States," *Commercial Advertiser* (New York), November 3, 1802, quotations from 2.

95. Jerry W. Knudson, "The Rage Around Tom Paine: Newspaper Reaction to his Homecoming in 1802," *New York Historical Society Quarterly* LIII (January 1969): 34–63, quotations from 49 and 40–41.

96. "Communications," *Republican Gazetteer* (Boston), November 3, 1802, quotations from 3.

97. *American Citizen* (New York), November 4, 1802, quotation from 3.

98. "Mr. Thomas Paine; Lancaster Intelligencer," *Morning Chronicle* (New York), November 8, 1802, quotation from 3.

99. Foner, *Tom Paine*, 261; and Young, "Paine, Jefferson," 265–67.

100. "Thomas Paine," *Republican Watchtower* (New York), November 17, 1809, quotations from 1; and "Thomas Paine," *American Citizen* (New York), November 15, 1809, 10:3002, quotation from 3.

CHAPTER 2

1. Eric Slauter, *The State as a Work of Art: The Cultural Origins of the Constitution* (Chicago: University of Chicago Press, 2009), 39–41; David Hackett Fischer, *The Revolution of American Conservatism: The Federalist Party in the Era of Jeffersonian Democracy* (New York: Harper and Row, 1965); Linda K. Kerber, *Federalists in Dissent: Imagery and Ideology in Jeffersonian America* (Ithaca: Cornell University Press, 1970) and *Women of the Republic: Intellect and Ideology in Revolutionary America* (Chapel Hill: University of North Carolina Press, 1980); Bernard Bailyn, *The Ideological Origins of the American Revolution* (Cambridge, MA: Harvard University Press, 1967), 281–301; Gordon S. Wood, *The Radicalism of the American*

Revolution (New York: Random House, 1991), 225, 233, 288–89; and Edmund S. Morgan, *Inventing the People: The Rise of Popular Sovereignty in England and America* (New York: W. W. Norton, 1988).

2. Thomas Jefferson to Spencer Roane, September 6, 1819, in *The Writings and Thomas Jefferson*, ed. Andrew A. Lipscomb and Albert Ellery Bergh, 20 vols. (Washington DC, 1903–14), 15:212. For the importance of Jefferson's election, see James Horn, Jan Ellen Lewis, and Peter S. Onuf, eds., *The Revolution of 1800: Democracy, Race, and the New Republic* (Charlottesville: University of Virginia Press, 2002).

3. *Connecticut Courant* (Hartford), July 7, 1800, 3.

4. Increase N. Tarbox, ed., *Diary of Thomas Robbins, 1796–1854*, 2 vols. (Boston: Beacon Press, 1886), quotations from 1:118 and 1:132.

5. John L. Brooke, "Consent, Civil Society, and the Public Sphere in the Age of Revolution and the Early American Republic," in *Beyond the Founders: New Approaches to the Political History of the American Republic*, ed. Jeffrey L. Pasley, Andrew W. Robertson, and David Waldstreicher (Chapel Hill: University of North Carolina Press, 2004), 207–50.

6. "Extract of a Letter from Robert G. Harper, to His Constituents," *The Carolina Gazette* (Charleston), June 5, 1800, 4; see also Ralph Ketcham, *Presidents Above Party: The First American Presidency, 1789–1829* (Chapel Hill: University of North Carolina Press, 1984).

7. Gary B. Nash, *The Unknown American Revolution: The Unruly Birth of Democracy and the Struggle to Create America* (New York: Viking Penguin, 2005), 448; and Stephen A. Marini, "The Religious World of Daniel Shays," in *In Debt to Shays: The Bicentennial of an Agrarian Revolution*, ed. Robert A. Gross (Charlottesville: University of Virginia Press, 1993), 239–77.

8. John Adams to Thomas Jefferson, June 30, 1813, in *The Adams-Jefferson Letters: The Complete Correspondence between Thomas Jefferson and Abigail and John Adams*, ed. Lester J. Cappon (Chapel Hill: University of North Carolina, 1959), 346–48.

9. Michael Lienesch, "Reinterpreting Rebellion: The Influence of Shays's Rebellion on American Political Thought," in Gross, ed., *In Debt to Shays*, 161–82, quotation from 178.

10. Paul Douglas Newman, *Fries's Rebellion: The Enduring Struggle for the American Revolution* (Philadelphia: University of Pennsylvania Press, 2004); quotations from 172 and 187.

11. Society of Tammany or Columbian Order, Committee of Amusement, Minutes, October 12, 1792, reprinted in *The Democratic-Republican Societies, 1790–1800: A Documentary Sourcebook of Constitutions, Declarations, Addresses, Resolutions, and Toasts*, ed. Philip S. Foner (Westport: Greenwood Press, 1976), 201.

12. "Resolutions Adopted Condemning the South Carolina Legislature, Jun 23, 1794," *City Gazette* (Charleston), June 28, 1794, reprinted in Foner, ed., *Democratic-Republican Societies*, 389.

13. David McCullough, *John Adams* (New York: Simon and Schuster, 2001), 493–507, quotations from 501 and 505.

14. "Celebration in Duchess County, State of New York," *Aurora General Advertiser* (Philadelphia), July 12, 1798, 3.

15. "For the Aurora, Friend Bache," *Aurora*, August 13, 1798, 3.

16. Quotations from "The Kentucky Resolutions of 1798," http://www.constitution.org/cons/kent1798.htm, last accessed June 19, 2011.

17. Ibid.

18. James C. Klotter, *The Breckinridges of Kentucky* (Lexington: University Press of Kentucky, 2006; orig. 1986), 20–22.

19. *Herald of Liberty* (Washington, PA), July 7, 1800, 3.

20. *Gazette of the United States* (Philadelphia), November 25, 1800, 3.

21. James E. Lewis, Jr., "'What is to Become of Our Government?' The Revolutionary Potential of the Election of 1800," in Horn et al., eds., *Revolution of 1800*, 3–29.

22. Richard J. Purcell, *Connecticut in Transition: 1775–1818* (Middletown: Wesleyan University Press, 1963; orig. 1918), 159–60.

23. *The American Mercury* (Hartford), March 17, quotations from 3.

24. Ibid., quotations from 3.

25. *Diary of Thomas Robbins*, quotation from 192.

26. Ronald P. Formisano, *The Transformation of Political Culture: Massachusetts Parties, 1790s–1840s* (New York: Oxford University Press, 1983); David Waldstreicher, *In the Midst of Perpetual Fetes: The Making of American Nationalism, 1776–1820* (Chapel Hill: University of North Carolina Press, 1997); Matthew Q. Dawson, *Partisanship and the Birth of America's Second Party, 1796–1800* (Westport: Greenwood Press, 2000); and Rachel N. Klein, *Unification of a Slave State: The Rise of the Planter Class in the South Carolina Backcountry, 1760–1808* (Chapel Hill: University of North Carolina Press, 1990), 259–62.

27. Nash, *Unknown American Revolution*; David A. Wilson, *United Irishmen, United States: Immigrant Radicals in the Early Republic* (Ithaca: Cornell University Press, 1998); David Barry Gaspar and David Patrick Geggus, eds., *A Turbulent Time: The French Revolution and the Greater Caribbean* (Bloomington: Indiana University Press, 1997); and Sarah J. Purcell, *Sealed with Blood: War, Sacrifice, and Memory in Revolutionary America* (Philadelphia: University of Pennsylvania Press, 2002).

28. François Furstenberg, *In the Name of the Father: Washington's Legacy, Slavery, and the Making of a Nation* (New York: Penguin Press, 2000), 26–28, 47–50, quotations from 48–49.

29. Catherine Allgor, *Parlor Politics: In Which the Ladies of Washington Help Build a City and a Government* (Charlottesville: University Press of Virginia, 2000), 19–20, quotation from 20.

30. Jeffrey L. Pasley, "The Cheese and the Words: Popular Political Culture and Participatory Democracy in the Early American Republic, in Pasley et al., eds., *Beyond the Founders*, 31–56.

31. Allgor, *Parlor Politics*, 24–26, quotation from 25; for preoccupation with deception in optics and art in the early republic, see Wendy Bellion, "Object Lessons: Pleasing Deceptions," *Commonplace* 3, no. 1 (October 2002), http://www.common-place.org/vol-03/no-01/lessons/bellion-2.shtml, last accessed June 20, 2011, and "Likeness and Deception in Early American Art" (PhD dissertation, Northwestern University, 2001).

32. Joyce Appleby, "Thomas Jefferson and the Psychology of Democracy," in Horn et al., eds., *Revolution of 1800*, 155–72; David Waldstreicher, "Why Thomas Jefferson and African Americans Wore Their Politics on their Sleeves: Dress and Mobilization between American Revolutions," in Pasley et al., eds., *Beyond the Founders*, 79–103; and Allgor, *Parlor Politics*, 4–47.

33. Appleby, "Jefferson and the Psychology of Democracy," quotation from 157.

34. Allgor, *Parlor Politics*, quotations from 43 and 28.

35. *New York Evening Post* 45, January 7, 1802, quotations from 3.

36. Allgor, *Parlor Politics*, quotation from 32; see also 259 n. 69.

37. Stephen Burroughs, *Sketch of the Life of the Notorious Stephen Burroughs containing the most enteresting* [i.e., interesting] *event of his life as given by himself* (Hudson: H and L Steels, 1809; orig. 1798), quotations from 3, 7, 25, 37, and 39; Stephen Mihm, *A Nation of Counterfeiters: Capitalists, Con Men, and the Making of the United States* (Cambridge, MA: Harvard University Press, 2007), 35–38.

38. Burroughs, *Sketch*, 41–48, quotations from 41–42 and 44.

39. Ibid., quotation from 55; and Stephen Burroughs, *A Sermon, delivered in Rutland, on a Hay-mow* (Northampton: T. M. Pomroy, 1807; orig. 1784?), quotation from 3–4.

40. Burroughs, *Sketch*, quotations from 55 and 104–5; and Mihm, *A Nation of Counterfeiters*, 38–59.

41. Mihm, *A Nation of Counterfeiters*; and Robert A. Gross, "The Confidence Man and the Preacher: the Cultural Politics of Shays' Rebellion," in Gross, ed., *In Debt to Shays*, 297–320.

42. Julia A. Stern, *The Plight of Feeling: Sympathy and Dissent in the Early American Novel* (Chicago: University of Chicago Press, 1997), 31–70; and Cathy N. Davidson, *Revolution and the Word: the Rise of the Novel in America*, 2d ed. (New York: Oxford University Press, 2004; orig. 1986), 217–21.

43. Susanna Rowson, *Charlotte Temple: A Tale of Truth*, 4th American ed. (Harrisburg: John Wyeth, 1801; orig. 1791), quotations from 58, 3, and 41.

44. Stern, *Plight of Feeling*, 10, 30, and 68.

45. Rowson, *Charlotte Temple*, quotations from 55 and 127.

46. Ibid., quotations from 175, 193, and 196.

47. Stern, *Plight of Feeling*, 34–35; see also Davidson, *Revolution and the Word*, 217–21; Amanda Porterfield, *Feminine Spirituality in America: From Sarah Edwards to Martha Graham* (Philadelphia: Temple University Press, 1980), 59–61.

48. "Preface," in *Memoirs of Mary Wollstonecraft Godwin, author of a Vindication of the Rights of Women* (Philadelphia: n.s., 1802), quotations from 1–2.

49. Clare A. Lyons, *Sex among the Rabble: An Intimate History of Gender and Power in the Age of Revolution, Philadelphia, 1730–1830* (Chapel Hill: University of North Carolina Press, 2006), 15, 65, 242–46, 264, 279–80, 288, 295, and 333.

50. Rosemarie Zagarri, *Revolutionary Backlash: Women and Politics in the Early American Republic* (Philadelphia: University of Pennsylvania Press, 2007), quotation from 86; see also Catherine Bell, *Ritual Theory, Ritual Practice* (New York: Oxford University Press, 1992).

51. Lee Travers, *Celebrating the Fourth: Independence Day and the Rites of Nationalism in the Early Republic* (Amherst: University of Massachusetts Press, 1997), 135–41, quotation from 136.

52. *Independent Chronicle* (Boston), July 4, 1805, quotation from 3; *Charleston Courier*, July 2, 1807, quotation from 3; see also Rosemarie Zagarri, "Women and Party Conflict in the Early Republic," in Pasley et al., eds., *Beyond the Founders*, 107–28.

53. Rosemarie Zagarri, "The Rights of Man and Woman," *William and Mary Quarterly*, 3d ser., LV (1998), 203–30; Kerber, *Women of the Republic*.

54. Ann Douglas, *The Feminization of American Culture* (New York: Farrar, Straus and Giroux, 1998; orig. 1977); Jane Tompkins, *Sensational Designs: The Cultural Work of American Fiction, 1790–1860* (New York: Oxford University Press, 1985); and Eva Cherniavsky, *That Pale Mother Rising: Sentimental Discourses and the Imitation of Motherhood in 19th-Century America* (Bloomington: Indiana University Press, 1995).

55. Zagarri, *Revolutionary Backlash*, 30–37, quotation from 35.

56. "Communication," *Vermont Gazette* (Bennington), November 16, 1798, 2; and Simon P. Newman, *Parades and the Politics of the Streets: Festive Culture in the Early American Republic* (Philadelphia: University of Pennsylvania Press, 1997).

57. Sean Wilentz, *Chants Democratic: New York City and the Rise of the American Working Class, 1788–1850* (New York: Oxford University Press, 2004; orig. 1984), 48 n. 51.

58. Adam Rothman, *Slave Country: American Expansion and the Origins of the Deep South* (Cambridge, MA: Harvard University Press, 2005), quotations from 103 and 123–24.

59. Klein, *Unification of a Slave State*, 211.

60. Travers, *Celebrating the Fourth*, 148–49.

61. "Resolutions Adopted on Jay's Treaty, September 28, 1975," *City Gazette* (Charleston), October 28, 1795, reprinted in Foner, ed., *Democratic-Republican Societies*, 400–409, quotations from 405 and 404.

62. Klein, *Unification*, 203–8.

63. Douglas R. Egerton, *Gabriel's Rebellion: The Virginia Slave Conspiracies of 1800 and 1802* (Chapel Hill: University of North Carolina Press, 1992), 28–39, quotation from 39.

64. Egerton, *Gabriel's Rebellion*, 66–115.

65. Gary B. Nash, *Forging Freedom: The Formation of Philadelphia's Black Community, 1720–1840* (Cambridge, MA: Harvard University Press, 1999), 144–78.

66. "From the Philadelphia *Freeman's Journal*," *Evening Post* (New York), July 12, 1804, quotations from 3; Nash, *Forging Freedom*, 176.

67. "Thursday; Second; Spruce; Walnut," *Evening Post* (NY), July 10, 1804, quotations from 3.

68. Shane White, "It Was a Proud Day": African Americans, Festivals, and Parades in the North, 1741–1834," *Journal of American History* 81, no. 1 (June, 1994): 13–50, quotations from 30.

69. McCullough, *John Adams*, 519–21, quotations from 521; Laurent DuBois, *Avengers of the New World: The Story of the Haitian Revolution* (Cambridge, MA: Harvard University Press, 2004); and Donald R. Hickey, "America's Response to the Slave Revolt in Haiti, 1791–1806," *Journal of the Early Republic* 2, no. 4 (Winter 1982): 361–79.

70. Kerber, *Federalists in Dissent*, 45–52; and Winthrop D. Jordan, *White over Black: American Attitudes Toward the Negro, 1550–1812* (New York: W. W. Norton, 1977; orig. 1968), 461–69.

71. Quotation in McCullough, *John Adams*, 480; and Kerber, *Federalists in Dissent*, 45–52.

72. Ronald P. Formisano, *Transformation of Political Culture*, 4.

73. John Lardas Modern, "Evangelical Secularism and the Measure of Leviathan," *Church History: Studies in Christianity and Culture* 77 (2008): 801–76; David Paul Nord, *Faith in Reading: Religious Publishing and the Birth of Mass Media in America* (New York: Oxford University Press, 2007); Candy Gunther Brown, *The Word in the World: Evangelical Publish-*

ing, Writing, and Reading in America, 1789–1880 (Chapel Hill: University of North Carolina Press, 2004); and Richard Rabinowitz, *The Spiritual Self In Everyday Life: The Transformation of Personal Religious Experience in Nineteenth-Century New England* (Boston: Northeastern University Press, 1989).

74. William Gribben, *The Churches Militant: The War of 1812 and American Religion* (New Haven: Yale University Press, 1973); and Charles I. Foster, *An Errand of Mercy; the Evangelical United Front, 1790–1837* (Chapel Hill: University of North Carolina Press, 1960).

75. Lyman Beecher, *A Plea for the West* (Cincinnati: Truman and Smith, 1835).

CHAPTER 3

1. John B. Boles, *The Great Revival: Beginnings of the Bible Belt* (Lexington: University Press of Kentucky, 1996; orig. 1972); Ellen Eslinger, *Citizens of Zion: The Social Origins of Camp Meeting Revivalism* (Knoxville: University of Tennessee Press, 1999); Paul Conkin, *Cane Ridge: America's Pentecost* (Madison: University of Wisconsin Press, 1990); and Bernard Weisberger, *They Gathered at the River: The Story of the Great Revivalists and Their Impact upon Religion in America* (Boston: Beacon Books, 1958).

2. Monica Nagar, *Evangelizing the South: A Social History of Church and State in Early America* (New York: Oxford University Press, 2008); Stephanie McCurry, *Masters of Small Worlds: Yeoman Households, Gender Relations, and the Political Culture of the Antebellum South Carolina Low Country* (New York: Oxford University Press, 1995); Christine Leigh Heyrman, *Southern Cross: The Beginnings of the Bible Belt* (Chapel Hill: University of North Carolina Press, 1997); Philip N. Mulder, *A Controversial Spirit: Evangelical Awakenings in the South* (New York: Oxford University Press, 2002); Rachel N. Klein, *Unification of a Slave State: The Rise of the Planter Class in the South Carolina Backcountry, 1760–1808* (Chapel Hill: University of North Carolina Press, 1990); and Cynthia Lynn Lyerly, *Methodism and the Southern Mind, 1770–1810* (New York: Oxford University Press, 1998).

3. David Hackett Fischer, *The Revolution of American Conservatism: The Federalist Party in the Era of Jeffersonian Democracy* (New York: Harper and Row, 1965); David W. Kling, *A Field of Divine Wonders: The New Divinity and Village Revivals in Northwestern Connecticut 1792–1822* (University Park: Pennsylvania State University Press, 1993); Randolph Roth, *The Democratic Dilemma: Religion, Reform, and the Social Order in the Connecticut River Valley of Vermont, 1791–1850* (Cambridge: Cambridge University Press, 1987); Clifford S. Griffin, *Their Brothers' Keepers: Moral Stewardship in the United States, 1800–1865* (New Brunswick: Rutgers University Press, 1960); Nancy F. Cott, *The Bonds of Womanhood: "Women's Sphere" in New England, 1780–1835* (New Haven: Yale University Press, 1977); Richard Douglas Shiels, "The Connecticut Clergy in the Second Great Awakening" (PhD dissertation, Boston University Graduate School, 1976); and Charles I. Foster, *An Errand of Mercy; the Evangelical United Front, 1790–1837* (Chapel Hill: University of North Carolina Press, 1960).

4. Kathryn Kish Sklar, "The Founding of Mount Holyoke College," in *Women of America: A History*, ed. Carol Ruth Berkin and Mary Beth Norton (Boston: Houghton Mifflin, 1979), 177–201, esp. 180–81.

5. Clare A. Lyons, *Sex among the Rabble: An Intimate History of Gender and Power in the Age of Revolution, Philadelphia, 1730–1830* (Chapel Hill: University of North Carolina, 2006);

and Kyle Roberts, "Urban Evangelicals: Popular Urban Belief in New York City, 1783–1845" (PhD dissertation, University of Pennsylvania, 2007); Christine Stansell, *City of Women: Sex and Class in New York, 1789–1860* (Urbana: University of Illinois Press, 1987); Terry D. Bilhartz, *Urban Religion and the Second Great Awakening Church and Society in Early National Baltimore* (Cranberry: Associated University Presses, 1986); Dee E. Andrews, *The Methodists and Revolutionary America, 1760–1800: The Shaping of an Evangelical Culture* (Princeton: Princeton University Press, 2000); and Bruce Dorsey, *Reforming Men and Women: Gender in the Antebellum City* (Ithaca: Cornell University Press, 2002).

6. Daniel Boorstin, *The Lost World of Thomas Jefferson* (New York: Beacon Press, 1960; orig. 1948).

7. Peter Kafer, *Charles Brockden Brown's Revolution and the Birth of American Gothic* (Philadelphia: University of Pennsylvania Press, 2004); and Bryan Waterman, *Republic of Intellect: The Friendly Club of New York City and the Making of American Literature* (Baltimore: John Hopkins University Press, 2007).

8. Waterman, *Republic of Intellect*, 233.

9. Fischer, *Revolution of American Conservatism*, 182–87.

10. Ron Chernow, *Alexander Hamilton* (New York: Penguin Books, 2004), 464, 582, and 728.

11. Charles Brockden Brown, *Jane Talbot* (Charleston: Bibliobazaar, 2006; orig. 1801), quotations from 110–11; Kafer, *Charles Brockden Brown's Revolution*, 85–86; and Bruce Burgett, "Masochism and Male Sentimentalism: Charles Brockden Brown's *Clara Howard*," in *Sentimental Men: Masculinity and the Politics of Affect in American Culture*, ed. Mary Chapman and Glenn Hendler (Berkeley: University of California Press, 1999), 205–25.

12. *Jane Talbot*, quotations from 57 and 58.

13. Ibid., quotations from 75–76.

14. Ibid., quotations from 100 and 232; and Cathy N. Davidson, *Revolution and the Word: The Rise of the Novel in America* (New York: Oxford University Press, 2004; orig. 1986).

15. *Jane Talbot*, quotations from 148 and 261.

16. William Dunlap, *The Life of Charles Brockden Brown together with selections from the rarest of his printed works, from his original letters, and from his manuscripts*, 2 vols. (Philadelphia: James P. Parke, 1815), quotations from 1:16, 1:57, and 1:69–72.

17. Dunlap, *Life of Charles Brockden Brown*, quotation from 2:68.

18. Brown, *Jane Talbot*, quotation from 67.

19. Dunlap, *Life of Charles Brockden Brown*, 2:67–68; Charles Brockden Brown, "To the Rev. Dr. J. B. Linn, Philadelphia, July 1804," reprinted in Dunlap, *Life of Charles Brockden Brown*, 2:110–12; Joseph Priestley, *A Letter to the Reverend John Blair Linn, A.M., A Pastor of the First Presbyterian Congregation in the City of Philadelphia in Defence of the Pamphlet, Entitled, Socrates and Jesus Compared by Joseph Priestley* (Northumberland, PA: Andrew Kennedy, 1803); and Joseph Priestley, *A Second Letter to the Revd. John Blair Linn, D.D., Pastor of the First Presbyterian Congregation in the City of Philadelphia, a Reply to his Defence of the Doctrines of the Divinity of Christ and Atonement by Joseph Priestley* (Northumberland, PA: Andrew Kennedy, 1803), quotation from 4–5.

20. Charles Brockden Brown, *An Address to the Congress of the United States, on the Utility and Justice of Restrictions upon Foreign Commerce. With Reflections on Foreign Trade in*

General, and the Future Prospects of America (Philadelphia: C. and A. Conrad and Co., 1809), quotation from vi.

21. Brown, *An Address to the Congress,* quotation from 87.

22. Ibid., quotations from v and vii.

23. Charles Brockden Brown, *The British Treaty* (Philadelphia: n.p., 1807; signed in London, December 1806, by Pinkney and Monroe, but refused ratification by President Jefferson, without consultation of the Senate), quotations from 6.

24. Ibid., quotations from 14 and 15.

25. Ibid., quotations from 10–12.

26. Ibid., quotation from 46.

27. Ibid., quotations from 91 and 261.

28. Donald G. Mathews, "The Second Great Awakening as an Organizing Process, 1780–1830: An Hypothesis," *American Quarterly* 21, no. 1 (Spring 1969): 23–43; and Roger Finke and Rodney Stark, "How the Upstart Sects Won America: 1776–1850," *Journal for the Scientific Study of Religion* 28, no. 1 (March 1989): 27–44.

29. *A Plan for establishing a chaplain, of the Presbyterian denomination, in the jail, hospital, and bettering-house, of the city of Philadelphia with, considerations in favour of such an establishment and, a short address to those to whom the whole is offered* (Philadelphia: R. Aitken, 1802).

30. Carroll D. Wright, *Historical Review of Wages and Prices, 1752–1860* (Boston: Wright and Potter, 1885), 63–65.

31. *A Plan for establishing a chaplain,* quotations from 4–6.

32. *Extracts from the Minutes of the General Assembly of the Presbyterian Church, in the United States of America, A.D. 1802* (Philadelphia: R. Aitken, 1802), 12–21.

33. *A Plan for establishing a chaplain,* quotations from 14 and 9.

34. Lyons, *Sex Among the Rabble,* 323–33, 359; map 1, 282–83.

35. Ibid., 328–29; table 22, 341; map 2, 346–47.

36. James Tagg, *Benjamin Franklin Bache and the Philadelphia Aurora* (Philadelphia: University of Pennsylvania Press, 1991); Andrew Shankman, *Crucible of American Democracy: The Struggle to Fuse Egalitarianism and Capitalism in Jeffersonian Pennsylvania* (Lawrence: University of Kansas Press, 2004); and J. Clark Archer, Stephen J. Lavin, Kenneth C. Martis, and Fred M. Shelley, *Historical Atlas of U.S. Presidential Elections 1788–2004* (Washington, DC: CQ Press, 2006), 39–42 and map 5.

37. "The Salutatory Oration delivered at the late Commencement of the Young Ladies' Academy of Philadelphia," *Aurora General Advertiser* (Philadelphia), January 1, 1795, quotations from 3.

38. *Salem Gazette,* August 25, 1798, quoted in Anson Ely Morse, "The Federalist Party in Massachusetts to the Year 1800" (PhD dissertation, Princeton University, 1909), 138.

39. Ernest Sandeen, *The Roots of Fundamentalism* (Chicago: University of Chicago Press, 1970).

40. Timothy Dwight, *The duty of Americans, at the present crisis, illustrated in a discourse, preached on the fourth of July, 1798* (New Haven: Thomas Green, 1798), quotations from 19–21; and Colin Wells advances a more benign interpretation of Dwight in *The Devil and Doctor*

Dwight: Satire and Theology in the Early American Republic (Chapel Hill: University of North Carolina Press, 2002).

41. Timothy Dwight, *A discourse on some events of the last century, delivered in the Brick Church in New Haven, on Wednesday, January 7, 1801* (New Haven: Ezra Read, 1801), quotations from 45; see also Timothy Dwight, *The Triumph of Infidelity, a poem* (Hartford: n.p., 1788), 16.

42. Edward D. Griffith, "An Account of a Revival of Religion in New Hartford, Conn, in the years 1798 and 1799," in *New England Revivals, as they Existed at the Close of the Eighteenth, and Beginning of the Nineteenth Centuries. Compiled Principally from Narratives First Published in the Connecticut Evangelical Magazine,* ed. Bennet Tyler (Boston: Sabbath School Society, 1846), quotations from 70–72 and 81; see also David W. Kling, *A Field of Divine Wonders: The New Divinity and Village Revivals in Northwestern Connecticut 1792–1822* (University Park: University of Pennsylvania Press, 1993).

43. Reverend Ammi R. Robbins, "An Account of a Revival of Religion in Norfolk, Conn., in the year 1799," in Tyler, ed., *New England Revivals,* quotations from 181 and 184–85.

44. Tyler, ed., *New England Revivals,* 85, 187, 155, 249, and 285.

45. Martha Tomhave Blauvelt, *The Work of the Heart: Young Women and Emotion, 1780–1830* (Charlottesville: University of Virginia Press, 2007); Anne M. Boylan, *The Origins of Women's Activism: New York and Boston, 1798–1840* (Chapel Hill: University of North Carolina Press, 2002); and Julia A. Stern, *The Plight of Feeling: Sympathy and Dissent in the Early American Novel* (Chicago: University of Chicago Press, 1997).

46. Giles H. Cowles, "An Account of a Revival of Religion in Bristol, Conn., in the year 1799," in Tyler, ed., *New England Revivals,* quotations from 205–7.

47. *Acts and Proceedings of the General Assembly of the Presbyterian Church in the United States of America in the year 1801* (Philadelphia: R. Aitken, 1801), quotation from 24.

48. *Extracts from the Minutes of the General Assembly of the Presbyterian Church, in the United States of America, A.D. 1802* (Philadelphia: R. Aitken, 1802), quotation from 6; Philip N. Mulder, *A Controversial Spirit: Evangelical Awakenings in the South* (New York: Oxford University Press, 2001), 147; and Isaac Watts, *The Psalms of David, Imitated in the Language of the New Testament, and Applied to the Christian Use and Worship,* ed. Timothy Dwight (New Haven: Hudson and Goodwin, 1803), quotations from 3 and 264.

49. James B. Finley, *Sketches of Western Methodism: Biographical, Historical, and Miscellaneous. Illustrative of Pioneer Life,* ed. W. P. Strickland (Cincinnati: R. P. Thompson, 1854), quotations from 205–6.

50. *Memorials of the Introduction of Methodism into the Eastern States: Comprising Biographical Notices of its Early Preachers, Sketches of its First Churches, and Reminiscences of its Early Struggles and Successes,* ed. A. Stevens (Boston: Charles H. Pierce, 1848), quotations from 426–27.

51. Elizabeth Drinker, "November 21, 1805," in *The Diary of Elizabeth Drinker: the Life Cycle of an Eighteenth-Century Woman,* ed. Elaine Crane (Boston: Northeastern University Press, 1994), quotations from 276.

52. Elisa Ann Everson, "'A Little Labour of Love': The Extraordinary Career of Dorothy Ripley, Female Evangelist in Early America" (PhD dissertation, Georgia State University, 2007), quotation from 215.

53. James McGready, "On the Divine Authority of the Christian Religion," "The Lord Jesus Christ a Mighty Conqueror," and "The Meeting of Christ and His Disciples," all reprinted in *The Posthumous Works of the Reverend and Pious James M'Gready, Late Minister of the Gospel, in Henderson, Kentucky*, ed. James Smith (Nashville: Lowry and Smith, 1833), quotations from 7, 43, 205–6.

54. James McGready, A Short Narrative of the Revival of Religion in Logan County, in the State of Kentucky, and the Adjacent Settlements in the State of Tennessee, from May 1797, until September 1800," in *New York Missionary Magazine* 4 (1803), quotation from 155; and James McGready, "Narrative of the Commencement and Progress of the Revival of 1800" (1801), in *Posthumous Works*, ix–xvi, quotations from xii–xiv; see also Boles, *Great Revival*, 47–59.

55. William H. Milburn, *Pioneers, Preachers and People of the Mississippi Valley* (New York: Derby and Jackson, 1860), quotations from 357.

56. Ibid., quotations from 359–60.

57. John G. Jones, *A Complete History of Methodism As Connected with the Mississippi Conference of the Methodist Episcopal Church, South* (Nashville: Southern Methodist Publishing House, 1887), 379–85, quotation from 385.

58. Bilhartz, "The Baltimore Awakening in Perspective," in Bilhartz, *Urban Religion and the Second Great Awakening*, 134–45.

59. Eslinger, *Citizens of Zion*, quotation from 231.

60. William E. Arnold, *A History of Methodism in Kentucky* (Louisville: Herald Place, 1935), quotations from 190–91.

61. James B. Finley, *Autobiography of Rev. James B. Finley; or, Pioneer Life in the West*, ed. W. P. Strickland (Cincinnati: R. P. Thompson, 1855), quotations from 240.

62. Ibid., 173–82, quotations from 173–4.

63. Boles, *Great Revival*, 162–63, quotation from 153.

64. Leigh Eric Schmidt, *Holy Fairs: Scottish Communions ad American Revivals in the Early Modern Period* (Princeton: Princeton University Press, 1989); Wigger, *American Saint: Francis Asbury and the Methodists* (New York: Oxford University Press, 2009), 313–28; and Andrews, *Methodists and Revolutionary America*, 221–39.

65. John H. Wigger, *Taking Heaven by Storm: Methodism and the Rise of Popular Christianity in America* (Urbana: University of Illinois Press, 2001; orig. 1998), 3–4.

66. Finley, *Sketches of Western Methodism*, quotation from 114.

67. See Boles, *Great Revival*; and David Hempton, *Methodism: Empire of the Spirit* (New Haven: Yale University Press, 2005).

68. Andrews, *Methodists and Revolutionary America*, 168–75 and 112–16; see also Wigger, *American Saint*; and Hempton, *Methodism: Empire of the Spirit*.

69. *Jane Talbot*, quotation from 196.

70. Andrews, *Methodists and Revolutionary America*, quotation from 118.

71. *Jane Talbot*, 229.

72. Richard S. Newman, *Freedom's Prophet: Bishop Richard Allen, the AME Church, and the Black Founding Fathers* (New York: New York University Press, 2008), 27–70, quotation from 70; see also Gary B. Nash, *Forging Freedom: The Formation of Philadelphia's Black Com-*

munity, 1720–1840 (Cambridge, MA: Harvard University Press, 1988); and Albert J. Raboteau, *A Fire in the Bones: Reflections on African American Religious History* (New York: 1999), 81–102.

73. Newman, *Freedom's Prophet*, 130; and Andrews, *Methodists and Revolutionary America*, 149–50, quotation from 149.

74. Richard Allen, ed., *A Collection of hymns and spiritual songs. From various authors* (Philadelphia: T. L. Plowman, 1801), quotation from 3.

75. John Saillant, *Black Puritan, Black Republican: The Life and Thought of Lemuel Haynes, 1753–1833* (New York: Oxford University Press, 2003).

76. Lemuel Haynes, *The Nature and Importance of True Republicanism: with a Few Suggestions, Favorable to Independence. A discourse, Delivered at Rutland, (Vermont,) the Fourth of July 1801.—It being the 25th Anniversary of American Independence* (Rutland: William Fay, 1801), quotations from 6–7; Lemuel Haynes, *Universal Salvation, A Very Ancient Doctrine: With Some Account of the Life and Character of its Author* (New Haven: Oliver Steele and Co., 1806), quotation from 8; and Lemuel Haynes, *The Important Concerns of Ministers, and the People of their Charge, at the Day of Judgment. Illustrated in a Sermon, Delivered at Rutland, Orange Society; August 22d, 1797, at the Interment of the Rev. Abraham Carpenter, their Worthy Pastor* (Rutland: Josiah Fay, 1798), quotations from 7–8.

77. Oscar F. Safford, *Hosea Ballou: A Marvellous Life-Story* (Boston: Universalist Publishing House, 1889), 85–95, quotation from 92.

78. Haynes, *Universal Salvation*, quotations from 3–5 and 8.

79. Ibid.

80. Hosea Ballou, *An Epistle to the Rev. Lemuel Haynes Containing a Brief Reply to his Sermon . . . Designed to Refute the Doctrine of Universal Salvation by Hosea Ballou* (Randolph, VT: n.p., 1806), quotation from 1.

81. Saillant, *Black Puritan*, quotations from 167.

82. Eslinger, *Citizens of Zion*, 175–80; James D. Essig, *American Evangelicals Against Slavery, 1770–1808* (Philadelphia: Temple University Press, 1982); and Charles F. Irons, *The Origins of Proslavery Christianity: White and Black Evangelicals in Colonial and Antebellum Virginia* (Chapel Hill: University of North Carolina Press, 2008); Christine Leigh Hyerman, *Southern Cross: The Beginnings of the Bible Belt* (Chapel Hill: University of North Carolina Press, 1997), 206–52; Andrews, *Methodists and Revolutionary America*, 123–54; Donald G. Mathews, *Slavery and Methodism: A Chapter in American Morality* (Princeton: Princeton University Press, 1965); Winthrop Jordan, *White over Black: American Attitudes toward the Negro, 1550–1812* (Baltimore: Pelican Books, 1969), 281–93; David Benedict, *A General History of the Baptist Denomination in America and Other Parts of the World*, vol. 2 (Boston: Manning and Loring, 1813); Asa E. Martin, *The Antislavery Movement in Kentucky Prior to 1850* (Louisville: Standard Printing, 1918); and William E. Arnold, *A History of Methodism in Kentucky* (Louisville: Herald Place, 1935), 266 and 315.

83. Sylvia R. Frey and Betty Wood, *Come Shouting to Zion: African American Protestantism in the American South and British Caribbean to 1830* (Chapel Hill: University of North Carolina Press, 1998); James T. Campbell, *Songs of Zion: The African Methodist Episcopal Church in the United States and South Africa* (Chapel Hill: University of North Carolina Press, 1998);

and Ann Taves, *Fits, Trances, and Visions: Experiencing Religion and Explaining Experience from Wesley to James* (Princeton: Princeton University Press,1999), 76–117.

84. McCurry, *Masters of Small Worlds*; Lyerly, *Methodism and the Southern Mind*; Monica Najar, *Evangelizing the South: A Social History of Church and State in Early America* (New York: Oxford University Press, 2008); and Klein, *Unification of a Slave State*; Adam Rothman, *Slave Country: American Expansionism and the Origins of the Deep South* (Cambridge, MA: Harvard University Press, 2005).

85. Jones, *A Complete History of Methodism*, quotations from 106 and 107.

86. Ibid., quotations from 199.

87. Henry Holcome, *The First Fruits in a Series of Letters* (Philadelphia: Ann Cochran, 1813), quotations from 63–65; see also David Benedict, *A General History of the Baptist Denomination in America and Other Parts of the World*, 2 vols. (Boston: Manning and Loring, 1813), 2:189–92; and *History of the Baptist Denomination in Georgia: With Biographical Compendium and Portrait Gallery of Baptist Ministers and Other Georgia Baptists* (Atlanta: Jas. P. Harrison, 1881), 48.

88. Charles William Janson, *The Stranger in America* (New York: Press of the Pioneers, 1935; orig. 1807), quotations from 101.

89. Ibid., quotations from 363, 365–66, and 383–84.

90. Lemuel Burkitt and Jesse Read, *A Concise History of the Kehukee Baptist Association from its Original Rise to the Present Time* (Halifax, NC: n.p., 1803), quotations from xviii–xix, xxv, 70, and 54.

91. Ibid., quotations from 140 and 144–45.

92. Ibid., quotations from 155 and 146.

CHAPTER 4

1. Sarah Knott, *Sensibility and the American Revolution* (Chapel Hill: University of North Carolina Press, 2009).

2. Alexander McLeod, *Messiah, governor of the nations of the earth, a discourse* (New York: T. and J. Swords, 1803), quotation from 24.

3. Elijah Parish, *A sermon, preached before the Massachusetts Missionary Society at their annual meeting, in Boston, May 26, 1807* (Northampton: E. W. Allen, 1807), quotations from 3–7.

4. For a different interpretation of the relationship between religion and democracy in the early nineteenth century, see Nathan O. Hatch, *The Democratization of American Christianity* (New Haven: Yale University Press, 1989).

5. Aurelius Augustinus, *Concerning the City of God against the Pagans*, trans. Henry Bettenson (Hammondsworth: Penguin Books, 1972; orig. 1467 in Latin), quotation from 842; Carlos Eire, *War Against the Idols: The Reformation of Worship from Erasmus to Calvin* (Cambridge: Cambridge University Press, 1986); Ruth M. Bloch, *Visionary Republic: Millennial Themes in American Thought, 1756–1800* (Cambridge: Cambridge University Press, 1985); and Stephen Marini, *Radical Sects of Revolutionary New England* (Cambridge, MA: Harvard University Press, 1982).

6. Roger Finke and Rodney Stark, *The Churching of America, 1790–1990: Winners and Losers in our Religious Economy* (New Brunswick: Rutgers University Press, 1992), 54–108; Roger Finke and Rodney Stark, "American Religion in 1776: A Statistical Portrait," *Sociological Analysis* 49, no. 1 (Spring 1988): 39–51; Edwin Scott Gaustad and Philip L. Barlow, *New Historical Atlas of Religion in America* (New York: Oxford University Press, 2001), 1–164; Dee Andrews, *The Methodists and Revolutionary America, 1760–1800* (Princeton: Princeton University Press, 2000), 4 and 259–61; and Christine Leigh Heyrman, *Southern Cross: The Beginnings of the Bible Belt* (Chapel Hill: University of North Carolina Press, 1997), 261–66.

7. Terry D. Bilhartz, *Urban Religion and the Second Great Awakening: Church and Society in Early National Baltimore* (Cranberry: Associated University Presses, 1986), 20.

8. Jeffry H. Morrison, *John Witherspoon and the Founding of the American Republic* (Notre Dame: University of Notre Dame Press, 2005), quotation from Witherspoon to John Adams, 34.

9. William Bentley, *The Diary of William Bentley, D.D., Pastor of the East Church, Salem, Massachusetts*, 4 vols. (Glouster, MA: Peter Smith, 1907; orig. 1907), 1:265–269, 1:276, 1:409, 1:432, and 1:425; and J. Rixley Ruffin, *A Paradise of Reason: William Bentley and Enlightenment Christianity in the Early Republic* (New York: Oxford University Press, 2008), 164.

10. *A platform of church discipline gathered out of the Word of God: and agreed upon by the elders: and messengers of the churches assembled in the Synod at Cambridge in New England To be presented at the churches and Generall Court for their consideration and acceptance, in the Lord* (Cambridge: Samuel Green, 1649), quotation from 1; see also Norman Pettit, *The Heart Prepared: Grace and Conversion in Puritan Spiritual Life* (Middletown: Wesleyan University Press, 1989; orig. 1966); H. Brooks Holifield, *The Covenant Sealed: The Development of Puritan Sacramental Theology in Old and New England, 1570–1750* (New Haven: Yale University Press, 1974); and Perry Miller, "The Marrow of Puritan Divinity," in Perry Miller, *Errand into the Wilderness* (Cambridge, MA: Harvard University Press, 1956), 48–98.

11. *A platform of church discipline*, quotations from 28.

12. Robert G. Pope, *Half-Way Covenant: Church Membership in Puritan New England* (Princeton: Princeton University Press, 1969).

13. Patricia U. Bonomi, *Under the Cope of Heaven: Religion, Society, and Politics in Colonial America*, rev. ed. (New York: Oxford University Press, 2003; orig. 1986), 61–72; and David D. Hall, *The Faithful Shepherd: A History of New England Ministry in the Seventeenth Century* (Chapel Hill: University of North Carolina Press, 1972).

14. Bloch, *Visionary Republic*, quotation from 80; and Harry S. Stout, *The New England Soul: Preaching and Religious Culture in Colonial New England* (New York: Oxford University Press, 1986), quotations from 307–8.

15. Joseph Haroutunian, *From Piety to Moralism: The Passing of the New England Theology* (New York: Henry Holt, 1932); and E. Brooks Holifield, *Theology in America: Christian Thought from the Age of the Puritans to the Civil War* (New Haven: Yale University Press, 2003).

16. Joseph Lyman, *The two olive trees, or, Zerubbabel and Joshua religion, the leading qualification of civil rulers and Christian ministers illustrated in a sermon, preached at Hatfield, Nov. 4, 1804, being the day preceding the choice of electors in Massachusetts also, God, the*

sure fundations [sic] *of confidence and joy a Thanksgiving sermon, delivered Nov. 29, 1804* (Northampton: William Butler, 1804), quotations from 12 and 13.

17. Edward A. Kendall, *Travels through the northern parts of the United States in the years 1807 and 1808* (New York: I. Riley, 1809), 4–7, quotation from 7.

18. Timothy Dwight, *A sermon preached at the opening of the Theological Institution in Andover; and at the ordination of Rev. Eliphalet Pearson, LL.D., September 28th, 1808* (Boston: McFarland, Mallory and Company, 1808), quotations from 8 and 17.

19. Dwight, *A sermon . . . at . . . Andover*, quotations from 15 and 16.

20. Ibid., quotations from 8–9 and 14.

21. Ibid., quotations from 26–27 and 32.

22. Ibid., quotation from 8; see also Holifield, *Theology in America*, 159–96; Mark A. Noll, *America's God: From Jonathan Edwards to Abraham Lincoln* (New York: Oxford University Press, 2002), 53–208; and Morrison, *John Witherspoon*, 2, 5, 42.

23. McLeod, *Messiah, Governor*, quotations from 33 and 7.

24. Jonathan Edwards, *A Treatise Concerning Religious Affections*, vol. 2, in *The Works of Jonathan Edwards*, ed. John E. Smith (New Haven: Yale University Press, 1959; orig. 1746); and Jonathan Edwards, *The Nature of True Virtue* (Ann Arbor: University of Michigan Press, 1960; orig. 1765).

25. Edmund S. Morgan, *Inventing the People: The Rise of Popular Sovereignty in England and America* (New York: W. W. Norton, 1988).

26. Morrison, *John Witherspoon*, 110–11.

27. *Constitution of the Presbyterian Church*, quotations from 137 and 35; for discussion of state laws against blasphemy, see David Sehat, *The Myth of American Religious Freedom* (New York: Oxford University Press, 2011), 1–7, 60–68, 175–76, and 217.

28. *Constitution of the Presbyterian Church*, quotation from 146.

29. Ibid., 139, 44, 105, quotation from 139.

30. Beriah Hotchin, *The doctrine of election considered and explained, in a sermon, delivered before the presbytery at New Lebanon, June 3, MDCCCI, and occasionally in different congregations elsewhere* (Hudson, NY: Ashbel Stoddard, 1801), quotations from 4–5.

31. Alexander McLeod, *The constitution, character, and duties of the Gospel ministry a sermon, preached at the ordination of the Rev. Gilbert McMaster, in the First Presbyterian Church, Duanesburgh* (New York: J. Seymour, 1808), quotations from 24 and 48.

32. Sarah Newman Connell Ayer, *Diary of Sarah Ayer, February, 1807, in Diary of Sarah Connell Ayer Andover and Newburyport, Massachusetts, Concord and Bow, New Hampshire, Portland and Eastport, Maine* (Portland, ME: LaFavor-Tower Co., 1910), quotations from 5, 26, and 30.

33. Ibid., quotations from 32 and 36.

34. Ibid., quotation from 53.

35. Ibid., quotation from 48.

36. Ibid., quotation from 78; for discussion of Sullivan, see Ronald P. Formisano, *The Transformation of Political Culture: Massachusetts Parties, 1790s–1840s* (New York: Oxford University Press, 1983), 68–72.

37. Ibid., quotation from 69 and 146.

38. William Bentley, *The Diary of William Bentley, D.D., Pastor of the East Church, Salem, Massachusetts,* 4 vols. (Gloucester: Peter Smith, 1962; orig. 1907), quotations from 1:252 and 1:409.

39. James O'Kelly, *The author's apology for protesting against the Methodist Episcopal Government* (1798), in *The Methodist Experience in America: A Sourcebook,* 2 vols., ed. Russell E. Richey, Kenneth E. Rowe, and Jean Miller Schmidt (Nashville: Abingdon Press, 2000), quotations from 2:113–5.

40. Thomas Coke and Francis Asbury, *The Doctrines and Disciplines of the Methodist Episcopal Church, in America* (Philadelphia: Henry Tuckniss, 1798), quotation from 42.

41. Ibid.

42. James Wilson, *Apostolic church government displayed; and the government and system of the Methodist Episcopal Church investigated. To which is added, an appendix, containing a concise dissertation on the nature and duration of the apostolic personal authority and office* (Providence: Bennet Wheeler, 1798), quotations from iv, vi, and 193.

43. Coke and Asbury, *Doctrines and Disciplines,* 161–63, quotations from 163 and 161.

44. Ibid., quotations from 86, 83, and 87.

45. William H. Milburn, *Pioneers, Preachers and People of the Mississippi Valley* (New York: Derby and Jackson, 1860), quotations from 367–69.

46. William Winans, "Autobiography of William Winans" (1850), typescript from Milsaps-Wilson Library, Milsaps College, quotations from 20.

47. James McGready, "The Meeting of Christ and his Disciples," 2:220–26, and "The Young Invited to Come to Christ," 2:262–78, both in *The Posthumous Works of the Reverend and Pious James M'Gready, Late Minister of the Gospel, in Henderson, Kentucky,* ed. James Smith (Nashville: Lowry and Smith, 1833), quotations from 2:224 and 2:275; and Leigh Eric Schmidt, *Holy Fairs: Scottish Communions and American Revivals in the Early Modern Period* (Princeton: Princeton University Press, 1989), 60–66.

48. John Griffing Jones, *A complete history of Methodism as connected with the Mississippi Conference of the Methodist Episcopal Church, South, 1799–1817,* 2 vols. (Nashville: Southern Methodist Publishing House, 1887), quotations from 1:66 and 1:41.

49. Christine Leigh Heyrman, *Southern Cross: The Beginnings of the Bible Belt* (Chapel Hill: University of North Carolina Press, 1997), 161–205, quotations from 169.

50. Sarah Jones, *Devout Letters: Or, Letters Spiritual and Friendly. Written by Mrs. Sarah Jones,* ed. by Jeremiah Minter (Alexandria: Jeremiah Minter, 1804), quotations from 74; see also Cynthia Lynn Lyerly, *Methodism and the Southern Mind, 1770–1810* (New York: Oxford University Press, 1998), 33.

51. Andrew Fuller, *The practical uses of Christian baptism a circular letter from the ministers and messengers of the several Baptist churches of the Northamptonshire Association, assembled at Northampton, June 15, 16, 1802, to the churches in their connexion composed by Andrew Fuller* (Burlington and Philadelphia: Stephen C. Ustnick and Thomas Ustnick, 1802), quotation from 6.

52. Statement attributed to John Dickins in O'Kelly, *Author's Apology,* quotation from 1:34.

53. *A summary of church discipline, shewing the qualifications and duties, of the officers and members, of a Gospel-church* (Charleston: Baptist-Association, 1783), quotation from 2.

54. Fuller, *Practical Uses*, quotation from 11.

55. David Benedict, *A general history of the Baptist denomination in America and other parts of the world* (Boston: Manning and Loring, 1813), quotations from 109 and 110.

56. Ibid., quotations from 91 and 159.

57. Henry Holcombe, *The First Fruits in a Series of Letters* (Philadelphia: Ann Cochran, 1812), quotation from 92.

58. William Warren Sweet, "The Churches as Moral Courts of the Frontier," *Church History* 2, no. 1 (March 1933), 3–21, esp. 11–12; see also William Warren Sweet, ed., *Religion on the American Frontier*, vol. 1, *The Baptists 1783–1830, A Collection of Source Material* (New York: Cooper Square Publishers, 1964; orig. 1931); Monica Najar, *Evangelizing the South: A Social History of Church and State in Early America* (New York: Oxford University Press, 2008); and Mark Dementi Kaplanoff, "Evangelizing the South: A Social History of Church and State in Early America" (PhD dissertation, University of Cambridge, 1979), 76–80.

59. Lemuel Read and Jesse Burkitt, *A concise history of the Kehukee Baptist Association from its original rise to the present time* (Halifax, NC: n.p., 1803), 52–57; Robert B. Semple, *A history of the rise and progress of the Baptists in Virginia* (Richmond: John Lynth, 1810), 97; see also *A summary of church discipline*, 41–47.

60. Semple, *Baptists in Virginia*, quotation from 79; see also *A History of Kentucky Baptists, from 1769 to 1885, Including More than 800 Biographical Sketches*, 2 vols. (Lafayette: Church History Research and Archives, 1976; orig. 1886), 1:183.

61. "August 10–12, 1805 Elkhorn Baptist Association KY," in Sweet, ed., *Religion on the American Frontier . . . The Baptists*, quotation from 508.

62. Elias Smith, *The day of judgment revealed by the king of glory and his servants collected from the records of his kingdom* (Exeter, NH: Henry Ranlet, 1805), quotation from 5.

63. Elias Smith, *A Letter to Mr. Daniel Humphreys, Sandemanian Teacher* (Portsmouth, NH: Gazette Office, 1804), quotation from 3.

64. *A summary of church discipline*, quotation from 8.

65. Benedict, *A general history*, quotations from 107–8, 37, and 39.

66. Stephanie McCurry, *Masters of Small Worlds: Yeoman Households, Gender Relations, and the Political Culture of the Antebellum South Carolina Low Country* (New York: Oxford University Press, 1995), 141–42, quotations from 141.

67. Curtis D. Johnson, *Islands of Holiness: Rural Religion in Upstate New York, 1790–1860* (Ithaca: Cornell University Press, 1989), 10.

68. Burkitt and Read, *A Concise History*, quotation from vii–viii; and Heyrman, *Southern Cross*, 161–205.

69. Ira Berlin, *Slaves without Masters: The Free Negroes in the Antebellum South* (New York: Random House, 1974), 66–68; and Heyrman, *Southern Cross*, 217–25.

70. Bloch, *Visionary Republic*, 185.

71. Elias Smith, *A Sermon on Baptism, Preached at Nortwood [i.e., Northwood], July 12, 1802, Delivered at the Baptizing of Mrs. Stokes* (Portsmouth, NH: N. S. and W. Peirce, 1802), quotations from 20 and 22; and Fuller, *Practical Uses*, quotations from 10 and 12.

72. Holcombe, *First Fruits*, quotation from 55; and Letter from Reverend David Lilly, August 23, 1802, in Benedict, *A general history*, 165–66, quotations from 166.

73. Burkitt and Read, *A Concise History*, quotations from 147 and 149.

74. Charles W. Janson, *The Stranger in America* (New York: Press of the Pioneers, 1935; orig. 1807), quotations from 105–7.

75. Joseph Washburn, "An Account of a Revival of Religion in Farmington, Conn., in the year 1799," in *New England Revivals, as They Existed at the Close of the Eighteenth, and the Beginning of the Nineteenth Centuries*, ed. Bennet Tyler (Wheaton: Richard Owen Roberts, 1980; orig. 1846), quotations from 172 and 176.

76. James Hall, *A narrative of a most extraordinary work of religion in North Carolina by the Rev. James Hall. Also a collection of interesting letters from the Rev. James M'Corkle. To which is added, the agreeable intelligence of a revival in South Carolina. Annexed to the above is an astonishing instance of the power of conscience: The folly of atheism and, A poem written by a young lady of Philadelphia, after the death of her father* (Philadelphia: William W. Woodward, 1802), quotation from 7.

77. *The Appearance of the Devil* (United States, 1801), quotations from 3–4 (not numbered).

78. Reverend Woodard, *The atheist confuted with an essay on eternity and advantageous thoughts on the duty of man* (Philadelphia: Thomas T. Stiles, 1806), quotations from 50–51.

79. Thomas Allen, *Submission to the will of God. A discourse, occasioned by the death of Thomas Allen, Jun., Esq., one of the representatives of this town in the General Court of this commonwealth, who departed this life at Boston, on Saturday, the 22d day of March, 1806, in the 38th year of his age; delivered at Pittsfield, March 30, 1806* (Pittsfield: Phineas Allen, 1806), quotations from 5, 7, and 8.

80. William Warren Sweet, *Religion on the American Frontier, 1783–1840*, vol. 2, in Sweet, ed., *The Presbyterians* (Chicago: University of Chicago Press, 1936), 697; and Ian R. Terrell, "Drink and Temperance in the Antebellum South: An Overview and Interpretation," *Journal of Southern History* 48, no. 4 (November 1982): 486.

CHAPTER 5

1. Thomas Jefferson to Spencer Roane, September 6, 1819, in *The Writings of Thomas Jefferson*, ed. Andrew Lipscomb and Albert Ellery Bergh, 20 vols. (Washington DC: 1903–4), 15:212; Ronald Formisano, "The Concept of Political Culture," *Journal of Interdisciplinary Culture* 31, no. 3 (Winter 2001): 393–426; Ronald Formisano, "Deferential-Participant Politics: The Early Republic's Political Culture, 1789–1840," *The American Political Science Review* 68, no. 2 (June 1974): 473–87; and Jeffrey Pasley, "1800 as a Revolution in Political Culture: Newspapers, Celebrations, Voting, and Democratization in the Early Republic," in *The Revolution of 1800: Democracy, Race, and the New Republic*, ed. James Horn, Jan Ellen Lewis, and Peter S. Onuf (Charlottesville: University of Virginia Press, 2002), 121–52; see also Sean Wilentz, *Chants Democratic: New York City and the Rise of the American Working Class, 1788–1850* (New York: Oxford University Press, 1984); Alan Taylor, *William Cooper's Town: Power and Persuasion on the Frontier of the Early American Republic* (New York: Alfred A. Knopf, 1995); Jeffrey L. Pasley, *The Tyranny of Printers: Newspaper Politics in the Early American Republic* (Charlottesville: University of Virginia, 2001); and Sean Wilentz, *The Rise of American Democracy: Jefferson to Lincoln* (New York: W. W. Norton, 2005).

2. Thomas Jefferson, "First Inaugural Address In the Washington, D.C.," Wednesday, March 4, 1801, http://www.bartleby.com/124/pres16.html, last accessed June 23, 2011.

3. William G. McLoughlin, *Isaac Backus and the American Pietist Tradition* (Boston: Little, Brown and Co., 1967), quotations from 229; and William G. McLoughlin, *New England Dissent 1630–1883: The Baptists and the Separation of Church and State*, 2 vols. (Cambridge, MA: Harvard University Press, 1971), 1:591–684, 2:785–766; see also Stephen A. Marini, *Radical Sects of Revolutionary New England* (Cambridge, MA: Harvard University Press, 1982); and Thomas S. Kidd, *God of Liberty: A Religious History of the American Revolution* (New York: Basic Books, 2010).

4. John Leland, *The history of Jack Nips. Containing arguments in opposition to infant-baptism—to civil authority in religious affairs—to preaching by rule, or, writing sermons—and to the proceedings of societies of the standing order, in a general taxation, &c.* (Exeter, NH: Stearns and Winslow, 1794), quotations from 10–11.

5. James Madison, "To the Honorable the General Assembly of the Commonwealth of Virginia A Memorial and Remonstrance," ca. June 20, 1785, in *The Papers of James Madison*, vol. 8, *10 March 1784–28 March 1786*, ed. Robert A. Rutland and William M. E. Rachal (Chicago: University of Chicago Press, 1973), quotation from 8:303; and "Editorial Note," in *Papers of James Madison*, 8:287–98, quotations from 8:298; see also Eric Slauter, *The State as a Work of Art: The Cultural Origins of the Constitution* (Chicago: University of Chicago Press, 2009), 276.

6. McLoughlin, *Isaac Backus*, quotation from 143.

7. Sumner B. Twiss, "Roger Williams and Freedom of Conscience and Religion as a Natural Right," Florida State University working paper cited with the author's permission; John Milton, *The Tenure of Kings and Magistrates: A Defence of the People of England* (1649), in John Milton, *Political Writings*, ed. Martin Dzelzinis, trans. Claire Gruzelier (Cambridge: Cambridge University Press, 1991); Jerome Huyler, *Locke in America: The Moral Philosophy of the Founding Era* (Lawrence: University of Kansas Press, 1995); George F. Sensabaugh, *Milton in Early America* (Princeton: Princeton University Press, 1964), 135–45; and John Witte, Jr., *The Reformation of Rights: Law, Religion, and Human Rights in Early Modern Calvinism* (London: Cambridge University Press, 2007).

8. John Locke, "An Essay on Toleration" (1667), in John Locke, *Political Essays*, ed. Mark Goldie (Cambridge: Cambridge University Press, 1997), quotations from 142, 136 and 138; John Locke, "Religion" (1681), in Locke, *Political Essays*, quotations from 278–79; and Roger Williams, *The Blood Tenent Yet More Bloody*, in *Roger Williams: His Contribution to the American Tradition*, ed. Perry Miller (New York: Atheneum, 1970), quotations from 185 and 191; see also Roger Williams, *The Bloody Tenent, of Persecution* (London, 1644).

9. Jefferson, *Notes*, quotation from 159.

10. Locke, "Essay on Toleration," quotations from 139.

11. Thomas Jefferson, *Notes on the State of Virginia*, ed. William Peden (New York: Norton Library, 1972; orig. 1787), quotation from 159; and John Leland, *Politics sermonized exhibited in Ashfield on July 4, 1806* (Springfield: Andrew Wright, 1806), quotation from 8.

12. John Leland, *The rights of conscience inalienable, and therefore religious opinions not cognizable by law* (Richmond: John Asplund, 1793).

13. Leland, *Politics sermonized*, quotations from 8 and 19.

14. Ibid., quotations from 8.

15. Paul Goodman, *The Democratic-Republicans of Massachusetts: Politics in a Young Republic* (Cambridge, MA: Harvard University Press, 1964), 94–95.

16. Thomas Jefferson to Gideon Granger, October 18, 1800, in *The Papers of Thomas Jefferson Digital Edition*, ed. Barbara B. Oberg and J. Jefferson Looney, main series, vol. 32 (Charlottesville: University of Virginia Press, Rotunda, 2008), http://rotunda.upress.Virginia .edu/founders/TSJN.html, last accessed June 23, 2011.

17. Paul Goodman, *The Democratic-Republicans of Massachusetts: Politics in a Young Republic* (Cambridge, MA: Harvard University Press, 1964), 94–95, quotation from 95.

18. "August 12, Elkhorn Baptist Association KY, August 10–12, 1805," in William Warren Sweet, ed., *Religion on the American Frontier*, vol. 1, *The Baptists 1783–1830, A Collection of Source Material* (New York: Cooper Square Publishers, 1964; orig. 1931), quotation from 1:508.

19. Leland, *Politics Sermonized*, quotations from 22; and McLoughlin, *Isaac Backus*, 229.

20. Jeffrey L. Pasley, "The Cheese and the Words: Popular Political Culture and Participatory Democracy in the Early Republic," in *Beyond the Founders: New Approaches to the Political History of the Early Republic*, ed. Jeffrey L. Pasley, Andrew W. Robertson, and David Waldstreicher (Chapel Hill: University of North Carolina Press, 2004), 31–56, quotations from 36 and 37.

21. Thomas Jefferson, "To James Madison, 2 March 1798," and "To Thomas Mann Randolph, Jr., 7 January 1793," in *The Papers of Thomas Jefferson Digital Edition*; and Thomas Jefferson to Dr. Joseph Priestley, Washington, March 21, 1801," in *The Life and Selected Writings of Thomas Jefferson*, ed. Adrienne Koch and William Peden (New York: Modern Library, 2004), quotations from 514; see also Frank Lambert, *The Founding Fathers and the Place of Religion in America* (Princeton: Princeton University Press, 2003), 265–87; and David L. Holmes, *The Faiths of the Founding Fathers* (New York: Oxford University Press, 2006), 79–98.

22. Philip S. Foner, ed., *The Democratic-Republican Societies, 1790–1800: A Documentary Sourcebook of Constitutions, Declarations, Addresses, Resolutions, and Toasts* (Westport: Greenwood Press, 1976); and Pasley, *Tyranny of Printers*.

23. "For the Aurora," *Aurora General Advertiser* (Philadelphia), June 24, 1799, 2588, quotations from 2.

24. "Communication," October 3, 1800, *Virginia Argus* (Richmond), quotations from 3; see also "Connecticut, Yale College," June 23, 1801, *Virginia Argus* (Richmond), 1.

25. "From the Carolina Gazette, on the Election of the President of the United States," November 24, 1800, *Herald of Liberty* (Washington, PA), quotations from 1.

26. "Politics. Old-South-No. XXVI. Considerations for the Clergy &People;" January 24–26, 1801, *Independent Chronicle* (Boston), quotations from 1.

27. "Electioneering-Both Sides," March 26–30, 1801, *Independent Chronicle* (Boston), quotations from 1.

28. "From the Commercial Advertiser. No. 11. to the President of the United States," *Connecticut Courant*, November 2, 1801 (Richmond), quotations from 1.

29. Jonathan J. Den Hartog, "Reassessing John Adams and the Rationalist Accommodation of Religion in the Revolutionary Era," unpublished paper, American Society of Church History Winter Meeting, January 8, 2010.

30. George Washington, *The president's address to the people of the United States, announcing his design of retiring from public life, at the expiration of the present constitutional term of the presidentship* (Philadelphia: D. Hogan, S. Longcope, and Co., 1796), quotations from 5–6, 10, and 11.

31. Jedidiah Morse, *The present situation of other nations of the world, contrasted with our own. A sermon, delivered at Charlestown, in the Commonwealth of Massachusetts, February 19, 1795; being the day recommended by George Washington, president of the United States of America, for publick thanksgiving and prayer* (Boston: Samuel Hall, 1795), quotations from 5–6.

32. Ibid., quotations from 6–7.

33. Richard Douglas Shiels, *The Connecticut Clergy in the Second Great Awakening* (PhD dissertation, Boston University, 1976); Randolph Roth, *The Democratic Dilemma: Religion, Reform, and the Social Order in the Connecticut River Valley of Vermont, 1791–1850* (Cambridge: Cambridge University Press, 1987); and Stephen C. Bullock, *Freemasonry and the Transformation of the American Social Order, 1730–1840* (Chapel Hill: University of North Carolina Press, 1996).

34. Jedidiah Morse, *A sermon, exhibiting the present dangers, and consequent duties of the citizens of the United States of America. Delivered at Charlestown, April 25, 1799. The day of the national fast* (Hartford: Hudson and Goodwin, 1799), quotations from 12 and 13.

35. *Connecticut Courant* (Hartford), August 8, 1800, quotations from 1; and Jefferson, *Notes on the State of Virginia*, quotation from 159.

36. Ron Chernow, *Alexander Hamilton* (New York: Penguin Books, 2004), 512–13, quotations from 513; see also Jefferson, *Notes on the State of Virginia*, 137–43.

37. Chernow, *Alexander Hamilton*, 607–9, quotations from 608 and 609.

38. "For the Chronicle," *The Independent Chronicle and Universal Advertiser* (Boston), May 12, 1800, quotations from 2.

39. "From the *Aurora* (June 27)," *The Times; and District of Columbia Daily Advertiser*, July 2, 1800, quotation from 2.

40. "For the Chronicle," *Independent Chronicle*, June 30, 1800, quotation from 2.

41. "Mr. Jefferson; Virginia," *The Times and District of Columbia Daily Advertiser* (Alexandria), April 21, 1800, quotations from 3.

42. Edward D. Griffin, *The kingdom of Christ a missionary sermon, preached before the General Assembly of the Presbyterian Church, in Philadelphia, May 23d, 1805* (Philadelphia: Jane Aitken, 1805), quotation from 25; see also Conrad Edik Wright, *The Transformation of Charity in Postrevolutionary New England* (Boston: Northeastern University Press, 1992); Clifton Jackson Phillips, *Protestant America and the Pagan World: The First Half Century of the American Board of Commissioners for Foreign Missions, 1810–1860* (Cambridge, MA: Harvard University Press, 1969); and Anne M. Boylan, *The Origins of Women's Activism: New York and Boston, 1797–1840* (Chapel Hill: University of North Carolina Press, 2002).

43. Dee Andrews, *The Methodists and Revolutionary America, 1760–1800: The Shaping of an Evangelical Culture* (Princeton: Princeton University Press, 200), 47–51, 190–94; and John Wigger, *American Saint: Francis Asbury and the Methodists* (New York: Oxford University Press, 2009), 97–109.

44. Francis Asbury, *The Journal of the Rev. Francis Asbury, bishop of the Methodist Episcopal Church, from August 1, 1771, to December 7, 1815*, 3 vols. (New York: N. Bangs and T. Mason, 1821), quotations from 3:124–25.

45. Andrews, *Methodists and Revolutionary America*, 192–94.

46. James O'Kelly, *A vindication of the author's Apology with reflections on the Reply, and a few remarks on Bishop Asbury's annotations on his Book of discipline* (Raleigh: Joseph Gales, 1801); William H. Williams, *The Garden of Methodism: The Delmarva Peninsula, 1769–1820* (Wilmington, Scholarly Resources, 1984); Russell E. Richey "The Formation of American Methodism: The Chesapeake Refraction of Wesleyanism," in *Methodism and the Shaping of American Culture*, ed. Nathan O. Hatch and John H. Wigger (Nashville: Abingdon Press, 2001), 197–221; and Nathan O. Hatch "The Puzzle of American Methodism," in Hatch and Wigger, eds., *Methodism and the Shaping of American Culture*, 38–39.

47. William E. Arnold, *A History of Methodism in Kentucky* (Louisville: Herald Place, 1935), 193; and Stanley Elkins and Eric McKitrick, *The Age of Federalism* (New York: Oxford University Press, 1993); see also Terry D. Bilhartz, *Urban Religion and the Second Great Awakening: Church and Society in Early National Baltimore* (Cranberry: Associated University Presses, 1986), tables 2, 3, 5, 6, and 11, 158–67.

48. Arnold, *History of Methodism in Kentucky*, 265.

49. Lowell H. Harrison, *John Breckinridge: Jeffersonian Republican* (Louisville: Filson Club Publications, 1969); and James C. Klotter, *The Breckinridges of Kentucky* (Lexington: University Press of Kentucky, 1986), 13–35.

50. Mary Cabell to Mary Hopkins Cabell Breckinridge, March 14, 1801, in *Breckinridge Family Papers*, Library of Congress.

51. Harrison, *John Breckinridge*, 15; and Breckinridge to Mary Hopkins Cabell Breckinridge, January 4, 1806, in *Breckinridge Family Papers*, Library of Congress.

52. Joseph C. Cabelle to John Breckinridge, from Union Hill, May 20, 1800, in *Breckinridge Family Papers*, Library of Congress.

53. Harrison, *John Breckinridge*, 33–34 and 64–65.

54. Archibald Stuart to John Breckinridge, January 3, 1800, in *Breckinridge Family Papers*, Library of Congress,

55. David Waldstreicher, *In the Midst of Perpetual Fetes: The Making of American Nationalism, 1776–1820* (Chapel Hill: University of North Carolina Press, 1997).

56. Carroll D. Wright, *History of Wages and Prices in Massachusetts: 1752–1885* (Boston: Wright and Potter, 1885), 62 and 65.

57. Harrison, *John Breckinridge*, 33 and 122–124.

58. John Breckinridge, "To the Inhabitants of the United States West of the Allegany and Apalachian Mountains," reprinted in "The Democratic Societies of 1793 and 1794 in Kentucky, Pennsylvania and Virginia," *The William and Mary Quarterly*, Second Series, vol. 2, no. 4 (October 1922): 239–43, quotation from 240; and Harrison, *John Breckinridge*, 15 and 55, quotation from 55.

59. Klotter, *Breckinridges*, 29–31, quotation from 30.

60. Harrison, *John Breckinridge*, 119.

61. Arnold, *History of Methodism in Kentucky*, 157–62, quotations from 162 and 159; and

George W. Ranck, *History of Lexington, Kentucky: Its Early Annals and Recent Progress* (Cincinnati: Robert Clarke and Co., 1872), 118–22.

62. Klotter, *Breckinridges*, 39–40 and 48.

63. Ibid., 46–55, quotations from 53 and 51.

64. Andrews, *Methodists and Revolutionary America*, 202–3; Hatch and Wigger, "Introduction," in Hatch and Wigger, eds., *Methodism and the Shaping of American Culture*, 17; John Wigger, *American Saint*, 190–95; John B. Boles, *The Great Revival: Beginnings of the Bible Belt* (Lexington: University Press of Kentucky, 1996; orig. 1972), 145–46; Nathan O. Hatch, *The Democratization of Christianity* (New Haven: Yale University Press, 1989), 49–56; and David Hempton, *Methodism: Empire of the Spirit* (New Haven: Yale University Press, 2005), 99–108.

65. Andrew R. L. Cayton, *Ideology and Politics in the Ohio Country, 1780–1825* (Kent: Kent State University Press, 1986), esp. 58–59; and Richard Carwardine, "Methodist Ministers and the Second Party System," in *Perspectives on American Methodism: Interpretive Essays*, ed. Russell E. Richey, Kenneth E. Rowe, and Jean Miller Schmidt (Nashville: Abingdon Press, 1993), 159–77.

66. Wigger, *American Saint*, 148–54, quotations from 148–49, 152, and 153; see also Cynthia Lynn Lyerly, *Methodism and the Southern Mind, 1770–1810* (New York: Oxford University Press, 1998); and Charles F. Irons, *The Origins of Proslavery Christianity: White and Black Evangelicals in Colonial and Antebellum Virginia* (Chapel Hill: University of North Carolina Press, 2008).

67. Asbury, *Journal*, quotations from 2:312.

68. Ibid., 3:9, 3:15, and 3:124, quotations from 3:15 and 3:124.

69. Arnold, *History of Methodism in Kentucky*, 143–45, 265–66, and 313–15. According to Arnold, there were "1,856 white and 114 colored" in the Western District of Kentucky and the Cumberland Valley in 1796, down by "203 white and 52 colored communicants" from 1792. In 1804, there were "9,082 whites and 513 colored" communicants in the Western District. See Arnold, *History of Methodism in Kentucky*, 143 and 265.

70. Christine Leigh Heyrman, *Southern Cross: The Beginnings of the Bible Belt* (Chapel Hill: University of North Carolina Press, 1997), 206–52, quotations from 237 and 236; see also Lyerly, *Methodism and the Southern Mind*, 119–45.

CHAPTER 6

1. "Supplemental Journal of Such Proceedings of the First Session of the Twelfth Congress, as, during the Time They Were Depending, Were Ordered to Be Kept Secret, and Respecting which the Injunction of Secrecy was afterwards Removed by Order of the House," 24 Annals of Congress (1812), quotation from 1587.

2. For reference to Clay as "Harry of the West" in the *Kentucky Gazette* in 1804, see Bernard Mayo, *Henry Clay: Spokesman of the New West* (Boston: Houghton Mifflin, 1937), 146.

3. Henry Clay, Washington *National Intelligencer*, April 14, 1812, reprinted in *The Papers of Henry Clay*, ed. James F. Hopkins, 10 vols. (Lexington: University of Kentucky Press), 1:645–48, quotations from 1:645 and 1:648. For reference to a "band of brothers," see "Congress, House

of Representatives, Tuesday November 29, Report of the Committee on Foreign Relations under Consideration," *The Reporter* (Lexington), January 16, 1809; see also "Proceedings and Debates of the Senate of the United States, at the First Session of the Twelfth Congress, begun at the City of Washington, Monday, November 4, 1811," 23 Annals of Congress (1811–12), 339.

4. Richard McNemar, *The Kentucky revival, or, A short history of the late extraordinary outpouring of the spirit of God, in the western states of America* [microform] *agreeably to Scripture promises, and prophecies concerning the latter day with a brief account of the entrance and progress of what the world called Shakerism* (Cincinnati: John W. Brown, 1807), quotations from 63 and 84; for discussion of dueling as both a ritual practice and rhetorical framework for political combat in the early republic, see Joanne B. Freeman, *Affairs of Honor: National Politics in the New Republic* (New Haven: Yale University Press, 2001).

5. "Supplemental Journal of Such Proceedings of the First Session of the Twelfth Congress, as, during the Time They Were Depending, Were Ordered to Be Kept Secret, and Respecting which the Injunction of Secrecy was afterwards Removed by Order of the House," 24 Annals of Congress (1812), quotations from 1587 and 1588; and Donald R. Hickey, *The War of 1812: A Forgotten Conflict* (Urbana: University of Illinois Press, 1995; orig. 1989), 29–30; see also Reginald Horsman, "On to Canada: Manifest Destiny and United States Strategy in the War of 1812," *Michigan Historical Review* 13, no. 2 (Fall 1987): 1–24; Robert V. Haynes, "The Southwest and the War of 1812," *Louisiana History: Journal of the Louisiana Historical Association* 5, no. 1 (Winter 1964): 41–51; and Donald R. Hickey, "The War of 1812: Still a Forgotten Conflict?" *Journal of Military History* 65, no. 3 (July 2001): 741–69.

6. "Supplemental Journal . . . of the First Session of the Twelfth Congress," 24 Annals of Congress (1812), 1589–91, quotations from 1589 and 1591.

7. Ibid., 1589–91, quotations from 1591.

8. "Map of the Seat of War, *Weekly Aurora* (Philadelphia), October 20, 1812, quotations from 203.

9. David Sehat, *The Myth of American Religious Freedom* (New York: Oxford University Press, 2011), 51–69; Daniel Walker Howe, *What Hath God Wrought: The Transformation of America, 1815–1848* (New York: Oxford University Press, 2007), 285–89; John Seelye, *Memory's Nation: The Place of Plymouth Rock* (Chapel Hill: University of North Carolina Press, 1998); Ann Uhry Abrams, *The Pilgrims and Pocahontas: Rival Myths of American Origin* (Boulder: Westview Press, 1999); and Michael Kammen, *Mystic Chords of Memory: The Transformation of Tradition in American Culture* (New York: Vintage, 1993).

10. Bertram Wyatt-Brown, *The Shaping of Southern Culture: Honor, Grace, and War, 1760s–1880s* (Chapel Hill: University of North Carolina Press, 2001).

11. Charles W. Janson, *The Stranger in America* (New York: Press of the Pioneers, 1935; orig. 1807), quotations from 310.

12. Margaret van Dwight, *A Journey to Ohio in 1810*, ed. Max Farrand (New York: Yale University Press, 1912), quotations from 14.

13. William Winans, "Autobiography of William Winans" (1850), typescript from Milsaps-Wilson Library, Milsaps College, quotations from 77.

14. Dwight, *Journey to Ohio*, quotations from 36, 38, and 39.

15. Winans, "Autobiography," quotations from 17.

16. James McGready, "Sermon IX: The Devices of Satan," in *The Posthumous Works of the Reverend and Pious James M'Gready, Late Minister of the Gospel, in Henderson, Kentucky*, ed. James Smith, 2 vols. (Nashville: Lowry and Smith, 1833), 1:275–85, quotations from 1:281.

17. McGready, "Sermon XV the Sinner's Guide to Hell," in Smith, ed., *Posthumous Works*, 1:230–41, quotations from 234–35.

18. Adam Rothman, *Slave Country: American Expansion and the Origins of the Deep South* (Cambridge, MA: Harvard University Press, 2005), 45, 94–95, quotations from 94 and 95.

19. Scaevola (Henry Clay), "To the Citizens of Fayette," *Kentucky Gazette*, February 28, 1799; for hardening strategies for managing slavery, see Christine Leigh Heyrman, *Southern Cross: The Beginnings of the Bible Belt* (Chapel Hill: University of North Carolina Press, 1997); Rachel N. Klein, *Unification of a Slave State: The Rise of the Planter Class in the South Carolina Backcountry, 1760–1808* (Chapel Hill: University of North Carolina Press, 1990); Adam Rothman, *Slave Country*; Charles F. Irons, *The Origins of Proslavery Christianity: White and Black Evangelicals in Colonial and Antebellum Virginia* (Chapel Hill: University of North Carolina, 2008); and Cynthia Lynn Lyerly, *Methodism and the Southern Mind, 1770–1810* (New York: Oxford University Press, 1998).

20. Anthony F. C. Wallace, *Jefferson and the Indians: The Tragic Fate of the First Americans* (Cambridge, MA: Harvard University Press, 1999); John Sugden, *Tecumseh: A Life* (New York: Henry Holt and Company, 1997); Robert M. Owens, *Mr. Jefferson's Hammer: William Henry Harrison and the Origins of American Indian Policy* (Norman: University of Oklahoma Press, 2007); Gregory Evans Dowd, *A Spirited Resistance: The North American Indian Struggle for Unity, 1745–1815* (Baltimore: Johns Hopkins University Press, 1992); Daniel K. Richter, *Facing East: A Native History of Early America* (Cambridge, MA: Harvard University Press, 2001); and Carroll Smith-Rosenberg, *This Violent Empire: The Birth of an American National Identity* (Chapel Hill: University of North Carolina Press, 2010), 207–49.

21. Sugden, *Tecumseh*, 138–42.

22. Sam Gill, *Mother Earth: An American Story* (Chicago: University of Chicago Press, 1987); and Sugden, *Tecumseh*, 153.

23. Sugden, *Tecumseh*, 226–36; Amanda Porterfield, "Tecumseh, Tenskwatawa, and the Relationship between Religion and Politics," in *Religion and the Life of the Nation: American Recoveries*, ed. Rowland A. Sherrill (Urbana: University of Illinois Press, 1990), 219–34.

24. Hickey, *War of 1812*, 19–24, Randolph quotation from 20.

25. Ibid., 20–22; and *Hartford Courant*, April 8, 1812, quotation from 3.

26. "State of Ohio," *Republican Star* (Easton, MD), February 2, 1812, quotations from 2; for Methodists in early Ohio politics, see James B. Finley, *Sketches of Western Methodism: Biographical, Historical, and Miscellaneous. Illustrative of Pioneer Life*, ed. W. P. Strickland (Cincinnati: R. P. Thompson, 1854), 260–77; and Andrew R. L. Cayton, *The Frontier Republic: Ideology and Politics in The Ohio Country, 1780–1825* (Kent: Kent State University Press, 1986).

27. "The Soldier's Return," *Republican Star*, December 1, 1812, quotations from 4.

28. James B. Finley, *Autobiography of Rev. James B. Finley, Or, Pioneer Life in the West*, ed. W. P. Strickland (Cincinnati: Cranston and Curts, 1853), quotations from 258 and 260–61; see also Christine Leigh Heyrman, *Southern Cross: Beginnings of the Bible Belt* (New York: Alfred A. Knopf, 1997), 206–52.

29. John C. Jones, *A Complete History of Methodism As Connected With The Mississippi Conference of the Methodist Episcopal Church, South*, vol. 1, *1799–1817* (Nashville: Southern Methodist Publishing Press, 1887), quotations from 114.

30. John Wigger, *American Saint: Francis Asbury and the American Methodists* (New York: Oxford University Press, 2009), quotations from 383.

31. Finley, *Sketches of Western Methodism*, 34–35, quotation from 35.

32. Thomas Baldwin, *The Knowledge of the Lord Filling the Earth. A Sermon, Delivered in Boston, June 4, 1812, Before the Massachusetts Bible Society, being their third anniversary* (Boston: Lincoln and Edmands, 1812), quotations from 17 and 21.

33. Robert J. Allison, *The Crescent Obscured: The United States and the Muslim World, 1776–1815* (Chicago: University of Chicago Press, 1995), quotations from 206 and 205.

34. William G. McLoughlin, *New England Dissent 1630–1883: The Baptists and the Separation of Church and State*, 2 vols. (Cambridge, MA: Harvard University Press, 1971), 2:831, quotation from 2:831.

35. Terry D. Bilhartz, *Urban Religion and the Second Great Awakening: Church and Society in Early National Baltimore* (Cranbury: Associated University Press, 1986), 20–27; and Paul A. Gilje, "The Baltimore Riots of 1812 and the Breakdown of the Anglo-American Mob Tradition," *Journal of Social History* 13, no. 4 (Summer 1980): 547–64.

36. Gilje, "Baltimore Riots," quotation from 549.

37. "A Mobocracy," *Federal Republican*, July 27, 1812, quotation from 2.

38. Hickey, *War of 1812*, 52–71; and Gilje, "Baltimore Riots," 553–54; see also Paul Gilje, *The Road to Mobocracy: Popular Disorder in New York City, 1763–1834* (Chapel Hill: University of North Carolina Press, 1987).

39. "Political Duty," *Republican Star*, July 21, 1812, quotations from 2.

40. "Mr. Madison's War," *New York Evening Post*, August 6, 1812, 3132, quotation from 2.

41. Gilje, *Road to Mobocracy*, 97–99 and 115.

42. "Democratic Consistency," *Hartford Courant*, August 8, 1812, quotation from 3.

43. "Heroism," *Carthage Gazette and Friend of the People* (Carthage, TN), June 5, 1811, quotation from 2; Consistency (author), "For the City Gazette," *City Gazette and Daily Advertiser* (Charleston), August 15, 1812, quotations from 2; and William Hull, "A Proclamation. Inhabitants of Canada!" *Democratic Republican* (Walpole, NH), August 10, 1812, quotation from 2.

44. Jacob Duché, *The duty of standing fast in our spiritual and temporal liberties, a sermon, preached in Christ-Church, July 7th, 1775. Before the First Battalion of the city and liberties of Philadelphia; and now published at their request* (Philadelphia: James Humphreys, 1775), quotations from 15 and iii; and Jay Fliegelman, *Prodigals and Pilgrims: The American Revolution Against Patriarchal Authority, 1750–1800* (Cambridge, MA: Cambridge University Press, 1982), esp. 98.

45. Mayo, *Henry Clay*, 335–41; and Freeman, *Affairs of Honor*.

46. "NON-INTERCOURSE," 21 Annals of Congress (February 1810), quotations from 579–80; and Norman K. Risjord, "1812: Conservatives, War Hawks and the Nation's Honor," *William and Mary Quarterly* 18, no. 2 (April 1961): 196–210.

47. "NON-INTERCOURSE," quotations from 581.

48. Robert V. Remini, *Henry Clay: Statesman for the Union* (New York: W. W. Norton, 1991), quotations from 2.

49. Josiah Quincy quoted in Edmund Quincy, *Life of Josiah Quincy of Massachusetts* (Boston: Ticknor and Fields, 1867), 255.

50. David S. Heidler and Jeanne T. Heidler, *Henry Clay: The Essential American* (New York: Random House, 2010).

51. Josiah Quincy quoted in E. Quincy, *Life of Josiah Quincy*, 129.

52. Timothy Dwight, *The folly, guilt, and mischiefs of duelling: a sermon, preached in the college chapel at New Haven, on the Sabbath preceding the annual commencement, September, 1804* (Hartford: Hudson and Goodwin, 1804), quotations from 15, 24, and 14.

53. *Hartford Courant*, September 15, 1812, quotations from 1.

54. Josiah Quincy, "Speech on Foreign Relations," reprinted in E. Quincy, *Life of Josiah Quincy*, 149.

55. Josiah Quincy quoted in E. Quincy, *Life of Josiah Quincy*, 160 and 159.

56. Mayo, *Henry Clay*, 204–8, 403, 408–9, quotations from 192 and 408; and Remini, *Henry Clay*, 79–82.

57. Mayo, *Henry Clay*, 408; Remini, *Henry Clay*, 78.

58. Mayo, *Henry Clay*, 230, 271, 277, 282, quotation from 408; John Randolph to George Hay, January 3, 1806, in Robert Dawidoff, *The Education of John Randolph* (New York: W. W. Norton, 1979), quotation from 187; and John Randolph to Francis Scott Key, May 10, 1813, in Dawidoff, *Education of John Randolph*, quotation from 198; see also Norman Risjord, *The Old Republicans: Southern Conservatism in the Age of Jefferson* (New York: Columbia University Press, 1965), 35, 163.

59. Sugden, *Tecumseh*, 259.

60. E. Quincy, *Life of Josiah Quincy*, 126–27, 143, and 266–68; and Henry Adams, *John Randolph* (Boston: Houghton Mifflin Company, 1898; orig. 1882), 65, 77, 90, 171–72, 260.

61. Remini, *Henry Clay*, 7.

62. "Additional Military Force," 25 Annals of Congress (1813), quotations from 664.

63. Hickey, *War of 1812*, 1–3 and 30, quotation from 30.

64. "Naval Establishment," 23 Annals of Congress (1812), quotation from 912.

65. McGready, "The Nature and Tendency of Unbelief," in Smith, ed., *Posthumous Works*, quotations from 155.

66. Jedidiah Morse, *A sermon, delivered at Charlestown, July 23, 1812, the day appointed by the Governor . . . to be observed in fasting and prayer . . . in consequence of a declaration of war with Great Britain* (Boston: Samuel Etheridge, 1812), quotations from 3; and William Gribben, *The Churches Militant: The War of 1812 and American Religion* (New Haven: Yale University Press, 1973), 20–27.

67. Sacvan Bercovitch, *The American Jeremiad* (Madison: University of Wisconsin Press, 1978).

68. Morse, "A Sermon, Delivered at Charlestown," quotations from 18.

69. Timothy Dwight, *A discourse, in two parts, delivered July 23, 1812, on the public fast, in the chapel of Yale College. By Timothy Dwight, D.D. L.L.D. president of that seminary. Published at the request of the students and others* (Utica: Ira Merrell, 1812), quotations from 15, 16, 43, and 44.

70. Timothy Dwight, *A discourse, in two parts, delivered August 20, 1812, on the national fast, in the chapel of Yale College* (New York: J. Seymour, 1812), quotations from 52 and 53.

71. Dwight, *A discourse . . . delivered August 20, 1812*, quotations from 29 and 43-44; and Jonathan Edwards, *A History of the Work of Redemption containing the Outlines of a Body of Divinity, in a Method Entirely New* (Worcester: Isaiah Thomas, 1808; originally a series of sermons preached in Northampton in 1739, ed. John Erskine, pub. Edinburgh, 1774).

72. Timothy Dwight, *A sermon, delivered in Boston, Sept. 16, 1813, before the American Board of Commissioners for Foreign Missions, at their fourth annual meeting* (Boston: Samuel T. Armstrong, 1813), quotations from 15, 18, and 3.

73. Richard J. Carwardine, *Evangelicals and Politics in Antebellum America* (New Haven: Yale University Press, 1993); Howe, *What Hath God Wrought*; Mark A. Noll, *America's God: From Jonathan Edwards to Abraham Lincoln* (New York: Oxford University Press, 2002), 161–346; Clifton Jackson Phillips, *Protestant America and the Pagan World: The First Half Century of the American Board of Commissioners for Foreign Missions, 1810-1860* (Cambridge, MA: Harvard University Press, 1969); and Amanda Porterfield, *Mary Lyon and the Mount Holyoke Missionaries* (New York: Oxford University Press, 1997).

74. Oh, say, can you see, by the dawn's early light,

What so proudly we hailed at the twilight's last gleaming?
Whose broad stripes and bright stars, thru the perilous fight,
O'er the ramparts we watched, were so gallantly streaming?
And the rockets' red glare, the bombs bursting in air,
Gave proof through the night that our flag was still there.
O say, does that star-spangled banner yet wave
O'er the land of the free and the home of the brave?

On the shore dimly seen through the mists of the deep,
Where the foe's haughty host in dread silence reposes,
What is that which the breeze, o'er the towering steep,
As it fitfully blows, half conceals, half discloses?
Now it catches the gleam of the morning's first beam,
In full glory reflected, now shines on the stream:
Tis the star-spangled banner: O, long may it wave
O'er the land of the free and the home of the brave!

And where is that band who so vauntingly swore
That the havoc of war and the battle's confusion
A home and a country should leave us no more?
Their blood has washed out their foul footsteps' pollution.
No refuge could save the hireling and slave
From the terror of flight or the gloom of the grave:
And the star-spangled banner in triumph doth wave
O'er the land of the free and the home of the brave.

O, thus be it ever when freemen shall stand,
Between their loved home and the war's desolation!

Blest with victory and peace, may the heav'n-rescued land
Praise the Power that hath made and preserved us a nation!
Then conquer we must, when our cause it is just,
And this be our motto: "In God is our trust"
And the star-spangled banner in triumph shall wave
O'er the land of the free and the home of the brave!

Quoted from http://kids.niehs.nih.gov/lyrics/spangle.htm.

INDEX

CPSIA information can be obtained
at www.ICGtesting.com
Printed in the USA
LVHW031637010421
683225LV00005B/1022

9 780226 271965